EXPANDING OUR LIGHT

THE PATH TO PERFECTION

DR. LAUREN J. BALL

ISBN 978-1-953223-47-0 (paperback)

Copyright © 2020 by Dr. Lauren J. Ball

All rights reserved. No part of this publication may be reproduced, distributed, or transmitted in any form or by any means, including photocopying, recording, or other electronic or mechanical methods without the prior written permission of the publisher. For permission requests, solicit the publisher via the address below.

Rushmore Press LLC
1 800 460 9188
www.rushmorepress.com

Printed in the United States of America

CONTENTS

Chapter 1:	The Light	1
Chapter 2:	The Pathway	13
Chapter 3:	Adulthood Versus Maturity	33
Chapter 4:	Perfection	37
Chapter 5:	Agency	49
Chapter 6:	A Question of Faith	58
Chapter 7:	Faith, the Power Within	70
Chapter 8:	Faith in Action	76
Chapter 9:	Repentance	81
Chapter 10:	Forgiveness	87
Chapter 11:	Baptism and the Basic Elements of Christ's Church	97
Chapter 12:	Obedience	121
Chapter 13:	Commandments and Beatitudes	129
Chapter 14:	Love and Charity	140
Chapter 15:	Meekness and Humility	150
Chapter 16:	Justice and Mercy	163
Chapter 17:	Honesty and Integrity	171
Chapter 18:	Compassion and Kindness	177
Chapter 19:	Loyalty	182
Chapter 20:	Prayer and Meditation	189
Chapter 21:	Destructive Syndromes	206
Chapter 22:	The Kamikaze Syndrome	211

Chapter 23:	Anger	217
Chapter 24:	Hatred and Prejudice	228
Chapter 25:	Greed	237
Chapter 26:	Procrastination	241
Chapter 27:	Idolatry	248
Chapter 28:	Pride	254
Chapter 29:	Afterthoughts	259
Chapter 30:	Living the Gospel of Jesus Christ Requires Us To	262

1

THE LIGHT

And God saw these souls that they were good, and he stood in the midst of them, and he said: These I will make my rulers; for he stood among those that were spirits, and he saw that they were good; and he said unto me: Abraham, thou art one of them; thou wast chosen before thou wast born.

And there stood one among them that was like unto God, and He said unto those who were with him: We will go down, for there is space there, and we will take of these materials, and we will make an earth whereon these may dwell;

And we will prove them herewith, to see if they will do all things whatsoever the Lord their God shall command them;" (Abraham 3:23–25; emphasis added)

When Moses came down from the mountain with the stone plates containing the Ten Commandments, he had a glow about him, a brightness that frightened the Israelites. (Exodus 34:29–34)

When Joseph Smith saw the Father and the Son, their light and glory was brighter than the noonday sun (Joseph Smith 1:17). We see about us every day people who seem to have an unusual brightness, a light that surrounds them and sets them apart from others.

It is a light that seems to come from within and radiates outward to form an aura about them. There is a kindness, a peace, an understanding quality they possess, which attracts many to them. It is the intention of this book to give us some of the tools we need to expand this sphere of light, which needs to be brightened and magnified in each of us, until, like our Savior and God the Father, it becomes brighter than the noon day sun.

Conversely, there are those who seem to be encircled about by darkness, which drives most people from them. These are they who have shunned the powers of light and righteousness. They go the ways of Satan, and seek to gratify themselves, and lust after the pleasures of the moment, regardless of whom they hurt. There is no place in their lives, whatsoever, for our Lord and Savior. Their agency has been used to choose the path of least resistance, the path of darkness and destruction.

We each generate and project our own sphere of light. In some of us, it is bright and lights up the surrounding area, and those within it, with truth, peace, and happiness. In some, it is a small sphere and very dim, casting long shadows of disharmony, contention, and confusion. It is also the intent of this book to help us intensify, increase the projection, and magnification of our own spheres of light and truth. This light, which emanates from people, depicts the righteous knowledge and intelligence they possess and use. These emanations will increase in brightness and intensity as we become more and more perfected, as we embrace the concepts of love, charity, humility, righteousness, etc. and expunge those destructive traits such as anger, greed, procrastination, pride, and other traits of unrighteousness.

If we increase the brightness of our spheres of influence each day by magnifying our stewardships here on earth, we will be doing as our Father in heaven has commanded. Our radiance can eventually become as bright as God's and reach outward to all those who seek righteousness and perfection. At some point in our existence, many of us stop and ponder the meaning of life and search inward for the answers to some of its most perplexing questions, which follow:

- Who am I?
- What am I?

- Why am I?
- Where did I come from?
- Why am I here?
- Where am I going when I leave here?
- What must I do to get there?

When seriously considered and searched, these are questions that lead to a quest for truth, knowledge, wisdom, intelligence, and comprehension. When answered with the truth and applied correctly, they have the ability to change our lives, allowing us to set and attain productive, righteous goals, which make us eternal winners in this spiritual quest called life. They also help us place in proper perspective, the need to set our ultimate goals on those spiritual values, which will allow us to reside with our Father in heaven, in His celestial kingdom once again, through repentance and continuing our quest for the perfection commanded of us in Matthew 5:48.

Each of these questions will be briefly answered here but only with simplified responses. To obtain an expanded understanding, the scriptures must be searched and studied daily and diligently. Fasting and prayerful meditation are also essential to grasping any of God's creations. If we truly want to have a lasting spiritual impact on others and ourselves, we must make a *serious commitment* to obey God's laws and commandments, accept and participate in all of His ordinances. We must truly follow Him as He has directed and commanded.

For some of the questions listed, an expanded answer will be given in these pages. A careful study of this book is designed to inspire the reader to set aside a portion of each day to meditate and ponder the knowledge God has given us in the scriptures to help us master our lives while here on earth.

Opening our minds to truth may be difficult but essential to our salvation as we strive for perfection, wisdom, knowledge, and righteousness. As we study, whether it is this or any other book, we should always ask God in fervent prayer for an understanding of its truths. We must then listen to the promptings and influences of the Holy Ghost for either confirmation or renunciation. The road to perfection is a glorious, righteous journey rather than something that can be attained in a short time period.

Only the Holy Ghost manifests all truth. When we assume that the answers we receive come from Him without first praying may very well misled us by the powers of darkness. God cannot lie! Lucifer is always misleading! So, when we try to understand the things of God without true humility, without an open mind, or without prayer and scripture study, we may well be misled.

God loves us all equally. He does not, however, love all of our actions equally. Therein lies the only difference between the sinner and the saint. It is this distinction that will ultimately determine which of the degrees of glory we will inherit for we will be judged our works and by our works what we have become with respect to what we could have become and the degree of our repentance.

We should seriously ponder in our hearts, the answers to these questions: Who am I? I am, in truth, a child of God! I am a distinct personality, separate from all others. I am the sum total of all the knowledge, experience, beliefs, belief systems, traditions, and the thoughts I have formed in this life. Before I came to earth, I was literally a spirit child of God, loved by Him and tutored under His direction.

What am I? I am what I have made of myself! By the choices I have made and by using my thoughts and actions. I have become a personality, physically, mentally, and spiritually unique. I am responsible for the "me" I have created (and will create) because God has given me the greatest of all gifts—the right to choose for myself what I want to be, good or evil, productive, non-productive, or counterproductive. This freedom to choose is known as *agency*. Though I have allowed others to influence some of my actions and mold my thinking, still, I am the one responsible for what I have become. I cannot foist the blame on others, not my parents, my peers, my siblings, or others who have played a part in my upbringing. When I reached maturity, I not only assumed the full responsibility for all of my thinking and actions, but I also relinquished the right to blame anyone else for what I have become or will become.

Where am I? I am on the planet earth and, in time, somewhere between the pre-existent spirit world and the paradise of the millennium. I am somewhere between total evil and total righteousness or perfection. I am in a state somewhere between forgiveness and unforgiveness, between complete repentance and total no repentance. I hope to be in a state of complete repentance before I die. I realize that I will be judged by what I have become, of what I have repented, and not whether the good I have accomplished outweighs the sins I have committed.

Why am I? I am because God created me and loves me. I am, so that by exercising my agency, in a righteous manner, I may again live with my heavenly Father. I am so that I may, through righteous endeavors, become a perfected being like God has commanded (Matthew 5:48). I am so that I might have joy and happiness.

Where did I come from? Before I was born into this world, I was a spirit child of God. I resided in the premortal spirit world, being taught those things needed to prepare me for this life. The things I learned and embraced of God's laws and commandments and the degree of my commitment and obedience to God's law helped to determine the status and circumstances into which I was born and helped to determine what opportunities and afflictions I would be afforded in this life to help me grow spiritually.

Why am I here? I am here to work out my salvation and exaltation. I am here to overcome temptation, to learn obedience, to gain all of the righteous knowledge and experience I can while in this world and to seek out the truth wherever I can find it. I am here to identify, overcome, conquer, and rise above all adversity and, with the help of God, to subdue the earth and all of my destructive traits and to learn total self-discipline. I am here to perfect my mind, body, and spirit to the maximum extent possible. I am here to become a productive and spiritually influential member of society. I am also here to help others in every way I can, especially to aid them in working out their salvation and in drawing close to God in every way.

Where am I going when I leave here? Initially, I will go to heaven where I will have a partial judgment. This will determine where I will be until the end of the millennium. After that, where I go depends largely on what I do while I am here on earth. "In our Father's house are many mansions." Where I go depends on how I have treated my fellow man, the degree of my perfection, the extent of my repentance, the degree I have embraced God's laws and commandments and accepted and participated in His ordinances. With an absolute and sure knowledge of Christ, I could be cast into outer darkness if I then choose to worship Satan completely. Or I could inherit one of the kingdoms of God: The telestial (the lowest), the terrestrial (or middle kingdom), or even the celestial kingdom (the highest). The Bible is replete with scriptures on the judgment. I will be judged according to my works, good or evil. The kingdom I will inherit depends on my thoughts and actions while here on earth. I alone am responsible for what I become because I have exercised my agency as I have desired and, therefore, I must be prepared to accept what God's judgment dictates. I must never forget that in spite of all I can do, and I must never quit striving; it is the redemption of Jesus Christ that makes it possible for me to work out my salvation and exaltation. Through repentance and enduring to the end, I can live with God and Christ again.

What must I do to get there? I must strive with all my strength, heart, mind, and soul to be obedient to all of God's commandments, and when I err, I must repent and I must put the things of God first in my life. I must be in a constant state of repentance, embrace the law of love and follow all the concepts God has given us in the scriptures. I must never forget that as a child of God, I owe my first loyalty to Him. I must serve mankind and learn to love as God has loved, unconditionally. I must make humility, meekness, and charity a very real part of my life. I cannot procrastinate the day of my repentance and receive the fullness of God's blessings or expect to have the same degree of perfection as those who don't. I must treat every day as a sacred gift from God and act accordingly.

This book is designed to help the reader set the goals necessary to gain the highest degree in the celestial kingdom. To aim for anything less would be to deny God, Christ, the Holy Spirit, and the glorious purpose for which they sent us here. It could also mean that we were too lazy and slothful to care if we even entered one of the kingdoms or that we were not interested in setting the goals that would expedite our progress and spiritual growth. I pray that we will accept nothing less than the best efforts for which we are capable.

Also, this book is a selection of basic and essential guideposts to help us understand why we are here and what spiritual paths we need to take to gain the greatest possible growth toward perfection—road markers with which we can identify regardless of who we are, what our backgrounds are, or from where we come.

My search to find these universal guidelines has taken me through the scriptures many times, through many good and revealing books and especially through much meditation and prayer. The answers have come slowly, one at a time, over a period of many years. Sometimes, the answers have come because of traumatic experiences in my life. Usually, they have come because of my persistence in pursuing and seeking them out, but I feel they have always come through inspiration from God.

To some, these guideposts may seem overly simplistic and of little value. Continued study and application, however, will reveal the tremendous impact they can have on our lives if correctly applied.

Certain assumptions are necessary to help understand this work. First, God placed man here for a specific purpose and mission. Second, this purpose must be consistent with the teachings in the scriptures. Third, this purpose must be attainable, easily understood, and be compatible with the commandments God has given us. When we accept and continue to strive to fulfill the purpose for which He placed us here, we will reap all the eternal blessings He has promised the obedient, the faithful, the righteous, and the repentant. If the reader does not believe in God, he still should not deny the value of following the precepts upon which this work is based. In so doing, his quality of life can be considerably improved, human suffering can be diminished, and his happiness and contentment can be increased far beyond his imagination. Embracing these concepts will help balance one's life and put his goals in the proper perspective, thus giving a worthy purpose to his or her life.

The following terms are defined to help the reader understand this material and appreciate the meaning intended by the author. These definitions may have, more or less, an expanded meaning when applied to matters outside this work.

> **Agency.** The God-given right to respond to the forces of good or evil and the willingness to accept the responsibility for God's rewards or punishments earned therein. In other words, the right to choose and to make decisions as we see fit for any given set of circumstances, whether they be good or evil or some shade in between.

There are those who seem unwilling to accept the responsibility for their agency; nevertheless, when they appear before the bar on judgment day, they will be held accountable for the development and use of their agency. They will be unable to place the blame on those of whom they have asked to make their decisions for them or for their responsibility.

Perfection. That which is without blemish, has all knowledge, truth, wisdom, intelligence, power, glory, faith, control, is absolutely just and merciful, and exemplifies all goodness, patience and long-suffering. A person possessing this quality of perfection will have subdued every nonproductive and counterproductive characteristic, trait, need, and attribute, and have complete control and discipline over their lives. He/she will have perfected every one of the productive characteristics, traits, needs, and attributes and having all the qualities, power, and glory that are exemplified in God and Jesus Christ.

Productivity. Those thoughts and actions which lead to righteous accomplishments and growth toward perfection.

Nonproductivity. Those thoughts and actions which are passive to our growth toward perfection and which encourages us to follow the path toward destruction.

Counterproductivity. Those thoughts and actions which lead to unrighteous acts and accomplishments and are destructive to our growth toward perfection.

The purpose of life. To embrace and act upon everything that will perfect our bodies, minds, and spirits and to follow the plan of salvation and exaltation as God has outlined in the scriptures and strive for entrance into the celestial kingdom (Matthew 5:48).

Personality. The unique individuality that embodies each person. It is molded by all of our experiences, thoughts, actions, characteristics, attributes, traits, and our mental, physical, and spiritual needs.

Characteristics. Those components that comprise our personalities, appetites, attitudes, attributes, emotions, habits, and talents.

Traits. Those components which comprise our characteristics such as love, hate, humility, greed, kindness, etc.

Basic needs. Those physical, mental, and spiritual needs we all have which, when developed properly, balance our personalities, keep us healthy, and help us become the most productive individuals within the range of our capabilities.

Intelligence. The ever-increasing ability to use in wisdom and righteousness our knowledge, experience, and agency. This helps us to mature and be perfected in all phases and states of our existence. It also helps to increase our control over our environment in a very productive way.

Determining the truth. There is a method of determining the truth of all things, whether from God, man, or Satan. This applies to books, scriptures, talks, which political candidate is right, or anything of which there is a question. When we approach God in prayer, desiring to know the truth of a question, it is often done in such a haphazard way that we are unable to discern the answer when it comes. We all have our prejudices, biases, and our closed minds to certain issues; and when we kneel to pray, these biases interfere with and cloud our minds. For instance, if I were in an organization charged with the hiring and firing of personnel and I was prejudiced against a certain race there would be few, if any, of that race working for me. Even if an applicant against whose race, religion, education, or other biases, against, which I was prejudiced, was the better qualified of other applicants and I prayed about which one I should hire, my prejudice would certainly cloud the issue.

The desire to know the truth or mind of God requires that we completely open our minds to all possibilities when we pray. If we entertain any doubts or possess any predetermined attitudes concerning the subject of the prayer, we will surely be misled by the powers of darkness. For more grave matters, we should also include a twenty-four-hour fast and a period of serious meditative preparation prior to prayer. Also essential is the suspension or elimination of all prejudice and negative feelings pertaining to the subject matter. We must open our minds to God's will and the truth.

Should I desire to know if the Bible is the word of God and I possess a predetermined opinion that it is untrue being so told by my parents or others, I may well be misled by my negative attitude and will probably never know the truth. On the other hand, if I do have a sincere desire to know and precede my prayer with fasting and meditation, open my mind to all possibilities and relinquish my prejudices, the Holy Ghost will then manifest the truth to me. I will have a positive feeling that the Bible is God's word. If it is not true, I will feel very negatively toward it.

It is always necessary to read, study, and pray about that of which we wish to know the truth. The Holy Ghost can then be with and manifest the truth to us. If the fasting and prayer is done with a sincere desire to know, with an open mind, and without positive or negative prejudice, an answer will come. If the fasting and prayer are accompanied by a closed mind, predetermined negative attitudes, or any kind of prejudice or bias, the powers of darkness will surely take over.

If we were to pray to know if a religious book is the word of God and possess a predetermined attitude that it is false, the answer is going to be tainted by that attitude. Also, if we pray with a preformed opinion that it is true, we may still be misled. This applies to anything we read. All of our preset ideas, opinions, and attitudes must be eliminated. Our minds must be completely open and receptive, or inspiration from God may not be manifested. The Holy Ghost works best when our minds are open, no prejudices exist, and there are no preformed attitudes or biases to interfere with the inspiration He brings into our minds.

It is not easy to remove prejudice and open our minds to the influence of the Holy Ghost. It is equally difficult to change attitudes or mindsets, which prevents our understanding and acceptance of the truth. If these changes are not made, we could lose souls. Learning to rely on God's inspiration and strength will help us overcome these destructive influences, and we can then differentiate between the influences of good and evil more easily. As a by-product, our faith will also grow stronger.

Many ecclesiastical leaders have told their congregations that the Book of Mormon is not the word of God, that it is not true, and that we need no other scripture besides the Bible. How, then, can we overcome this mindset, this prejudice? We can start by acknowledging the possibility of it being true. If we make the mistake of saying that God could never have revealed this book to the prophet Joseph Smith on this continent, we are stating that we know the mind of God, that we are confining His actions to our beliefs or what we read in other scriptures, and we are saying that we know what is best for mankind not what is best for God. We are trying with our limited and ineffectual minds to define God's plans for mankind. Can we, in wisdom, state that God has given the world no more revelation than that found in the Bible and that He will give no more in the future? How do we know all He has done in the past or what He will do in the centuries to come? Are we in possession of all of the knowledge about Him and His plans for us? Are we really misinformed enough to believe that we know all there is to know about God, that He has revealed all He is going to reveal? This is God's world, not ours. Moses stated after seeing God and being exposed to some of His plans that "man is nothing." God does what He wants to do, and when anyone presupposes that He has done all He is going to do, they err greatly. I cannot and will not place limitations on what I believe God has done or not done or will do. I have studied, prayed, and accepted as truth the revelations He has given us. There appears to be a period of about two thousand years that we had no revelation. This does not mean there wasn't any or that there won't be any in the future. God can do what he pleases, when He pleases. I am not about to second-guess Him and put my salvation on the line. When our minds are open to truth, we can receive either confirmation or denial of the issues at stake, especially if we are sincere in our desire to know and follow the law of fasting and prayer. In making our decision about any book we question, we read and study it first, then fast, meditate, and pray to heavenly Father for the truth.

It is difficult for many of us to understand or accept the possibility of being deceived by Satan and the powers of darkness.

Satan influences us in every way he can. He will not only put temptation into our paths and minds but he will also inspire us with destructive and false revelation. His repertory for deceiving mankind is virtually unlimited and endless. His access to our minds is just as real as the manifested power of the forces for good. It must be this way or our freedom of choice, our agency, would be impaired. That is why the method for receiving inspiration from God has very strict guidelines. When not followed explicitly, we open the door for Satan to influence the answer to our prayers. If we follow these guidelines, we can know the truthfulness or falsity of all things.

In summary, these are the steps to receive inspiration from God and determine the truth of all things:

- Create a desire to know the truth concerning God's works here on earth.
- For things that may affect our salvation, fast and meditate for at least twenty-four hours prior to prayer.
- Begin and end the fast with sincere unprejudiced prayer.
- Develop an open mind and cast aside all positive or negative biases and predetermined attitudes.
- Pray with a humble, sincere, and contrite heart and with a genuine desire to know and have manifest to us the truthfulness about that for which we are praying. Include in our prayer that we will feel a burning in our bosom if truth exists and that negative thoughts will be present if it does not exist. Wait quietly and meditatively for the answer to come. Sometimes, it takes time for an answer to come. Don't be impatient, just keep praying and meditating and the answer will come. God loves us all and He will not let us down. Sometimes, a trial of our faith will precede the answer; but if we are persistent, it will come.

Just know that God's knowledge, wisdom, and intelligence is so far above ours that we never have the right to question His actions. He has total control of all of His creations, and what negativity He allows to happen to us is probably because we need to become repentant as individuals, communities, states, and nations. Our God-given adversities are here to help us grow spiritually.

2

THE PATHWAY

It is my belief that the greatest purpose for which man was placed on earth comes from Christ when he commandment us: "Be ye therefore perfect, even as your Father which is in Heaven is perfect" (Matthew 5:48). "Therefore I would that ye should be perfect even as I, or your Father who is in heaven is perfect" (3 Nephi 12:48). These two scriptures establish man's greatest and most noble goal and points the direction for the application of his greatest effort.

To better understand what is meant by perfection, let us look to our Father in heaven to whom Christ referred when he said, "Be ye perfect." First, God and Christ are resurrected beings having perfect bodies that do not age, which do not become ill, or become traumatized in any way. The glory and perfection of their bodies exceeds our limited understanding. They have perfect control over their bodies, minds, and the universe. Every cell in their bodies works in perfect celestial harmony with every other cell for whatever demands may be placed on them. Inasmuch as all illness can be traced back to their cells; therefore, God and Christ cannot become ill as their cells all function perfectly and never age or die. To completely clarify the meaning of perfection for deity, they have a perfect knowledge of everything, past, present, and future. This far exceeds what *little* knowledge we humans have. Even if we had all of the knowledge present in all of the books in every library in the world, we would not even come close to having God's knowledge. Add intelligence to the equation and the difference between God's intelligence and ours widens the gap even more. God's intelligence is infinite as is his knowledge. Add to this mix wisdom, which is infinite, and the gap widens enormously. Lastly, we must add power and glory to this combination, and we can barely begin to understand what we have to become to be perfect. Therefore, we must understand that perfection is not possible in this life. It is only possible after we are resurrected and celestialized. This doesn't mean that we shouldn't give our best efforts in becoming as perfect in this life as we possibly can. We can be perfect in paying our tithes and offerings, in filling our church and civic callings, attendance at our meetings, etc. Perfection then becomes a journey, not only in this life, but also during the millennium.

First, this ultimate physical perfection is not completely within the grasp of our mortal bodies, but we must learn the laws that govern our health and strive toward the perfection thereof as best we can with our limited knowledge. We must study the laws of nutrition, exercise, sleep, rest, and work, and abide by them. Only then can we expect to have good health and vitality. There are many other factors that affect our health, such as genetically inherited traits. When we place our faith on the prescription drugs given by the medical profession, in preference to relying on the great healing powers of deity through the priesthood, we show where our faith lies. It is a must that we adhere to the word of wisdom which is God's blessing to help us become as physically perfect as possible. Our bodies can be free from illness and pain to the extent that these factors and birth allow. By embracing all of the laws of health, we form the patterns that will allow us to work toward and ultimately gain the physical perfection our Father in Heaven has promised.

Our spirits as well as our minds and bodies need to be obedient. We should strive to lead righteous lives, accepting all church ordinances and callings gladly, and endure to the end to become as perfect as possible in this life.

Secondly, God has a perfect mind. To make His decisions and reach His goals, He has perfection in His thought processes. He has perfect control over the physical and spiritual universes and over the two great forces within it, the forces of good and evil. Again, we understand, only in a very limited way, the awesome power of His mind as it controls this universe and our destinies. To paraphrase a latter-day scripture, "As man is now, God once was, and, as God is now man may become," again, letting us know that this perfection is within our grasp, although not entirely in this mortal life.

God once made the statement, "This is my work and my glory, to bring to pass the immortality and eternal life of man" (Moses 1:39). From this we see that He has not left us to fight the battle alone. He has furnished us with an ultimate plan that, when followed, will guide us toward perfection. He has given us laws and commandments that are designed to help us grow spiritually and discipline ourselves. Ultimate control and discipline are part of the perfection we should be striving for. If we choose to ignore these laws and commandments, we miss out on the blessings associated with them. Not only that, we confine ourselves to a life of misery here on earth and in the eternities to come. There is a law irrevocably decreed in heaven before the foundations of this world upon which all blessings are predicated, "And when we obtain any blessing from God, it is by obedience to that law upon which it is predicated" (Doctrine and covenants, Section 130:20–21).

Perhaps the greatest gift God has given us is our agency, without which there could be no struggle or growth toward perfection. Can you imagine a life in which we have no right to make our own decisions, a life in which we are told what to believe, how to worship, who to worship, what jobs we must take, etc.? In such an environment, there could be no good or evil, no sin, no punishment, and no growth. We cannot grow without challenge and adversity. We would live in a form of slavery, neither knowing nor caring that perfection was possible. Where would be the challenge that allows us to grow? Where would be the incentive for excellence? As a result, we would progress neither as nations nor as individuals. We would still live in caves because there would be no incentive to live elsewhere. This is the life Satan would have forced us to live if Christ's plan had not been accepted. Agency is probably the most precious gift we have and Satan still attempts to wrest it from us. We must protect this great gift with all the weapons Christ has given us. If we do, we will not lose it.

Another great gift is adversity, which is necessary for our agency to be viable. Without it there could be neither struggle nor growth. It must be present to form a balance between the forces of good and evil. Without these powers, there could be no progress toward the perfection to which God has commanded. Righteously controlling our thinking enhances our power to choose that which is right and good.

> Thought is the essence of our deliberate creation of the awareness of self and the ideas and concepts created by our minds with the help of God, The Holy Ghost, and our Guardian Angels. It is the basis of the creation of self, and the demand to be recognized as a distinct, worthwhile, entity. Our thought processes are subject to the time-line awareness of experiences. (Memories) Thought and experience are the processes that create change. Each day is an awareness period in our lives, which reflects the changes we have undergone. Each day of our lives is different from every other day, and consequently the experiences of each day makes of us a different individual than we were the day before. Some days create a profound change, others only minute changes. Therefore, we become a different individual each day, and are at present, a composite of all the individuals that have been created and dis-created by us through the years. Each day we have lived, or had awareness, has had an impact on what we think and do, sometimes for the advancement of our spiritual growth and sometimes for its retardation. Some events, when repeated day after day in our childhood, and through-out life, have such an effect on our thoughts and minds that they literally control our actions in the form of compulsions, for the rest of our lives. (Dr. L. J. Ball)

Our minds use the combined knowledge and experience of spirit and body and the promptings of those spirits on the other side, some of which are guardian angels assigned to help us in this life and those spirits controlled by Satan that directs us toward destruction. Our thoughts come from physical memories starting at birth and extending to the present and spiritual memories that extend backward in time, essentially to infinity.

The mind is that intelligence that utilizes knowledge from both the spiritual and physical worlds but seems to have expression only in the physical. In reality, our thoughts and experiences are recorded in both the physical and spiritual brains or all life memories would be erased upon death, and life would be meaningless and useless to us. The mind could be further described as the "I am," or the intelligent awareness that makes the statement, "I exist." Everything that exists in both the physical and spiritual realms are extensions or expressions of the processing of thought and all sensory and psychic information by both the physical and spiritual brains. Therefore, everything that appears to exist does so only as our creation, for us, in our minds. This does not mean that things don't exist outside of ours mind, but rather, our awareness of the existence of things are impressions of our minds based on our past experiences, sensory inputs, and thoughts. Without our mind and our awareness, nothing could exist for us.

Most things we do in this life is preceded by thought. All of our beliefs, belief systems, and traditions are the result of judgments we have made from our sensory input and our thought processes. Since no one else controls our thinking, we become totally responsible for what we have created ourselves to be or allowed others to create us into what they would have us be. What we accept as reality is, indeed, reality for us. If our reality included our being able to walk on water, we could do so. Our limitations are set by the judgments of our thoughts and sensory input. Re-judge our thoughts and we change our reality.

Look at this world in which we live and view it from the eyes of an aborigine who has never seen our world. The planes, the cars, our phones, the computers, and all of the other amenities of life we enjoy would appear impossible to him while we take them for granted. Unlimited thinking or thought opens the limitless possibilities of the mind's potential. The mind is man's most powerful tool. "As a man thinketh in his heart, so is he." "Nothing is impossible to him who believes." These are biblical references that are intended to extend man's abilities if he will but grasp and hold on to the concept that nothing is impossible.

Why does there appear to be such a discrepancy between science and religion?

This is because man does not comprehend them in their proper perspective. Science is only man's feeble attempt at understanding, measuring, explaining, and experimenting with God's creations and laws and trying to comprehend his physical environment. In the final analysis, there will be no discrepancy. Man is incapable of grasping, but a very small portion of the whole of God's creations therefore all of man's measuring and theorizing will never be complete until God reveals to us his entire creation.

To perfect our minds, we must keep our physical bodies healthy by obeying the laws of health. This will help to give us clear minds with which to think. "For as he thinketh in his heart, so is he" (Proverbs 23:7). Our thoughts control our goals, desires, attitudes, appetites, emotions, habits, talents, wants, and certain needs such as our desire for sex. Therefore, the controlling of our mind is the key to our perfection. There is no greater power on earth than that of a well-disciplined mind—one that is open, righteous, productive in its designs, and goal oriented toward perfection—and which acts through God's limitless powers and laws.

Man's greatest accomplishments had their beginnings in the mind. Man's greatest evils also started there. To a large extent, the direction he takes depends upon preaccepted values and predetermined decisions. It also depends on his present response to the forces of good and evil in exercising his agency. The most arduous task man can and should undertake in this life is that of becoming as perfect as possible. To gain a greater insight, we must examine the meaning of perfection.

The commandment, to be perfect, pertains to our complete being and personality. It would be meaningless if it were unattainable. To be reachable, a method must be provided, not only to show us the way but also to help and guide us every step of the way. It is the intent of this book to motivate us to study the scriptures, seek God's help by praying to help clarify the meaning of some concepts, which can help us become perfect.

Embracing the commandment that the perfection of our minds, bodies, and spirits is the ultimate purpose, for which man was placed on earth, is necessary to our understanding of the roles we should assume in this life. It is necessary that we accept the fact that perfection cannot be accomplished by any other means than those outlined by God's teachings. Otherwise, the seeker of perfection will be misled by the teachings of man and the lure of earthly pleasures, which are many and attractive enough to deceive and pull us away from our ultimate goal of attaining perfection.

We must recognize and accept the truth that there are two forces at work in this world: the forces of good and the forces of evil. These two forces influence us in every decision we make, first in the mind, then in action. God has given us our agency to respond to whichever force we choose. Sometimes, our choice to respond is influenced by actions taken years or even generations ago. We, or a progenitor, has selected certain ways of reacting to specific situations such as disciplining our children or responding to anger or fear, etc. Having embraced a given response and then having it reinforced down through the years and ages creates in us a pattern that is passed from parent to child, sometimes for generations. Many bad traditions passed from parent to child go unrecognized and are, more often than not, considered to be productive to our growth, but the opposite is true.

Each of us should closely examine the way we love and discipline our children, such as the things we say in front of them and how we respond to anger, fear, or other emotions. We are molding our children's habits so they are not only affected now but may also affect lives for generations to come. We may be treating our children the way our great-great-grandparents treated their children. If our traditions are counterproductive or destructive to their spiritual growth, we need to break the cycle now and be rid of them forever. If they are productive, we need to encourage and magnify their development. Every conscious or unconscious response we make to these two great forces falls into one of the following three categories:

- Productivity: Our thoughts and the actions taken under the umbrella of God's laws, commandments, and ordinances, which helps us and others to grow and progress toward perfection.
- Nonproductivity: Our thoughts and actions which are passive to our growth toward perfection.
- Counterproductivity: Our thoughts and actions which are destructive to our struggle toward perfection.

The pursuit of counterproductive activities will ultimately guarantee our enslavement and destruction, denying agency both to us and to others. It embraces the forces of evil, those thoughts and temptations which entice and promise great happiness and joy but which deliver nothing but pain and destruction. Counterproductivity embraces all destructive thoughts and actions, denying God's teachings.

All of our actions are not necessarily preceded by thought. Some are reactions to habit. Some result from influences or pressures from the forces of good or evil on any of the seven basic characteristics: appetites, needs, attitudes, attributes, emotions, habits, and talents. When we allow ourselves to respond to any of these characteristics in a destructive manner over a period of time, they become automatic and have the ability to cause an action not preceded by thought. The forces of evil can also influence our actions by directly stimulating any basic emotion, element, characteristic, trait, or attribute. In this way, our behavior becomes controlled in a nonproductive or counterproductive way without conscious effort. Our productive behavior is also influenced in these same ways and should be encouraged so that we may develop and improve our righteous endeavors. The seven basic characteristics are each made of many traits, which will be discussed later.

Our mortal perfection can be complete only when all seven characteristics have been purged of the non and counterproductive or destructive components such as hate, greed, selfishness, anger, etc. and are then replaced with love, charity, humility, serenity, etc. When trying to help others with their growth, we must always look inward first because human nature causes us to "look through a glass darkly," in other words, the aberrations in our own personality may cause us to have a distorted view of others, and even ourselves, at times. Some people have no ability to see any imperfection within themselves. Someone who has been taught racial prejudice from childhood will have a very difficult time being objective about anything pertaining to that race. How can we help someone grow when we harbor some prejudice in our hearts concerning them?

Another problem many of us express is that we accept normal as being acceptable. To be normal is to be approved by us and our society. Herein lies one of Satan's greatest traps. If being normal is acceptable to everyone, then why try for excellence or perfection? When we are different, society may label us as prudes, as "better than thou" or self-righteous. "After all," they reason, "how can we have fun if we can't smoke, drink, carouse, gossip, etc.?"

The state of being normal may shift between perfection and imperfection. In one society, killing, rape, greed avarice, etc., may be acceptable and normal but not acceptable in another. In this period of time and society, "normal" is shifting away from perfection. The pendulum can be made to swing the other direction, only if enough of us begin again to work toward perfection, thus making the pressure felt in our society, to drive "normal" in the direction of righteousness. I believe that being normal or average is not acceptable to God. Should it be acceptable to us?

By applying the principles of productivity, nonproductivity, and counterproductivity to every aspect of our lives gives us a yardstick by which we can determine if we are on the path to perfection. We also have a measure to determine whether the organizations to which we belong—clubs, churches, groups, towns, states, countries, etc.— are helping or hindering us in attaining our righteous goals.

If perfection of the mental, physical, and spiritual states of each individual personality as set forth by the laws and commandments of God is not the prime motivating force of these organizations, they are a cancer and are destructive to our progress. Every effort should be made to change the direction in which their control takes us. It should be toward helping us become more productive, more loving, having more freedom, etc. At the very least, we need to ensure that they are ineffective in their attempt to direct our personal progress down a road we do not wish to take.

In our quest for perfection we, as individual personalities, must strive to make these seven basic characteristics totally productive. Each of these characteristics has many elements that need to be identified and analyzed, and through the use of all means available, changed when necessary to become more productive and unifying. These characteristics have already been identified, and many of their associated elements will be identified later in this chapter.

The perfection process is never easy and encompasses every aspect of our daily lives. It is a process that will be slow for some and fast for others. Lucifer will introduce discouragement into our efforts every step of the way. There will be times when we may feel it is not worth the effort. This again is Satan's promptings. We must not heed them. Instead, we should learn to pray continually for our Lord to give us strength, wisdom, and intelligence to sustain us and help us at all times, every minute of every day to overcome Satan's evil influences. Remember, God will allow adversity to come into our lives when we ask for strength. He will often allow things to be very rough, all to help in our growth and sanctification.

In striving toward perfection, we each need to eradicate nonproductive and counterproductive elements or traits through a continuing program of identification, analysis, and selection. It is easy to identify the nonproductive and counterproductive elements on which we must work. Most of us know which areas our attention is needed the most. We should first concentrate our efforts on these areas, and as they are expunged, we then go to those which are less pressing. The original list we prepare may contain many destructive elements in need of attention. If we attempt to work on all of them at once, we will become discouraged and probably give up.

When accompanied by fasting and prayer, there are two universal laws that can help us in the perfection process. The first one is into that area, in which we expend the greatest energy, the greatest results will occur. If we expend our energies on a diversity of things, little will be accomplished. It's like trying to build fifty houses at once, very little progress will be made and we soon become disheartened. However, if we were to expend all our efforts on just one or even two houses, we could see the progress and would get a great amount of satisfaction in watching them mature to completion. The same applies to the perfection process. Select one or two destructive components at a time to work on and we can see the progress and feel the satisfaction and joy of overcoming. Work on each element for a period of two or three months or until that element has been conquered and replaced by its opposite productive element. For example, if we want to rid our personality of hatred for someone, we must go through the steps of repentance; and through forgiveness, this hate will surely be replaced with love.

The other law closely associated with the first is the accomplishment of any productive goal can only be realized by creating a burning desire then gaining the specialized knowledge and expertise required to attain that goal. Then, use concentrated and persistent effort to accomplish it, always with the help of God. If we want to teach, we must gain the knowledge and expertise required before we will even be considered. Would one go to a physician who had never been to school? Certainly not! Would one attempt to be a farmer without gaining the knowledge and expertise required? We would certainly fail if we tried.

What is the difference then to attempt the greatest task God has commanded of us—our perfection? We first, must create the desire, then must gain the specialized knowledge and skill, and must be persistent. The winner is the one who keeps on trying regardless of the obstacles. The loser will fail because he may prefer to bypass the ridicule associated with losing by not even trying.

There is one last ingredient that must be present before we can become involved with the attainment of any goal, and that is self-dissatisfaction. This is the condition wherein we find ourselves so dissatisfied with an aspect of our lives that we decide to act on that dissatisfaction and do whatever is necessary to make a meaningful change. Self-dissatisfaction may be a spontaneous decision or it may be cultivated. In most cases, it must be cultivated because we, for the most part, are already mostly satisfied with ourselves or we are already in the process of making the changes.

The cultivation of self-dissatisfaction may be accomplished in several ways. First, we must compare all of our characteristics with those of a known perfected being—Jesus Christ—and identify those traits on which we need to work. To do this, we can make a graph (or number line) ranging from a minus nine to zero for the counterproductive traits and from zero to a plus nine for the productive traits. Then, with all honesty, we should rate ourselves for each of the traits listed. This will help in making a determination of the degree of our perfection. For each destructive component we choose to work on, list them in a separate 3"×5" card. A list of many destructive characteristics or traits that often need our effort has been provided at the end of this chapter. To make the list more complete and personalized, the reader may add other destructive characteristics or traits. Next comes an analysis of why we feel the way we do and which of the characteristics are involved. Until we understand why we react to the identified stimuli, it will be extremely difficult to generate enough desire to make the change; therefore, our efforts are unlikely to bear fruit.

After we have made our analysis and understand why we react as we do, we are ready for the next steps, which are prayer, meditation, affirmations, and if necessary, fasting. (Meditation is a thoughtful pondering of the problem.) Again, we should concentrate our efforts on one or two traits at a time or we will be overwhelmed by the magnitude of what we want to accomplish and nothing will get done.

When we take a close look at our imperfections, our dissatisfaction with them should be great enough to help us change. If this desire is intense enough to encourage us to act in a positive manner, we have acquired self-dissatisfaction. If the desire is not strong enough to help us take the necessary steps to change, then more intense prayer and sincere meditation may be required. To ensure that we are satisfied with our lives as they are is one of Satan's greatest endeavors; another is apathy.

We should never be satisfied unless we know we are perfected. In conjunction with prayer, fasting, and meditation the tool *auto-suggestion* may also be used to help accomplish our goals.

Autosuggestion or affirmation is the suggestion of the mind to itself of ideas that produce actual results and changes. It also helps to solidify our commitment to accomplish our goals and reinforce our prayers and meditation. When I use affirmation, I write my goal on a 5"×8" card. Let us assume that we lack self-confidence. The goal then, is to build self-confidence (a destructive element that needs to be eliminated). On a 5"×8" card, place the following: My goal is to increase my self-confidence and to increase my ability to get things done.

> With the infinite help and power of God, Jesus Christ, the Holy Ghost, and with unwavering faith, gratitude, and their unconditional love for me and me for them, I now choose to increase my confidence each day until I am able to accomplish my goals with no resistance. I will now definitely act on this important affirmation from this moment on and forever. So be it.

This is one basic format for increasing the effectiveness of perfecting the traits of righteousness and love.

If you are conquering one of the components of unrighteousness the following affirmation is very effective.

> With the infinite help and power of God, Jesus Christ and the Holy Ghost, and with intense faith, gratitude, and their unconditional love for me and me for them, I now choose to expunge and eliminate the unrighteous trait of anger from my personality. I will now definitely act on this important affirmation with unwavering faith, determination, and irreversible willpower from this moment on and forever. So be it.

Every morning upon arising and every night before going to bed, the selected affirmations should be read aloud with meaning and intensity at least four or five times to gain the maximum benefit. Then, with sincerity, we must get down on our knees and pray to our Heavenly Father for success in our endeavors.

This, still, isn't enough. We must do things that build self-confidence. We should remove all obstacles that control our performance, stretch the limits of our abilities, and take on and complete new and challenging activities and projects and our self-confidence will mature and grow toward perfection.

This same principle applies to each of the traits listed at the end of this chapter. Notice the examples on the 5"×8" card. There is nothing negative and nothing counterproductive listed. Care should be taken as we write on these cards that nothing negative or destructive is used.

Again, as we read our cards aloud to ourselves, we should read them with emotion, with feeling, and with intensity and conviction. This will give meaning and impact to our subconscious mind where the change must occur. The principle works most effectively when used in this manner. To make it even more effective, record and play it as a sleep learning technique. This same technique may be used to gain self-dissatisfaction.

Here are some other suggestions you may wish to add to your affirmations.

- I am becoming healthier every day.
- I am becoming slimmer and more vibrant every day.

- I will have unlimited energy today.
- I will be free from anger today.
- I am free from the desire to punish myself.
- I have no desire to be punished by others.
- I will sleep and rest well.
- I will be free of debt.
- I am free of fear.
- I am free of self-doubt.
- I am loving, kind, and understanding.
- I am honest.

We should bear in mind that the success of our endeavors depends on the degree of our commitment and the intensity of our desire to succeed.

Our Lord has informed us that His purpose is the everlasting and eternal life of man. Won't He then be more joyous if we are closer to perfection when we approach the judgment seat than if we make little or no effort? I'm sure there are other ways to promote self-dissatisfaction. If this method doesn't work, then search for one that will. Don't quit. The world is full of those who give up. To surrender is to follow Satan.

The following is a chart giving a partial list of productive and counterproductive components. It may be added to as the spirit directs. Each of us has our own individualized problems to overcome to humble us and help us grow. Add these to the list and use the same techniques listed above to gain control over them.

The continual elimination of nonproductive and counterproductive (unrighteous) characteristics or traits and replacing them with productive (righteous) characteristics or traits constitutes the ultimate law of repentance, which I believe is necessary to inherit the highest kingdom of God. Repentance is the second of the five basic principles of the gospel or requirements that must be embraced before we can return to and live with God again. The first four basic principles are outlined in the Fourth Article of Faith: (*History of the Church*, Vol. 4, pp. 535–541).

1. Faith in our Lord Jesus Christ.
2. Repentance.

3. Baptism by immersion by one holding the proper authority for the remission of sin.
4. The laying on of hands by one having the proper authority for the gift of the Holy Ghost.
5. Continued obedience to God's laws and commandments.

These principles will be discussed at length later in this book. Most of us have a tendency to shy away from wanting to know our standing regarding our perfection with respect to Christ. Perhaps it is because if we knew and felt we weren't perfect enough, we would have to do something about it. The following lists have been designed to allow us to look within ourselves and get a general idea of just how perfect or imperfect we actually are on a scale of one to nine.

To gain this knowledge, you should rate yourself for each of the productive (righteous) and the counterproductive (unrighteous) or destructive elements listed. Be as objective and honest as possible, and if more input is needed, have a close family member, spouse, father, mother, etc., also give you a rating. This will give you a good correlation and may also let you know that others do not necessarily share your view of yourself. This can have a very devastating effect on you if you are not prepared for it. Accept their rating in love and not anger. They are just trying to do as you have asked. They are also trying to be objective. You would not want them to lie, would you?

Approximately two months after you have made your first evaluation, it is time for another. Go through the complete process again, not just the one or two elements you have been working on. Things change, people change, our views of ourselves change, and other's assessments of us change. Again, be as objective as possible; and if you feel it is necessary, let the same person who evaluated you the first time do it again. Then, compare the two evaluations and see if there has been any progress. A lack of self-esteem may color your self-evaluation, so try and pick times when you feel as good about yourself as possible. This will make the rating as honest as it can be. If there are other factors that may influence the outcome of your evaluation; take them into consideration. Make it viable so it can be depended upon.

Remember that we are all children of God and that we must always rely on His arm not man's. He has all knowledge, all intelligence, all wisdom, and all power. Therefore, as mere humans with our very limited knowledge, intelligence, wisdom, and very little power, we should never question His actions as He controls everything in our universe and all life on earth. The reasons for God's action or inaction concerning us or this world are so far beyond our comprehension that we must accept what He does without complaining. Be thankful for His guidance, inspiration, and revelations, which will bring us back to Him. Agency is so important to Him that He will not violate ours in the face of all of the afflictions, ailments, and trials we must pass through, especially when our prayers are sincere and warranted.

The self-evaluation listed below is accomplished by putting the number that most honestly applies to our current standing on each of these productive traits: 1 is low and 9 is high. Place the number above the trait that you select. If you have little trouble with #1 being active in church activities and responsibilities, place the number that most applies in intensity above it.

When you select the one or two traits that most need your attention, create an affirmation following the basic format listed above for each trait then follow the procedure as noted.

RIGHTEOUS, PRODUCTIVE, UNIFYING TRAITS
(Components of Love)

Active___ Ambitious___ Appreciative___ Aware___ Benevolent___
Charitable___ Clean___ Committed___ Compassionate___
Confident___ Considerate___ Consistent___ Courageous___
Creative___ Dedicated___ Discerning___ Durable___
Empathetic___ Equality___ Faith___ Forgiving___ Friendly___
Goal oriented___ Gentle___ Godly___ Helpful___ Honest___
Honorable___ Hopeful___ Humble___ Humorous___ Industrious___
Inquisitive___ Has integrity___ Intents___ Just___ Kind___
Knowledgeable___ Loving___ Loyal___ Meek___ Merciful___
Meditative___ Modest___ Moral___ Motivated___ Obedient___
Organized___ Patient___ Persistent___ Prepared___ Prompt___
Pure___ Repentant___ Resilient___ Resolute___ Responsible___
Reverent___ Righteous___ Sacrificing___ Self-disciplined___
Self-esteemed___ Self-reliant___ Sensitive___ Serene___ Sharing___

Spiritually stable___ Steadfast___ Strong___ Studious___
Success oriented___ Surrendering___ Tactful___ Temperate___
Thoughtful___ Trusting___ Virtuous___ Watchful___.

UNRIGHTEOUS, COUNTERPRODUCTIVE, OR DESTRUCTIVE TRAITS
(Components of hate)

These are qualities of being. Give yourself a rating of –1 to 9, 9 being the least acceptable. If you're having real trouble with anger assign 9 to it. If you have little trouble with it, assign 1 to it. Continue with the evaluation until you have assigned a number to each of the destructive traits. For instance, with Anger, 7 would indicate that you have a real problem with it. Never select more than two components of hate at a time to expunge.

Anger___ Apathy___ Avarice___ Blindness___ Callousness___
Cheating___ Contemptible___ Contentious___ Controlling___
Cowardly___ Cruel___ Denying___ Devilish___ Dishonest___
Disloyal___ Disobedient___ Disorderly___ Disorganized___
Disdainful___ Destructive___ doubtful___ Dreadful___
Enslaving___ Envying___ Evil-minded___ Yielding___
Gossiping___ Greedy___ Hostile___ Hardhearted___
Hateful___ Intolerant___ Irreverent___ Irresponsible___
Insincere___ Jealous___ Lazy___ Lying___ Lustful___
Malevolent___ Malicious___ Mean___ Merciless___ Negative___
Not meditative___ Not persistent___ Not seeking___ Polluting___
Prejudiced___ Prideful___ Procrastinating___ Revengeful___
Sad___ Selfish___ Self-centered___ Sloppy___ Slothful___
Strife oriented___ Surrendering to evil___ Tactless___ Thankless___
Thoughtless___ Uncaring___ Unchaste___ Uncommitting___
Uncreative___ Undedicated___ Undependable___ Undiscerning___
Undisciplined___ Unempathetic___ Unenduring___ Unforgiving___
Unlawful___ Unmotivated___ Unprayerful___ Unprepared___
Unrepentant___ Unrighteous___ Unskilled___ Unsuccessful___
Unsure___ Unteachable___ Untrustworthy___ Unvirtuous___
Vacillating___ Weak___.

We should use these lists humbly, prayerfully, and with a real intent to perfect ourselves as best we can under our current circumstances to the extent that we can return to and live with our Eternal Father in heaven.

As the 5"×8" cards are used, try to visualize yourself as having reached your goal, creating mental images of yourself as being in a state of perfection concerning the traits you are working on. This will greatly increase the effectiveness of your efforts. Also, you should constantly approach your Father in heaven in sincere prayer and with humility. Satan will endeavor to stop your progress at all costs, so just reading this work and agreeing with its concepts is not enough. We should reread and consistently apply on a daily basis the steps outlined herein.

The following are the ten steps of growth to the kingdom of God. Those not desiring eternal marriage for both men and women may bypass step 10. Since steps 7 and 8 are dealing with priesthood, they apply only to men and are bypassed by women. Bear in mind that bypassing step 10 only allows us to obtain the lower of the three degrees in the celestial kingdom.

Partaking of the everlasting covenant of eternal marriage can allow you to attain the highest degree in the celestial kingdom. These are the 10 steps:

1. Recognize the existence of God and the need for obedience.
2. Have a desire for spiritual growth, salvation, and exaltation.
3. Acquire faith in God, His son Jesus Christ, and the Holy Ghost.
4. Undergo the process of repentance and make it a personal daily activity.
5. Undergo the ordinance of baptism for the remission of sins by one who has the authority.
6. Receive the gift of the Holy Ghost by the laying on of hands by one who has the authority.
7. Receive the Aaronic priesthood by ordination through the proper line of authority and obey all laws and covenants pertaining to it (males only).

EXPANDING OUR LIGHT

8. Receive the Melchizedek priesthood by ordination and through the proper line of authority and obey all laws and covenants pertaining to it (males only).
9. Receive your endowments in the holy temple of God.
10. Be sealed to your mate and offspring for time and all eternity in the holy temple of God. Always be repentant, faithful, and obedient to God's laws and commandments.

There is no other pathway to the kingdom of God. There is no way to bypass any of these steps (except as mentioned above) and achieve the celestial kingdom.

Below are ten components necessary to grow from step to step:

1. Trust in, rely on, and obey God's commandments and have faith in Christ, God, and the Holy Ghost. Recognize your sins, repent, be baptized, receive the Holy Ghost, and participate in all of the saving temple ordinances.
2. When you sin and possess imperfections, go through the process of repentance. Do not procrastinate the day of your repentance.
3. Increase your knowledge daily, especially righteous knowledge.
4. Perform righteous activities daily; do the right thing because it is the right thing to do.
5. Always serve God and mankind unselfishly on a daily basis.
6. Be charitable; love God and mankind.
7. Be humble, patient, kind, meek, compassionate, honest, have integrity, and be truthful at all times and in all places.
8. Seek for that which is good, righteousness, and beautiful.
9. Always be prayerful.
10. Seek for excellence in all endeavors; persevere to the end.

Here are eleven of the most-used paths leading away from the celestial kingdom.

1. Disobey God's laws and commandments.
2. Have an inordinate desire for fun, games, and pleasure.
3. Have an inordinate desire for wealth and power.

4. Be selfish, greedy, prideful, dishonest, hateful, and prejudicial.
5. Have uncontrolled lustful thoughts and actions.
6. Fail at self-discipline.
7. Fail to attempt to perfect your talents, productive traits, and characteristics.
8. Place any activity or organization between you and the pathway to God.
9. Embrace any religion, cult, or organization which is in opposition to the Gospel of Jesus Christ.
10. Always give in to temptation, never repent, and never help your fellow man.
11. Ignore the need for baptism and all of the saving ordinances.

> "When you are in any contest, you should work as if there were - to the very last minute - a chance to lose it."
> —Dwight D. Eisenhower,
> Commander of the European Theater of
> Operation during World War II.

The perfection of our righteous traits and characteristics cannot be accomplished completely in this earth life but should be considered a sacred journey throughout life and during the millennium where the perfection of our spirits, minds, and bodies will be completed, preparing us for the celestial kingdom and godhood.

3

ADULTHOOD VERSUS MATURITY

As I have studied it out in my mind, I believe that spiritual growth embodies the differences between adulthood and maturity. To reach adulthood, all one must do is grow old. Being an adult doesn't mean that a person has any special gifts or that he is righteous or evil. It merely means that he has grown to be an adult. He doesn't have to be anything but what he is. He can be a murderer, rapist, robber, philanderer, or whatever. He can also be a great spiritual leader, artist, tycoon, or just about anything and still be an adult, which means he can express any of the righteous or unrighteous traits and characteristics and still be an adult.

To be a totally complete mature human being entails being self-disciplined and so self-assured that no matter what others say about, do to, or think of you, you remain unruffled and unaffected. Your self-confidence is not challenged and you have a very high self-esteem, but are not prideful. Your faith has been developed to the maximum extent possible in this life. You can accomplish most anything you set your mind to do. You have an infallible faith in God, His Son Jesus Christ, the Holy Ghost, and the atonement. You do not judge individuals by their actions. Your love for mankind is unconditional. You are always kind, considerate, humble, meek, patient, have unquestionable integrity, and express all of the righteous components and traits. You have complete confidence in all you do. Anger, greed, hate, envy, and all other unrighteous traits controlled by Satan have been overcome, conquered, and risen above and expunged. The unrighteous elements are not expressed or suppressed but have been eradicated from your personality. I know of no one that has progressed this far. Most of us fall somewhere in between complete maturity or perfection and adulthood.

Love, humility, compassion, tenderness, kindness, helpfulness, and all other righteous characteristics and traits are expressed and displayed as part of your persona.

Webster's New World Dictionary defines mature as:

1. Full grown, as plants or animals, ripe as fruit.
2. Fully developed, *perfected*, etc. ...
3. Of a state of full development: as, of *mature* age. ...(italics added for emphasis)

The word *perfected* stands out because Mathew 5:48 gives us the commandment: "Be ye therefore perfect, even as your Father which is in heaven is perfect." I believe this commandment "to become perfect" is to strive above all other commandments except for love and charity. We need to be even with God and Christ. Since maturity and perfection are close to synonymous, it would enhance all of us to work to perfect all of the elements of righteousness and expunge all of the elements of unrighteousness. In so doing, we become closer to perfection and maturity. We then become more like our Heavenly Father and our Savior Jesus Christ.

To become mature and perfect is not an easy task. One must learn to completely control his or her thoughts, actions, and words to be completely in accord with God's and Christ's teachings and commandments.

It matters not how much monetary success we have in this life if our spiritual life does not equal or surpass it.

It matters not how little monetary success we have if we don't have spiritual growth.

There is nothing as important as spiritual growth in this life. Once we truly understand this and embrace the concept, our lives can or will make some magnificent changes.

In other words, spiritual growth becomes more important than any other endeavor in this life, except to love the Lord thy God with all thy might, mind, and soul and to love thy neighbor as thyself.

Lucifer will do anything and everything, twenty-four hours a day, every day, to thwart our spiritual growth. He wants us to be miserable in hell with him where we have eternity to realize what we have or have not done.

To thwart Satan and his minions in their endeavors to make of us his slaves, we need to recognize and expunge every single nuance and element of evil lurking behind every thought and action we experience. We should also examine what effect they have on our physical, spiritual, mental, and emotional states and the deleterious effects they have on our everyday lives. We must also recognize that every righteous thought and action counters and eliminates our evil thoughts and actions as we repent. It behooves us to learn to hate with every fiber of our beings the evils that exist in this world and what they can do to us if we remain uncaring or accepting of them. Don't hate the perpetrators, just the evils. We should then wipe clean each and every thought and action that Satan has prompted us to condone or act upon. Also, we should eliminate each and every thought inspired by him and avoid the actions associated with them.

We must learn to hate these evil promptings to the extent that even the very appearance of their presence in our minds can't be tolerated.

God's children are challenged every second of every day with afflictions, temptations, problems, sickness, illnesses of every sort, and obstacles that would create a plethora of evil responses. It is not that we have these trials and tribulations but how we respond to them that is important. We can play the victim (poor me) or we can do what God would have us do—take the challenges as strength and character builders and overcome, conquer, and rise above them with the help of God, Christ, the Holy Ghost, and our guardian angels. When we give in to Satan's influences, we become susceptible to greater and more lethal evils. Choosing this path leads to our enslavement and makes it much more difficult to regain our place with God in the eternal world.

Our mansions could be with God in His kingdom, or if we choose, we may decide to be in hell with Lucifer.

This life is a very serious matter—we can fight with our Lord and Savior Jesus Christ or we can become indentured and fight with Satan against the light of Christ.

We can choose to be soldiers for whichever side we lean toward—light or darkness, happiness or misery, eternal progression or eternal anguish where spiritual growth no longer exists and what knowledge, wisdom, and intelligence we have is of no value.

We could learn to be patient in our afflictions, adversities, and challenges; they can make us strong if we tolerate them well.

Remember, John the Baptist prepared the way for Christ's ministry. Satan is trying to prepare the way for our destruction before Christ's second coming.

4

PERFECTION

In chapters 4 through 20, this document will discuss the meaning of some of the righteous, productive, and unifying components or traits of love listed in chapter 2. It will help the reader understand the depth of influence these characteristics and traits have on our daily activities and should help us continue to perfect our lives so we can reside with God in the celestial kingdom.

The perfection that Christ commanded of us is the state which exists when we are spotless; without blemish; have all knowledge, all truth, all wisdom, all intelligence, all power, all glory; are in complete control over our lives; and are absolutely just and merciful and exemplifies all goodness and righteousness. It is that state for which all men and women should strive and direct a goodly part of their energies. It is to become like God and Christ.

Throughout the scriptures, God has given us the commandment to be perfect. He does not give us commandments we cannot obey or which are beyond our capabilities. He never promises that obedience to His commandments will be easy. He does give us the guidelines that help to accomplish what He commands. Some commandments, like perfection, are given as a journey to be strived for as best we can in our sojourn here on earth, with the possibility of reaching it during the millennium.

> And it came to pass that I, Nephi, said unto my father: I will go and do the things which the Lord hath commanded, for I know that the Lord giveth no commandments unto the children of men, save he shall prepare a way for them that they may accomplish the thing which he commandeth them. (1 Nephi 3:7) Book of Mormon

Many of the big obstacles to perfection are our wants and desires. We all get caught up in the desire to own things and to accumulate things which make us prideful. Pride need not be counterproductive, but often we use it to raise ourselves above others. "I have something you don't have" or "mine is better than yours, so I am better than you." It is very difficult to continually keep our desires on a spiritual plane; in fact, it is impossible. We conduct our lives with a dependency on physical things like homes, cars, food, telephones, etc. Perhaps the key is to keep the physical and spiritual needs in perspective, balanced, and tuned to each other. The house becomes a home in which spiritual values are stressed instead of being a showplace where physical objects are displayed and worshiped and even used as elevators for our social standing.

Cars are another status symbol, as are boats and many other collectibles. Wouldn't it be much better to collect controls like control over anger, greed, hatred, prejudice, malice, etc.? These spiritual collectibles have eternal values and eternal uses. As we view the bigger picture which has the greater value: a showy car or control over our counterproductive traits? Satan makes it easy for us to use these destructive traits, and none of them will take us down the road to perfection. He will make the roads seem attractive. Roads that promise much happiness and joy but deliver nothing but misery. If there is any question about whether a decision will bring us closer to or further from perfection, we must ask ourselves this question, "Is this choice or decision productive to my growth toward perfection or not?" If there is any question about the answer, then pray about it and rely on the Lord for the answer. Essentially, pride is the exclusion of God in the obtaining of our wants, needs, and desires. If God is included in obtaining anything, pride goes by the wayside.

If the process of perfection were not needed as so many of today's Christian religions believe, why are there so many scriptural references to it?

Perfection, when examined from an eternal perspective, is the complete control or discipline of all our nonproductive and counterproductive characteristics, destructive elements, and attributes and traits and the complete acceptance and expression of all of the traits and elements of love and righteousness. What a gift to be able to present to our Heavenly Father!

The roots for the perfection process are found in love—love for God who has given us the opportunity to prove ourselves through obedience, love for our fellow man (without which there could be no perfection), and love for ourselves. Without self-love, it is impossible to generate a desire for perfection. Do we love ourselves enough to conquer anger, hatred, fear, etc.? If we have little love for ourselves, then we should repent of something we have done wrong, and we may be living in a sea of self-pity, guilt, worthlessness, and low self-esteem. Self-pity may be satisfying in a sick sort of way and will inevitably come between us and our strive for perfection. Can you imagine God embracing the concept of self-pity? The more we know about our capabilities and our personalities, the more we can act on the knowledge we have and the closer we come to perfection.

Satan has a million sidetracks in our everyday living, especially in the religions that teach us how to conduct our lives but not how to perfect ourselves. Why then are there so many references in the scriptures relating to perfection? Some are merely references and some are commandments that we cannot ignore. If we believe the Bible, both the Old and the New Testament, to be the word of God, we should not ignore so important a concept as becoming perfect. Below, I have included other scriptures that are related to the subject to expand our understanding and help us know that God's plan includes us all and that there is always hope.

Since there is no way we can become completely perfect in this life, we can become as perfect as this life will allow. We can be obedient to God's laws and commandments and participate in all His ordinances. I'm sure this is what He meant when He commanded us to be perfect.

Here are many of the available scriptural references pertaining to perfection:

> These are the generations of Noah: Noah was a just man and perfect in his generations, and Noah walked with God. (Genesis 6:9)

> And when Abram was ninety years old and nine, the Lord appeared to Abram, and said unto him, I am the Almighty God; walk before me, and be thou perfect. (Genesis 17:1)

> Thou shalt be perfect with the Lord thy God. (Deuteronomy 18:13)

> But thou shalt have a perfect and just weight, a perfect and just measure shalt thou have: that thy days may be lengthened in the land which the Lord thy God giveth thee. (Deuteronomy 25:15)

> He is the Rock, his work is perfect: for all his ways are judgment: a God of truth and without iniquity, just and right is he. (Deuteronomy 32:4)

> As for God, his way is perfect; the word of the Lord is tried: he is a buckler, to all them that trust in him. (2 Samuel 22:31)

> Let your heart therefore be perfect with the Lord our God, to walk in his statutes, and to keep his commandments, as at this day. (1 Kings 8:61)

> For it came to pass, when Solomon was old, that his wives turned away his heart after other gods: and his heart was not perfect with the Lord his God, as was the heart of David his father. (1 Kings 11:4)

> For the eyes of the Lord run to and fro throughout the whole earth, to shew himself strong in the behalf of them whose heart is perfect toward him. Herein thou hast done

foolishly: therefore from henceforth thou shalt have wars. (2 Chronicles 16:9)

There was a man in the land of Uz, whose name was Job; and that man was perfect and upright, and one that feared God, and eschewed evil. (Job 1:1)

The law of the Lord is perfect, converting the soul: the testimony of the Lord is sure, making wise the simple. (Psalms 19:7)

Out of Zion, the perfection of beauty, God hath shined. (Psalms 50:2)

But the path of the just is as the shining light, that shineth more and more unto the perfect day. (Proverbs 4:18)

Be ye therefore perfect even as your Father which is in Heaven is perfect. (Matthew 5:48)

Therefore I would that ye should be perfect even as I, or your Father who is in heaven is perfect. (3 Nephi 12:48)

Jesus said unto him, if thou wilt be perfect, go and sell that thou hast, and give to the poor, and thou shalt have treasure in heaven: and come and follow me. (Matthew 19:21)

The disciple is not above his master: but every one that is perfect shall be as his master. (Luke 6:40)

And that which fell among thorns are they, which when they have heard, go forth, and are choked with cares and riches and pleasures of this life, and bring no fruit to perfection. (Luke 8:14)

And he said unto them, Go ye, and tell that fox, Behold, I cast out devils, and I do cures today and tomorrow, and the third day I shall be perfected. (Luke 13:32)

As thou hast sent me into the world, even so have I also sent them into the world.

And for their sakes I sanctify myself, that they also might be sanctified through the truth.

Neither pray I for these alone, but for them also which shall believe on me through their word;

That they all may be one; as thou, Father, are in me, and I in thee, that they also may be one in us: that the world may believe that thou has sent me.

And the glory which thou gavest me I have given them; that they may be one, even as we are one:
I in them, and thou in me, that they may be made perfect in one; and that the world may know that thou hast sent me, and hast loved them, as thou hast loved me. (John 17:18–23)

Now I beseech you, brethren, by the name of our Lord Jesus Christ, that ye all speak the same thing, and that there be no divisions among you; but that ye be perfectly joined together in the same mind and in the same judgment. (1 Corinthians 1:10)

And I, brethren, when I came to you, came not with excellency of speech or of wisdom, declaring unto you the testimony of God.

For I determined not to know anything among you, save Jesus Christ, and him Crucified.

And I was with you in weakness, and in fear, and in much trembling.

And my speech and my preaching was not with enticing words of man's wisdom, but in demonstration of the Spirit and of power:

That your faith should not stand in the wisdom of men, but in the power of God.

Howbeit we speak wisdom among them that are perfect: yet not the wisdom of this world, nor of the princes of this world, that come to nought: (1 Corinthians 2:1–6)

But when that which is perfect is come, then that which is in part shall be done away. (1 Corinthians 13:10)

EXPANDING OUR LIGHT

Having therefore these promises, dearly beloved, let us cleanse ourselves from all filthiness of the flesh and spirit, perfecting holiness in the fear of God. (2 Corinthians 7:1)

...Be perfect; be of good comfort; be of one mind; live in peace; and the God of love and peace shall be with you. (2 Corinthians 13:11)

And he gave some, apostles; and some, prophets; and some, evangelists; and some, pastors and teachers;
For the perfecting of the saints, for the work of the ministry, for the edifying of the body of Christ:
Till we all come in the unity of the faith, and of the knowledge of the Son of God, unto a perfect man, unto the measure of the stature of the fullness of Christ: (Ephesians 4:11–13)

Not as though I had already attained, either were already perfect: but I follow after, if that I may apprehend that for which also I am apprehended of Christ Jesus.
Brethren, I count not myself to have apprehended: but this one thing I do, forgetting those things, which, are behind, and reaching forth unto those things which are before,
I press toward the mark for the prize of the high calling of God in Christ Jesus.
Let us therefore, as many as be perfect, be thus minded: and if in anything ye be otherwise minded, God shall reveal even this unto you. (Philippians 3:12–15)

Whom we preach, warning every man, and teaching every man in all wisdom; that we may present every man perfect in Christ Jesus: (Colossians 1:28)

Put on therefore, as the elect of God, holy and beloved, bowels of mercies, kindness, humbleness of mind, meekness, longsuffering;
Forbearing one another, and forgiving one another, if any man have a quarrel against any: even as Christ forgave you, so also do ye.

And above all these things put on charity, which is the bond of perfectness. (Colossians 3:12–14)

Epaphras, who is one of you, a servant of Christ, saluteth you, always labouring fervently for you in prayers, that ye may stand perfect and complete in all the will of God. (Colossians 4:12)

Night and day praying exceedingly that we might see your face, and might perfect that, which is lacking in your faith? (1 Thessalonians 3:10)

All scripture is given by inspiration of God, and is profitable for doctrine, for reproof, for correction, for instruction in righteousness:

That the man of God may be perfect, thoroughly furnished unto all good works. (2 Timothy 3:16–17)

For it became him, for whom are all things, and by whom are all things, in bringing many sons unto glory, to make the captain of their salvation perfect through sufferings. (Hebrew 2:10)

And being made perfect, he became the author of eternal salvation unto all them that obey him; (Hebrew 5:9)

Therefore leaving the principles of the doctrine of Christ, let us go on unto perfection; not laying again the foundation of repentance from dead works, and of faith toward God, (Hebrew 6:1)

If therefore perfection were by the Levitical priesthood, (for under it the people received the law,) what further need was there that another priest should rise after the order of Melchizedec, and not be called after the order of Aaron? (Hebrew 7:11)

Which was a figure for the time then present, in which were offered both gifts and sacrifices, that could not make him that did the service perfect, as pertaining to the conscience;

Which stood only in meats and drinks, and divers washings, and carnal ordinances, imposed on them until the time of reformation. (Hebrew 9:9–10)

For the law having a shadow of good things to come, and not the very image of the things, can never with those sacrifices which they offered year by year continually make the comers thereunto perfect.

For then would they not have ceased to be offered? Because that the worshippers once purged should have had no more conscience of sins. (Hebrew 10:1–2)

And ye have forgotten the exhortation which speaketh unto you as unto children, My son, despise not thou the chastening of the Lord, nor faint when thou are rebuked of him:

For whom the Lord loveth he chasteneth, and scourgeth every son whom he receiveth.

If ye endure chastening, God dealeth with you, as with sons; for what son is he whom the father chasteneth not? (Hebrew 12:5–7)

To the general assembly and church of the firstborn, which are written in heaven, and to God the judge of all, and to the spirits of just men made perfect, (Hebrew 12:23)

Make you perfect in every good work to do his will, working in you that which is well pleasing in his sight, through Jesus Christ; to whom be glory for ever and ever. Amen. (Hebrew 13:21)

[4] But let patience have her perfect work, that ye may be perfect and entire, wanting nothing.

[5] If any of you lack wisdom, let him ask of God, that giveth to all man liberally, and upbraideth not; and it shall be given him.

[6] But let him ask in faith, nothing wavering. For he that wavereth is like a wave of the sea driven with the wind and tossed.

¹⁷ Every good gift and every perfect gift is from above, and cometh down from the Father of lights, with whom is no variableness, neither shadow of turning.

²⁵ But whoso looketh into the perfect law of liberty, and continueth therein, he being not a forgetful hearer, but a doer of the work, this man shall be blessed in his deed. (James 1:4–6, 17, 25)

But wilt thou know, O vain man, that faith without works is dead?

Was not Abraham our father justified by works, when he had offered Isaac his son upon the alter?

Seest thou how faith wrought with his works, and by works was faith made perfect?

And the scripture was fulfilled which saith, Abraham believed God, and it was imputed unto him for righteousness: and he was called the Friend of God.

Ye see then how that by works a man is justified, and not by faith only.

Likewise also was not Rahab the harlot justified by works, when she had received the messengers, and had sent them out another way?

For as the body without the spirit is dead, so faith without works is dead also. (James 2:20–26)

For in many things we offend all. If any man offend not in word, the same is a perfect man, and able also to bridle the whole body. (James 3:2)

But the God of all grace, who hath called us unto his eternal glory by Christ Jesus, after that ye have suffered a while, make you perfect, stablish, strengthen, settle you. (v)

But whoso keepeth his word, in him verily is the love of God perfected: hereby know we that we are in him. (1 John 2:5)

There is no fear in love; but perfect love casteth out fear: because fear hath torment. He that feareth is not made perfect in love. (1 John 4:18)

O how great the plan of our God! For on the other hand, the paradise of God must deliver up the spirits of the righteous, and the grave deliver up the body of the righteous; and the spirit and the body is restored to itself again, and all men become incorruptible, and immortal, and they are living souls, having a perfect knowledge like unto us in the flesh, save it be that our knowledge shall be perfect.

Wherefore, we shall have a perfect knowledge of all our guilt, and our uncleaness, and our nakedness; and the righteous shall have a perfect knowledge of their enjoyment, and their righteousness, being clothed with purity, yea, even with the robe of righteousness. (2 Nephi 9:13–14)

Wherefore, ye must press forward with a steadfastness in Christ, having a perfect brightness of hope, and a love of God and of all men. Wherefore, if ye shall press forward, feasting upon the word of Christ, and endure to the end, behold thus saith the Father: Ye shall have eternal life. (2 Nephi 31:20)

And now, beloved, marvel not that I tell you these things; for why not speak of the atonement of Christ, and attain to a perfect knowledge of him, as to attain to the knowledge of a resurrection and the world to come? (Jacob 4:12)

Or otherwise, can ye imagine yourselves brought before the tribunal of God with your souls filled with guilt and remorse, having a remembrance of all your guilt, yea, a perfect remembrance of all your wickedness, yea, a remembrance that ye have set at defiance the commandments of God? (Alma 5:18)

The spirit and the body shall be reunited again in its perfect form; both limb and joint shall be restored to its proper frame, even as we now are at this time; and we shall be brought to stand before God, knowing even as we know now, and have a bright recollection of all our guilt. (Alma 11:43)

And now, the plan of mercy could not be brought about except an atonement should be made; therefore God himself atoneth for the sins of the world, to bring about the plan of mercy, to appease the demands of justice, that God might be a perfect, just God, and a merciful God also. (Alma 42:15)

For behold, the Spirit of Christ is given to every man, that he may know good from evil; wherefore, I show unto you the way to judge; for every thing which inviteth to do good, and to persuade to believe in Christ, is sent forth by the power and gift of Christ; wherefore ye may know with a perfect knowledge it is of God. (Moroni 7:16)

That which is of God is light, and continueth in God, receiveth more light; and that light groweth brighter and brighter until the perfect day. (D & C 50:24)

Ye are not able to abide the presence of God now, neither the ministering of angels; wherefore, continue in patience until ye are perfected. (D & C 67:13)

5

AGENCY

Agency is one of the most important principles of the gospel and, indeed, one of our most cherished gifts from God. He is not a God of force but a God of love and power. In His great omnipotent wisdom, He has granted us our agency—the right to make choices, not just between good and evil but to make any choice we see fit, whether between the lesser of two evils or between righteous selections. Agency is our complete freedom of choice. We should always be willing to accept the results and responsibilities for the actions stemming from the choices we make, whether they are good or evil and whether we receive reward or punishment, health, or illness.

If we deliberately cut off a finger, we must be willing to live without the finger. If we smoke tobacco, then we must be willing to accept the poor health and even death with which it is associated. As a general rule, when we disobey the laws of health and become ill, we go to our physician and say, "Make me well." Physicians cannot make us well. Our bodies have built-in systems that heal when it malfunctions, if the internal environment is operating properly. Physicians can sometimes relieve the suffering by giving medication that removes the symptoms or pain and, in some cases, may induce the healing process. He may excise the organ or tissue that is causing our pain. This isn't making us well. To be well, we must be completely free of any disease process and free from any pain or distress and every cell in our bodies must be capable of functioning within the limitations imposed on it by the normal requirements of the environment in which we live. As we examine and exercise our agency, we should accept the inevitable responsibility with which it is associated.

We are responding to the power of good when we obey God's commandments, embrace His ordinances, and accept all the concepts taught by Christ and the prophets. Conversely, when we go against Christ's teachings and commandments, we are responding to the satanic forces of evil. Without these two opposing forces, agency would have no value. There could be no progress toward the perfection commanded of us in Matthew 5:48.

The destruction of our agencies is one of the major objectives of Satan, and its preservation should be one of our greatest endeavors in this life.

Many people have asked, "If it is true that God is a God of love, why then does he permit so much pain and suffering among mankind?" This is a worthy question that requires an intimate understanding of the principle of agency.

God does not often directly interfere with an individual's agency. If He did, He would be violating His own law which gives us the right to use our agency in any manner we desire. If He did interfere, we would no longer have our agency and this world would have no reason to exist. Men are the products of their own right and wrong decisions. God does have a hand in our lives in the broad sense that He gives us guidelines, inspiration, personal revelation, and our agency to make our own choices, always maintaining an essential balance between the promptings of the Holy Ghost and those of Lucifer's.

Let us take the case of a person involved in an automobile accident. A driver has lost control of his car on a snow-packed highway, plunging the car down an embankment to the bottom of a canyon. The driver had several opportunities to make different decisions regarding the accident. He had at least six different choices that influenced the outcome. The ones causing the accident are shown here. First, he could have stayed home, knowing a bad storm was brewing. Second, when the roads became treacherous, he made the decision to continue driving instead of pulling over to wait out the storm or he could have turned back. Later, driving through the swirling snow, the driver made yet another bad choice. When the car started to skid, he could have done one of two things: apply the brakes (amplifying the skid) or remove his foot from the accelerator and turn the wheels to the direction of the skid to help him regain control of the car. He chose the first, ending up in the hospital with multiple fractures and severe internal injuries. As in this situation, he was the victim of his own wrong decisions. God granted him that right. He made the choices that ultimately caused the accident, and then he had to live with the results of those decisions. God has the power to intervene, but to do so would have violated the agency of the driver. Lessons learned from the accident would then have been nonexistent. When asked in faith for God to intervene, He may do so at times.

But, you say, what about sickness, war, and all the other suffering to which mankind is subjected? In the case of sickness, in a majority of cases it is man himself through his habits, his lack of health knowledge, his choice of diet and exercise, and getting involved with illegal substances and other recreational drugs that ultimately bring on the illness. There are exceptions, of course, but for the most part, if mankind obeyed the laws of God and of health, he would have little suffering. If all mankind in every nation on earth obeyed the Golden Rule, there would be no wars, no contentions nor arguments, and no lessons needed to be learned.

True, many people are caught in the middle and are victims of the vile or negligent acts or greed of others. It is true that most of us dislike seeing others suffer. Seeing a loved one in pain and suffering tugs at our heartstrings and certainly does make us ask, "Could a just God allow this to happen?" The answer, obviously hard or impossible for the world at large to understand, is even difficult for knowledgeable church members to grasp. One reason is that we, as mere humans, need to feel pain in this life to help us understand in a very limited way the terrible pain our Savior experienced in the garden of Gethsemane and the agony of the cross. It also serves to humble us. Who knows better when we need humbling than our Savior?

God's knowledge is omnipotent, infinite, and eternal as is His intelligence, wisdom, power, and glory. His knowledge is so far above ours that we can, in no way, understand why He does what He does. We must accept on faith that what He does is truth, and is best for these, His human creations. We have no right nor the knowledge, wisdom, and intelligence to question it. To do so puts us on the downhill road to apostasy.

No one knows the mind and will of God. His reasons for allowing things to happen are many and varied. The ramifications of an event or series of events could only be known by Him in His great omnipotent wisdom and power. Sometimes, a person is allowed to suffer great hardships and pain for the purpose of attaining spiritual growth, gaining experience, and knowledge to increase his wisdom, faith, and understanding and to test his faith and give him strength. God even let His Son die on the cross, to suffer like no other has ever suffered, thus we are forever blessed and indebted to them both. So when we suffer, just remember the suffering Christ went through and be thankful for the blessings associated with it.

God often allows wars to chasten His people and bring them to repentance.

One of the best scriptures to explain the mind of God in these matters is sections 121 and 122 in the Doctrine and Covenants where the prophet Joseph Smith is suffering mighty afflictions both personally and for the church. He offered a prayer to God for an answer. This is such a beautiful and "answering" scripture, and it is recommended that you read these two sections. Condensed and paraphrased, it goes something like this:

> While in jail, Joseph turned to God in humble prayer, asking the reasons for His suffering both to himself and his people who were being persecuted and driven from place to place. The Lord told him in effect, "My son, complain not. I have given you these things so you may gain experience, to learn, grow - and develop into a stronger person. Do you suppose that you are suffering, even as I, when I hung on the cross to die and bear the sins of all mankind? It is for your own learning and understanding, my Son, that you suffer these things. Nor have you yet reached the depths of the sufferings of Job - for your friends have not contended against you as they did Job."

Read both sections (D & C 121 and 122) for a clearer and better understanding of the problem. These scriptures also help to explain the war question.

The battleground for the forces of good against the forces of evil begins in our minds. Our actions are the manifestations of winning or losing the battles consistently being fought there. A man's agency then becomes a tool for whichever force appeals to him the most. Worldly goods and possessions have great appeal for most of us, and consequently, we often choose the path of least resistance or the path that appeals to our friends whom we don't want to offend.

Christ said, "Seek ye first the Kingdom of God, and his righteousness; and all these things shall be added unto you" (Matthew 6:33). Seeking the kingdom of God does not encompass seeking out those things that bring us the greatest physical or mental pleasure but rather seeking for those things that bring us the greatest spiritual progress, growth, and joy—having charity in our hearts, being humble, serving mankind, etc. In fact, seeking the kingdom of God can be and often is a very painful and difficult process. God never promised us that this life would be a Garden of Eden. He sent us here to prove ourselves; to overcome, conquer, and rise all adversities, problems, illnesses; and to do whatsoever God asks and requires of us. He did promise us that He would do whatever was necessary to help us to work out our salvation. Sometimes, especially when we are not on the right path, He will bring severe adversity into our lives to humble and chasten us so that we are guided along the path He has provided.

Choosing between spiritual joy and physical pleasure is exercising our agency. Our Lord and Savior would have us use our agency wisely, righteously, and productively at all times.

It is extremely important to recognize that the battles between right and wrong, good and evil are being fought within our minds and for the minds and spirits of mankind. Since we know that our minds and spirits are at stake, we should always closely examine what we put into them. As we increase the pollution of our minds, we decrease our control over it; and we will eventually lose it to the force of evil if we are not careful.

There are thousands of ways to pollute our minds. Many seem innocent yet carry a dramatic impact such as the soap operas, most of the television programs, movies, hundreds of magazine pictures and articles, pornography, gaming, etc. There is not one branch of media that hasn't been touched in one way or the other by the forces of evil. To put it more bluntly, the magazine owners and editors, the producers, the directors, the writers, and many others have virtually sold out to Satan, as have many of our politicians who have become one of his major tools for the destruction of God's children and the nations around the world.

The major tool we have to fight these terrible forces of evil is the righteous use of our agency. Using it passively is just as bad as using it destructively. How can we use it righteously? Pray daily, read the scriptures, study and meditate on the ways of God, embrace His laws of love and charity, and be obedient to His commandments. "For where your treasure is, there will your heart be also" (Matthew 6:21). In other words, make every decision a righteous decision.

Since the battle for the minds and souls of men occurs in the mind and since this is where our decisions are made, utilizing our agency in learning to control and channel our minds should be one of the major endeavors in this life. It will also be our greatest asset when channeled in the direction of righteousness. The more control we have, the more power we have and the greater our satisfaction. God has perfect control. Therefore, His power is ultimate and perfect. Satan also has great power. His power, however, is neither perfect nor ultimate but is limited in its scope and power by God.

Our personalities are multifaceted and multidimensional. They comprise our physical, mental, spiritual, and emotional attributes. The power of personalities has been felt in this world since its creation and will continue to be felt as long as it exists. The amount of power our personalities have depends on the degree of our perfection, the amount of righteous knowledge we have acquired, and the influence for good we have on others and ourselves.

The road to our perfection is directly related to the desires, attitudes, and motivations we demonstrate and to how productive are our thoughts and actions. It is also relative to the goal of perfecting our personalities in making decisions and forming plans. The most important question we should always ask ourselves is "Are our thoughts and actions productive, nonproductive, or counterproductive for our growth toward perfection?" If we can always make them productive, we are using our agency in a righteous manner. We will all be held accountable directly to God for the use of our agency and also for the use of our time. Agency is a sacred gift from God; we should treat it as such.

Our purpose and mission in this life cannot be fulfilled unless our thoughts and actions are productive to our growth toward perfection. Our agency, then, must be protected with every possible tool at our disposal. Our response to the forces of good is a conscientious effort toward attaining perfection.

Perfection, as is possible on earth, is accomplished only when all nonproductive (unrighteous) and counterproductive (unrighteous) traits and characteristics have been purged from our personalities, all of our destructive actions expunged and erased by repentance, and the productive traits are embraced and magnified to their fullest extent.

If the ultimate aim or goal of a society or organization within the society is not the uplifting and perfecting of its members but instead tends to destroy or eliminate their agency, that society's or organization's freedoms and liberties should be reorganized to allow for and promote growth toward their spiritual goals.

A society, organization, or nation cannot long remain free unless the goals of perfection and agency are nurtured and protected by the individuals within them and the ruling body controlling the laws pertaining to them. The ultimate responsibility then falls back on each individual within the society to maintain and magnify these precious gifts from God. They are part of the stewardship He has charged each of us to protect and preserve. We can't wait for the next person to protect and preserve our agency and freedoms. These wonderful gifts are too precious to place in the hands of those who might destroy them.

A nation or society whose individuals and/or ruling body allow or promote the destructive forces within it to work toward enslavement and the suppression of rights will ultimately suffer the loss of freedom exemplified by an enslaved people. Much of our agency would be reduced or taken from us, and our growth toward perfection would be slowed or halted.

Contemplate the following scriptures to help further your understanding of the greatest principle of the gospel, *agency*:

Behold, I set before you this day a blessing and a curse; A blessing, if ye obey the commandments of the Lord your God, which I command you this day:

And a curse, if ye will not obey the commandments of the Lord your God, but turn aside out of the way which I command you this day, to go after other Gods which ye have not known. (Deuteronomy 11:26)

And if it seem evil unto you to serve the Lord, choose you this day whom ye will serve; whether the gods which your fathers served that were on the other side of the flood, or the gods of the Amorites, in whose land ye dwell: but as for me and my house, we will serve the Lord. (Joshua 24:15)

And Elijah came unto all the people, and said, "How long halt ye between two opinions? If the Lord be God, follow him: but if Baal, then follow him..." (1 Kings 18:21)

For it must needs be, that there is an opposition in all things. If not so, my first-born in the wilderness, righteousness could not be brought to pass, neither wickedness, neither holiness nor misery, neither good nor bad. Wherefore, all things must needs be a compound in one; wherefore if it should be one body it must needs remain as dead, having no life neither death, nor corruption nor incorruption, happiness nor misery, neither sense nor insensibility. (2 Nephi 2:11)

I say unto you that if ye should serve him who has created you from the beginnings, and is preserving you from day to day, by lending you breath, that ye may live and move and do according to your own will, and even supporting you from one moment to another - I say, if you should serve him with all your whole souls yet ye would be unprofitable servants. (Mosiah 2:21)

And it must needs be that the devil should tempt the children of men, or they could not be agents unto themselves; for if they should never have bitter they could not know the sweet. (D & C 29:39)

> For the power is in them, wherein they are agents unto themselves. And inasmuch as men do good they shall in nowise lose their reward. (D & C 58:28)
>
> The Lord said unto Enoch: Behold these thy brethren; they are the workmanship of mine own hands, and I gave unto them their knowledge, in the day I created them; and in the Garden of Eden, gave I unto man his agency; (Moses 7:32)

According to the use of his agency, man will realize his salvation or his destruction. The choice is his.

6

A QUESTION OF FAITH

Faith is the power by which all things are created and accomplished. It is the power by which all things exist and by which all people are moved to action. Therefore we, as a race of doers, need to understand every facet of its *profound* potential—how it works, how to develop it, and how to use it to make our lives more meaningful so we, too, can become great achievers *for righteousness* in this world. (From the teachings of Prophet Joseph Smith in the seven discourses on faith. Italics denote an addition not in the original context.)

God has encouraged us to develop and use our faith in righteousness. It can change our lives, bringing us productivity and happiness and keeping us in harmony with God's teachings. Part of our stewardship here on earth is learning to use the power of faith to control our every thought and action and to subdue all things.

There are two basic categories of faith: spiritual and temporal. *Spiritual faith* is broken into two subcategories: faith in God and faith in our ability to call down the powers of heaven when needed. *Temporal faith* is also broken into two subcategories: faith in our fellow man and faith in our ability to accomplish our goals.

Our salvation depends on our understanding and the application of the essentials of faith. The success of any endeavor depends on how well we apply its principles. The development of these principles is discussed in chapter 7. This chapter will help us understand how to apply our faith in calling down the powers of heaven.

> And the Lord said, "If ye had the faith as a grain of mustard seed, ye might say unto this sycamine tree, "be thou plucked up by the root, and be thou planted in the sea; and it should obey you: (Luke 17:6)

How many of us yearn to have such faith? What would we be willing to sacrifice to have the elements obey our commands?

The scriptures are replete with examples of indomitable faith in action. Moses parting the Red Sea, Joshua making the sun and moon stand still for a day, Christ bringing Lazarus back to life, His resurrection, etc. What must we give to have such faith?

I read an article somewhere about a lady's club which invited a concert pianist to play for them. At the conclusion of the concert, one of the ladies approached the pianist and stated, "I would give anything to be able to play with such skill." She was chagrined when the pianist answered, "No you wouldn't. You would not spend the required time at practice—six to eight hours a day, for years. If you really had the desire you would have already became an accomplished pianist."

That's the way it is with faith. We would like God to zap us with an invincible faith so we too could perform some of these great miracles. We would be willing to give almost anything to master this great power, except what God required for us to do—continual fasting, prayer, developing humility, insatiable desire, meekness, being charitable, putting aside our prejudices, always obeying His commandments, learning the principles of management, etc.

Faith is a gift from God. To receive this gift, we must know we are worthy and be in a spiritual state in which we know that God can trust us to use it wisely, righteously, and productively and to help not only ourselves but others who are in need.

The question then becomes, have I conducted my life in a manner in which God can trust me to use it wisely and righteously?"

Do we resist the devil's promptings to the extent that God can trust us enough to bless us with the faith required to use it righteously? Man has the propensity to use many of God's blessings and gifts in unrighteous manners. I believe that we must prove ourselves worthy before he will trust us enough to bless us with this very powerful blessing.

When we put our faith in medications in preference over using the great healing powers of God, we show where our faith lies. If our faith is not strong enough to rely on the powers above, then we must rely on what God has given us in mild herbs, supplements, and foods to treat our maladies. As a last result, we go to the medical profession and other healers for the relief of our maladies.

We must follow the law of repentance for our sins and remain in this state so guilt and doubt will not interfere with our ability to use our faith. We should give the long hours of study, prayer, fasting, and meditation required to build our faith to the level of all of our olden prophets and those presently available. These men were and are righteous. Their hearts were and are always with God. They knew what was required of them and voluntarily gave it. They were willing to make any sacrifice to become more intimate with His laws and teachings. They were also willing to give up their desire for the comforts and riches of the world. Possessions and collectables produce little temptation for the prophets as they have no real eternal value. God requires no less from us if we expect to gain the same level of faith for which they were noted. Before granting us this power, God must be sure that we will use it righteously, wisely, and not for personal gain or unrighteousness. In other words, we must earn the gift.

Would we be willing to relinquish some of our recreational time to know God better? He would like nothing more than for us to start *sacrificing* some of our time to increase our faith. Make more time for prayer, study and ponder the scriptures, and meditate on the things of God. Make more time for our families and time to serve mankind. We are encouraged to sacrifice our desire for unneeded worldly possessions.

Faith does not come easily but only to those who are persistent and worthy. We can expect very little if we give up when the first obstacles are placed in our paths. We are a fun-loving and a fun-oriented society. We love our TVs, phones, hunting, gaming, fishing, and our golfing; in fact, we have created or allowed others, including Satan, to create within us the desire to be entertained every minute of every day. To change our attitudes from this concept is not easy. We have developed a desire for our comforts, to having fun and excitement. If it's not fun pleasurable or exciting, I'm not interested. If it doesn't stimulate me in some way, it is not worth the trouble to incorporate it into my life.

We have become a world of puppets controlled by oratorical speeches, advertising, and the desire to be excited by new things, drugs, sex, pornography, etc. We allow the media and many other people to manipulate our desires, our thinking, emotions, even our education, our wants, and our needs. In one moment we can't pray to God for an increase of our faith but we can have time to watch some inane program on TV that promotes murder, sex, thievery, etc. (I'm putting myself into this category also.) If we truly want to have an increase our faith, we must maintain the standards set for us in the scriptures. Our pursuit of faith will be tried. God will know if we are serious in its pursuit.

Knowledge is the precursor to faith. It need not be sure knowledge, but a belief in something or someone. If we have no knowledge of God, we cannot exercise faith in Him. The more information we acquire about Him and His mission for mankind the easier it is to rely on Him for the redemption he has promised, thus increasing our faith in His abilities to bring us salvation and other righteous gifts. Therefore, the more knowledge we have of God, the greater will be our potential for using our faith in calling down the powers of heaven.

It matters not how much knowledge we acquire in this world if we don't use it to benefit mankind and ourselves. In the end, it will avail us nothing. Even if we were given all of God's knowledge but never used it, we would be denying the power of faith and it would lead to our destruction. We have a responsibility to use the knowledge we acquire not only for ourselves but also for the benefit of others. This expands our faith and our ability to achieve. God holds us accountable for how we use it. The more knowledge we obtain and use it for righteous purposes, the more our faith will grow and more knowledge will be given to us. Faith, then, depends on an accumulation of and a continual righteous use of knowledge.

Faith has enemies: doubt, fear, anger, guilt, deception, feeling unworthy, feeling undeserving, frustration, prejudice, worry, etc.

The greatest of these are doubt, guilt, and fear, which we will discuss later in this book.

The greatest destroyer of faith is doubt. The two cannot coexist. Because all of God's creations are accomplished by faith, doubt cannot be a part of His nature or all of His creations would cease to exist. Doubt can become a part of our nature, a part of our persona, which may prevent us from doing God's work. Creating doubt in about our ability to accomplish something is a major deception used by Satan to prevent us from becoming winners or developing our faith. When doubt about our capability creeps in, we must recognize that we are listening to the powers of darkness. When we fail to succeed in attaining some goals, it is so easy to castigate ourselves or blame others. What we should do is to examine the method used to achieve our unattained goal and change to another method that may be more successful. Blaming others and ourselves is a national pastime and should never become part of our repertory. It is self-defeating and comes from Satan.

It is not easy to conquer doubt. Satan would have us believe that we can do nothing. He would make us all losers if we permitted. In some of us, doubt becomes an ingrained habit that defies all attempts at removal. The only way I know to get rid of it is to start doing things we haven't done before and things that build our self-confidence. By removing the obstacles to productivity, we increase our confidence and our ability to get things done. As we gain in self-confidence, our doubts begin to fall by the wayside and our faith increases proportionately. No matter what the obstacle is, whether it is doubt or something else, we must always rely on the hand of God. There is no other way. When we fail to reach a goal, we must not lose faith but use the experience as a stepping-stone to strengthen our resolve. The loser will quit, but the winner will use every righteous method at his disposal until he succeeds. Each day, we should stretch the limits of our endeavors and soon we will have replaced our doubts with the faith of accomplishment. Thomas Edison tried over a thousand methods to produce a lightbulb before he finally succeeded in producing one that worked. Tenacity helps in building our faith.

Sometimes, we have doubts about our worthiness to receive God's blessings. Mostly, this is unresolved guilt. If so, we must go to our branch president, bishop, or stake president and confess the sins that are holding us back and preventing our faith from growing. The degree of our repentance will determine the degree of our salvation and exaltation and the building of our faith.

When we obey God's commandments, we know we are doing the right thing and internal conflict will not be present. When we read the scriptures, pray, or help our fellow man, we know it is right and our faith will grow and mature. If we are aware of the commandment to keep the Sabbath Day holy and we watch a football game on Sunday in preference to attending our meetings, there is a reasonable doubt that we are being obedient and faith will not grow. This same principle applies to all of God's commandments; disobedience creates doubt about our worthiness to call on the powers of heaven, thus diminishing our faith.

Guilt exists because of unresolved sin. To resolve it, we must repent. After taking the steps of repentance, we must receive conformation of God's forgiveness through Christ. This affirms our faith in Christ by acknowledging it is only through Him that we can be forgiven. Then, we must allow Him to work in our lives by letting Him assume the burden of our sins. We must never retain them unto ourselves, as so many of us do, but accept His forgiveness in true humility and thanksgiving.

When we nurture or retain guilt, our repentance is not complete. We have not allowed Christ to assume our entire burden. He will only take our load and relieve us of our guilt to the extent that we allow.

Fear is the last of the counterproductive traits discussed here. Others may apply, which should also be expunged. They must be eliminated on an individual basis when applicable.

Fear is so widespread and comes in such a variety of guises that it is difficult to discuss them collectively. They are so diverse that to do so would not do them justice, so I have selected a few that I feel apply to us all and will discuss some methods that may help to allay them.

Fear often produces such an emotional strain that we may lose the ability to think clearly, and we can't conjure up the faith to combat it. To develop the intense faith needed to cope with all fearful situations is not impossible. However, the monumental task need not be accomplished immediately. It must be taken a step at a time or we may become discouraged and feel it is not worth the effort.

When Daniel was thrown into the lion's den, he had the faith that he would be delivered and he was. Had he relinquished his hold on faith, he would surely have been devoured. How did he manage to overcome the innate fear of being eaten alive? How did he curb his emotions so that faith was the dominant factor? He had what most of us do not have, implicit trust in the Lord. Had this faith wavered, his story would have had a different ending. Do we have implicit faith in God? Do we waver in the face of serious adversity? To develop and sustain the level of faith needed to meet all of life's challenges takes an enormous amount of effort. To each kind of fear, we have our own individual response. Some of us take it in stride, others worry.

Worry is the nurturing of every possible mishap of which we can conceive. If a loved one is late getting home we fret about an accident, kidnapping, molestation, etc. Some people agonize over things so much they become incapacitated. If we develop an unwavering faith and trust in God, we no longer need to worry. This is the answer to most of our fears. Developing this degree of faith and trust in God that when adversity arises we will know with a sure certainty that He will be there to help us. Even when some great adversity or calamity does happen such as an accident that takes the life of a loved one, we can know that it is part of God's plan and that there is no need to blame Him or anyone else for it and no need to hate Him for the rest of our lives. The problem is developing a *complete* trust in God, a trust that will take into account every possibility, a knowledge that He does indeed know what is best for everyone living and dead. When we remove all the elements from our minds that are not conducive to developing faith, such as doubt, fear and guilt, we build a base upon which it can be perfected.

The key is learning to place complete trust in God's ability to help us regardless of the circumstances. The knowledge that He can do it is there, but the belief that He will do it depends on whether we feel we deserve it or that we are worthy of it. When we are not in perfect harmony with all His teachings, when we are not in a state of complete repentance, we feel that we don't deserve to have His help, so it usually isn't forthcoming. Often, we are blessed when we believe we are not worthy or don't deserve it. This can cause great stress in our lives, but if we lead worthy lives as Daniel did, we would deserve the ability to call down the powers of heaven when the need arose. Worthiness is a requisite part of faith. Without it we are unable to accomplish those spiritual tasks necessary for our growth toward perfection.

The growth of faith also depends on our ability to rid ourselves of any counterproductive trait that is its enemy. Each of these traits produces their own problems. No one has the ability to expunge them without God's help. To admit that we are always in need of His help is not easy to do. It takes an act of great humility to acknowledge that we always need Him; our pride is at stake. Nevertheless, in humility, we must seek God's help for each trait we intend to perfect or eliminate. There is no other way, and He will only help us to the extent that we ask and allow.

Obedience to God's laws and commandments is another important factor before faith can grow. Disobedience always has its penalties. The most serious is a partial severance from God's influence. This severance is manifest by diminished inspiration, guilt feelings, and being in disharmony with God's laws and commandments. Often, we are uneasy in the presence of someone who is living close to the gospel, who is doing those things we have neglected. Disobedience is sin and causes unresolved guilt, which is an enemy to faith.

Faith in God can only grow through obedience to His laws, repentance, and by righteous thoughts and actions. These factors depend on how great our commitment is to them and how open we are to His message. We need to completely open our hearts and minds to Him. The only way this is possible is through scripture study, prayer, obedience, fasting, repentance, baptism, meditation, by serving our fellow man, and by accepting the redemption He has offered us. To serve man is to serve God.

Consider these facts:

1. The degree to which we let the Holy Ghost influence us is directly proportional to the amount of faith we have in God.
2. The more we obey God's commandments, the greater our growth in faith will be.
3. The degree of our repentance is proportional to the degree of God's forgiveness. Christ cannot forgive us if we won't forgive ourselves or if we don't ask for it.

4. The degree of our belief in God's forgiveness is proportional to the amount of faith we have in Him.
5. Self-worth is directly proportional to self-forgiveness and the degree of our repentance.
6. If we cannot forgive ourselves, we have not repented. We have not given our complete burden over to Christ.
7. Faith is directly proportional to knowledge.
8. If our repentance is complete, we will have peace of mind, joy in our hearts, a feeling of being in harmony with God and His teachings, and the Holy Spirit will manifest His love and forgiveness.
9. If we totally turn our sins over to Christ, we have acknowledged our belief that only He can atone for them. Thus, our faith has grown.
10. The development of our faith should be close to the top of our list of priorities because it is the foundation of all creations, accomplishments, growth, and our very existence.
11. If faith did not exist, there could be no salvation, no baptism, no priesthood, no church, no gospel, and no life.
12. As we expand the limits of our righteous beliefs, our faith will grow and our knowledge will be firmer.
13. Obedience to God's laws and commandments and participation in His ordinances are necessary for the inheritance of His kingdom and the growth of our faith.

The law of repentance was given to help us regain God's presence. When used as an on-going, daily spiritual experience (to erase our sins and refrain from committing them again), we stay in tune with the spirit and remain close to God. Therein lies the path to our success in achieving entrance into the celestial kingdom where we will reside with God throughout the eternities.

Ponder the following scriptures concerning faith:

> And Jesus answering saith unto them, Have faith in God.
> For verily I say unto you, That whosoever shall say unto this mountain, Be thou removed, and be thou cast into the sea; and shall not doubt in his heart, but shall

believe that those things which he saith shall come to pass; he shall have whatsoever he saith.

Therefore I say unto you, what things soever ye desire, when ye pray, believe that ye receive them, and ye shall have them. (I feel it is much easier to believe that we will receive them if we lead a worthy life and we know we deserve them.) (Mark 11:22–24)

My brethren, count it all joy when ye fall into divers temptations;
Knowing this, that the trying of your faith worketh patience.
But let patience have her perfect work, that ye may be perfect and entire, wanting nothing.
If any of you lack wisdom, let him ask of God, that giveth to all men liberally, and upbraideth not; and it shall be given him.
But let him ask in faith, nothing wavering. For he that wavereth is like a wave of the sea driven with the wind and tossed. (James 1:2–6)

But Aaron said unto him: If thou desirest this thing, if thou wilt bow down before God, yea, if thou wilt repent of all thy sins, and will bow down before God, and call on his name in faith, believing that ye shall receive, then shalt thou receive the hope which thou desirest. (Alma 22:16)

And when they shall have received this, which is expedient that they should have first, to try their faith, and if it shall so be that they shall believe these things then shall the greater things be made manifest unto them.
And if it so be that they will not believe these things, then shall greater things be withheld from them, unto their condemnation. (3 Nephi 26:9–10)

⁶ And now I Moroni, would speak somewhat concerning these things; I would show unto the world that faith is things which are hoped for and not seen; wherefore, dispute not because ye see not, for ye receive no witness until after the trial of your faith.

⁷ For it was by faith that Christ showed himself unto our fathers, after he had risen from the dead; and he showed not himself unto them until after they had faith in him; wherefore, it must needs be that some had faith in him, for he showed himself not unto the world.

⁸ But because of the faith of men he has shown himself unto the world, and glorified the name of the Father, and prepared a way that thereby others might be partakers of the heavenly gift, that they might hope for those things which they have not seen.

⁹ Wherefore, ye may also have hope, and be partakers of the gift, if ye will but have faith.

¹⁰ Behold it was by faith that they of old were called after the holy order of God.

¹¹ Wherefore, by faith was the law of Moses given. But in the gift of his Son hath God prepared a more excellent way; and it is by faith that it hath been fulfilled.

¹² For if there be no faith among the children of men God can do no miracle among them; wherefore, he showed not himself until after their faith.

¹³ Behold, it was the faith of Alma and Amulek that caused the prison to tumble to the earth.

¹⁴ Behold, it was the faith of Nephi and Lehi that wrought the change upon the Lamanites, that they were baptized with fire and with the Holy Ghost.

¹⁵ Behold, it was the faith of Amman and his brethren which wrought so great a miracle among the Lamanites.

¹⁶ Yea, and even all they who wrought miracles wrought them by faith, even those who were before Christ and also those who were after.

¹⁷ And it was by faith that the three disciples obtained a promise that they should not taste of death; and they obtained not the promise until after their faith.

¹⁸ And neither at any time hath any wrought miracles until after their faith; wherefore they first believed in the Son of God.

¹⁹ And there were many whose faith was so exceedingly strong, even before Christ came, who could not be kept from within the veil, but truly saw with their eyes the things which they had beheld with an eye of faith, and they were glad.

²⁰ And behold, we have seen in this record that one of these was the brother of Jared; for so great was his faith in God, that when God put forth his finger he could not hide it from the sight of the brother of Jared, because of his word which he had spoken unto him, which word he had obtained by faith.

²¹ And it is by faith that my fathers have obtained the promise that these things should come unto their brethren through the Gentiles; therefore the Lord hath commanded me, yea, even Jesus Christ.

²⁷ And if men come unto me, I will show unto them their weakness. I give unto men weakness that they may be humble; and my grace is sufficient for all men that humble themselves before me; for if they humble themselves before me, and have faith in me, then will I make weak things become strong unto them.

²⁸ Behold, I will show unto the Gentiles their weakness, and I will show unto them that faith, hope and charity bringeth unto me—the fountain of all righteousness.

²⁹ And I, Moroni, having heard these words, was comforted, and said: O Lord, thy righteous will be done, for I know that thou workest unto the children of men according to their faith.

³⁰ For the brother of Jared said unto the mountain Zerin, Remove—and it was removed. And if he had not had faith it would not have moved; wherefore thou workest after men have faith.

³¹ For thus didst thou manifest thyself unto thy disciples; for after they had faith, and did speak in thy name, thou didst show thyself unto them in great power. (Ether 12:6–21, 27–31)

FAITH, THE POWER WITHIN

Through the ages, there have been those who have left their mark on history for good or evil. Every generation has had them. Some have given the world its greatest advancements. Others have been known for their inhumanity to man, leaving torture, pain, misery, and death in their wake. There have been the Edisons, Bells, Ptolemys, Franklins, etc. who have benefited mankind. The Hitlers, Napoleons, Genghis Khans, the Stalins, etc. have also left their evil marks. All of these men possessed the power to attain their goals, to reach out and affect the destiny of the human race.

What is this power? Can we obtain it? What are the laws that govern it? If we now possess it, how can we learn to use it in a beneficial, righteous, and positive way? For what purposes should this power be used? The answers to these questions will be examined as we progress through this chapter.

> There is a law irrevocably decreed in Heaven before the foundations of this world, upon which all blessings are predicated and when we obtain any blessing from God, it is by obedience to that law upon which it is predicated."
> (D & C 130:20–21)

From this we learn that there are laws controlling all blessings. Conversely, there are laws governing all disobedience.

Therefore, the blessings or trials we receive are because of the laws we have obeyed or disobeyed or in which we need added strength. We cannot change the law because it is ordained by God. There would be no justice for mankind if it were accomplished in any other manner.

We all have within us the embryonic seeds of greatness. The major difference between the great achievers and the rest of us is the degree of faith we have developed, self-confidence, and if we feel we deserve it. Faith gets things done regardless of the opposition. It is a gift from God, and we all use it to one degree or another. Man's every accomplishment is the result of faith. Every goal reached is because of its use. Even the least of us have developed a portion of this power. Its potential staggers the imagination. Most people choose the path of least resistance in life, developing only a fraction of its inherent power.

Faith is a gift from God. To receive it, we must feel worthy and we must be in a state that we know that God can trust us to use it wisely, righteously, and productively and that it will be used to help others. The question then becomes, have I conducted my life in a manner that God can trust me with its use?

When coupled with the powers of heaven, this inner strength or faith has an infinite and eternal capacity and a limitless number of uses. It is by and through the combined use of these powers that all destructive traits are eliminated, and the ultimate perfection of our mental, physical, emotional, and spiritual traits are enhanced.

This power is comprised of several components. First, its base is all the true knowledge and experiences we have acquired in our lifetimes. Second, it is the wise and intelligent use of this knowledge and experience. Third, it is the courage to act, overcome, conquer, and rise above all our adversities with the help of God to subdue our fears, anxieties, doubts, and worries. The sum of these traits either prevents us from accomplishing anything or allows us to set and attain any goal. This power is literally the power to do, to accomplish, and to be great. *It is faith.*

The laws that govern it are simple. They are the laws of usage and deserving. When we know we are worthy and deserve a blessing or an accomplishment, it will come to us through persistence. When we believe we don't deserve it, our efforts are seldom up to the task of completion. We make excuses and we procrastinate, and the blessings of achievement are never forthcoming. Therefore, everything we do depends on repentance and keeping ourselves worthy, knowing that we can do it, and knowing we deserve what we ask for through prayer and what we set out to accomplish.

Since everything we do is a result of using this power, then the more we do, the more it will grow. The less it is used the less effective it becomes. The more often we reach our goals and perfect the activities surrounding them, the stronger it becomes. Our self-esteem and self-worth flourishes as more of our goals are completed. This makes us more self-assured and confident allowing even more to be accomplished. This self-assurance is a manifestation of the growth of the power within. In other words, the more we increase our activities, the more we realize our true potential. As our self-confidence increases our ability to command the environment around us is magnified. This is another manifestation of the growth of this great power. Simply put, the controlling law is "use it or lose it." My own definition is: do it and growth occurs, don't do it and our abilities diminish.

Another necessity in developing our faith is the constant assimilation of true and righteous knowledge. Without knowledge, faith cannot exist. God gives us the knowledge upon which faith is based through study and accomplishment. He is the ultimate giver of our faith, which originates with and through Him. It is given to us as we earn it. It then behooves us to always include God in our lives every second of every day and be obedient to His laws and commandments.

Concentration and the focus of effort in any single area or activity will result in the accomplishment of any goal or endeavor and create an increase in the growth of faith. The great athletes, actors, entrepreneurs, businessmen, chess masters, and statesmen, as well as other great accomplishers use this method to become proficient in the area of their interest. Care must be taken to balance all facets of our lives with growth activities involving our personalities physically, mentally, emotionally, and spiritually.

There is a danger of making idols of our profession, vocation, or other interests. "Seek ye first the kingdom of God and his righteousness; and all these things shall be added unto you" (Matthew 6:33). This scripture lets us know where our major goal should be. When followed, there is no longer the danger of making idols of anything. Bear in mind that this power will grow only to the limitation of our endeavors; otherwise, our abilities will begin to diminish. Our achievements are restricted only by the limitations that we place on ourselves. If we believe we can do it, we can. If we think we can't, we won't. Only our negative, confined thinking (our lack of faith) limits what our achievements can be.

We should set our goals early in life. To be viable, they should be based on gospel principles and other acceptable knowledge. Most of these goals should be of an eternal nature which helps us reach God's highest kingdom. Faith is one of God's ordained tools designed to help us attain our goals. Coupled with the powers of heaven, fasting, prayer, scripture study, and obedience to God's laws, there is no righteous goal we cannot reach. Faith will then grow within us and become a great strength for good in our world and society. A righteous goal is a goal that benefits not only us but mankind as well.

Satan uses every possible weapon to make us stray from the paths God has created. To stray from these paths enslaves us, reduces or eliminates our agency, and keeps us from the eternal presence of our Father in heaven. We, too, must use every available tool to prevent his enslavement which keeps us from God's kingdom. If we ask these two questions before we make any decision to action, Satan will have little or no influence on our lives.

- Will this decision result in an action that is productive to my growth toward perfection?
- Will it help me attain the celestial kingdom?

The primary purpose for faith should be to work out our salvation and exaltation in and through the perfection process. It is especially influential in helping those within our circle of light and influence to attain the ultimate purpose for which man was created, to be with God eternally.

Fear and doubt are among the greatest destructive elements that place limitations on us as we begin to develop our faith. The fear of failing stops about 90 percent of us before we get started. Is it so much easier to forget the whole thing than to face this possibility?

Other limitations we place on ourselves are procrastination and lack of motivation. We become too lazy to expend the energy necessary to set and reach goals or accomplish a desired undertaking. It is much easier to be entertained by television, gaming, golfing, fishing, etc. I'm not saying we shouldn't completely eliminate these activities but to use them sparingly and righteously as a balance. We all need the enjoyment they bring into our lives, but not so much so that we neglect the most important thing in it: our goal of attaining the celestial kingdom. This we have to earn by overcoming our limitations, setting and attaining righteous goals, etc. We cannot earn it by taking the paths of least resistance or by coasting through life.

God is all knowing and all-powerful. He did not receive His knowledge and power by placing limitations on Himself, only by removing them. He also received it by eliminating all the nonproductive and counterproductive characteristics and traits from His personality by subduing and controlling all of His wants and needs. He received it by total self-discipline and self-control and by embracing and perfecting all of the righteous traits. We cannot attain this same status until we have done the same.

This is our life. God has given it to us to do with as we will. We can make it beautiful or miserable. We can make it spiritually productive or evil. We have the faith within us to make it evil, mediocre, or great. The choice is ours. By using our faith, *we can make things happen*, we can watch things happen, or we can just sit back, relax, and wonder what happened. Again, the choice is ours.

When life is over, all that we are and all that we take with us into the next phase of our existence is because of the choices we have made here—our own decisions. This is our life; we have made of it what it is by our choices and decisions coupled with our inner drive. The decisions we have allowed others to make for us also have an effect on what we have become. Ultimately, we do what we want to do what is acceptable to our desires. If our desires are righteous, then our actions will reflect it. If they are unrighteous, our actions will also reflect that. Handicaps have little to do with it. Many physically crippled and handicapped people have become great leaders, great achievers, and great thinkers, not letting anything deter them from their goals. Each of us has the power to do the same. No one can make us do it or do it for us. No one *else* is responsible or can be blamed. We choose to be what we are. We each choose our own destiny for better or for worse with God's help or without it. The choices we make are either righteous or unrighteous. To succeed like the *great ones,* we must all overcome, conquer, and rise above those traits and characteristics that prevent our accomplishments, all with the help of God.

The following steps may help us with our choices. Follow them and watch the power within (faith) grow.

1. Create within our minds a burning desire to work out our salvation and exaltation through the perfection process.
2. Use the power within, our faith, to create those things which are beautiful, beneficial, and productive for the entire human race, including ourselves.
3. Use it to overcome the imperfections, the destructive habits, and all that is nonproductive or counterproductive in our lives.
4. Develop it for use in reaching all our righteous goals and improving our talents.
5. Use it to control our wants, needs, appetites, and the degenerative influences of the world around us.
6. Use it to subdue and discipline every aspect of our lives and to overcome each counterproductive trait one at a time, and watch our faith grow.
7. And finally, we should use it to increase our enthusiasm and exuberance for living. Use it to create a positive attitude about everything, about our jobs, our home life, and our church activities and responsibilities. Use it to magnify our productive traits and to expand the limitations of all that we think and do.

8

FAITH IN ACTION

Planet Earth is a battleground for the war between the forces of good and evil. Some battles we win, some we lose. The war won't be over until the beginning of the millennium when Christ comes to claim His own. Those who have joined with Christ and won the most battles, enduring until the end, are they who are ranked with the forces of good. Those who have not heeded His word, who have procrastinated the day of their repentance, and have not taken seriously their sojourn here on earth, are they who have joined with the ranks of Satan.

Two of the most important objectives in this life are repentance and perseverance. We must keep trying; even when we go astray once in a while and strive with all the strength God has given us to endure to the end. If we give up when we have committed some grievous sin, Satan has won. When God placed us here, He knew we would make mistakes. That is why He gave us the law of repentance through the atonement of Christ Jesus. When we sin, He wants us to repent, to learn from the experience and renew our efforts to be more perfect. The person who makes mistakes is trying. Show me a man who doesn't make mistakes and I'll show you a man who is not trying. Only God and Christ are perfect.

Life's battles are not just being fought in a one-to-one basis. The local and state governments, our country and even the world is involved. God has given the human race temporary stewardship over this planet. Included in this stewardship is the responsibility of keeping this world and us free from pollutants. In part, they are thievery, adultery, pornography, promiscuity, violence of all kinds, gaming, and in fact anything that is contrary to our growth toward perfection.

When we, as world citizens, allow any destructive elements to exist without a fight, we are aligning ourselves with the evil one and, therefore, will share our guilt with the initiators. When we sit back, watch the evils of the world grow, and convince ourselves it is not our fight, then it isn't. Have we not then joined Satan's ranks?

We cannot expect God to fight our battles for us unless we first do all we can to make this world a more righteous place. We must fight evil in every form it takes using the powers of heaven, our faith or inner power, and all other weapons at our disposal, putting forth our greatest efforts to win. This is our responsibility. When enough of us put our whole hearts into the fight, then, and only then, will God give us the help we request. Remember when Moses and the Israelites wandered in the wilderness for forty years? When they were of one accord and lived in harmony with God, He helped them. When they didn't, He withdrew His support. They were just as guilty of complacency and lack of faith as we are today. These are among the greatest sins on earth; we just sit back and let the world go by making no effort to get involved with the many worthy causes that could make this a more harmonious and righteous world in which to live.

As individuals we are capable of changing much more than we believe we can. United, we could have an unbelievable impact on the evils that exist in the world. It would be wonderful if we all were united and organized. Without organization, nothing of any consequence has ever been accomplished. We can be assured that Satan is organized. How else could he accomplish the great evils the world has witnessed throughout its history?

How many of us approve of abortion or pornography or sex and violence we see on TV and in other media. The question should not be whether we approve or disapprove of what is there but whether or not God considers it evil. The only way to find out is to go to the Scriptures and read the commandments He has given us which defines His position. Our opinion (of what is right or wrong) is immaterial. We will be judged on what God has taught concerning sin, not on what we believe it should be. His words are explicit, true, and shouldn't be toyed with by man. Yet this is what many try to do. As a nation, we have made up our own minds as to what constitutes sin, not allowing for God's word on the subject. It is not right for man to assume that he, not God, has the right to determine what is and is not sin. When we do so, the standard soon becomes, "anything goes," and sin would exist only if man, not God, made the determination.

What have we, individually or collectively, done about the many evils that exist in our country and the world? Have we written letters asking for change, made telephone calls stating our position, and encouraged others to do so? Our apathy indicates that we either approve of or at least don't disapprove of to the extent that we are willing to take action against it.

The evils of the world exist largely because *good people* allow it. On judgment day, we may not be found guiltless when we have allowed laws to be passed protecting the rights of evildoers, even encouraging their destructive actions, allowing their degenerate influences to exist above the law. By following the channels of the law, we, the citizens of the United States, the world, and members of our churches have an obligation to use the powers of heaven, our faith, and all other available weapons to organize and create the necessary changes.

"State and religion shouldn't mix!" How often we hear this statement? It's like saying that milk and cream shouldn't mix. Our states and countries consist of the same people who make up all of our respective religions. They are inseparable. What should be separated is the influence of any church from controlling the governments or governments trying to force their edicts on our churches. When the founding fathers formulated the Constitution and the Bill of Rights, their intent was not to control school prayer or other simple issues that should be handled at the local level. How can issues such as school prayer influence or control the governmental process in any way except to make it more productive and viable? A righteous people are prayerful, law-abiding citizens.

It is Satan's ploy to create this separation and deception. He would like nothing better than to take God's laws and commandments out of our civil law. If he could accomplish this, we would be living in a state of slavery, anarchy, and completely subjected to the will of the governments. The communist nations of the world are good examples of Satan's plan in action. Our freedoms would be diminished or taken from us. Our agency would be affected and our growth toward perfection would be slowed or halted.

We can no longer allow ourselves the luxury of watching others *do it*. We can no longer remain passive and be free of the responsibility and guilt associated with Satan's attempts at enslaving us. We can no longer afford to give up our religious and other freedoms because we fear what the government or some organization might do. Our fealty, first and foremost, is to God and Christ and obedience to their commandments.

I am reminded of the episode in New York City a few years ago, where several people ignored a young woman as she was attacked and raped. I'm sure that most of the witnesses didn't approve. They simply didn't want to get involved. They just stood by and allowed it to happen; some even watched. There was another situation, in Boston I believe, where six or seven men raped a woman on a pool table while others cheered them on. For not helping these young women, do you not believe the onlookers should share the guilt of the perpetrator? When judgment day comes, I believe, we will be judged not only for unrepentant sins but also for the good we could have done but didn't.

There are sins of commission and sins of omission. Our responsibility is not just to ourselves but also to the whole human race. We need to take this responsibility seriously if we expect to make any inroads against the evils perpetrated against us by those who would rather follow Satan than God. When we sit by and accept these atrocities being done to others doing nothing, I believe that we will be held partially accountable. In order to be free of the blood of this generation, we must do what we can to *fight* evil wherever we find it. We must fight as individuals, as groups, states, and as nations. It is our moral obligation and duty to organize, with God at the helm, against wickedness and be a powerful force for good.

When God and His forces fight the final battle at the end of the millennium, there will be exceptional organization. Without it nothing can exist. Wars cannot be fought nor can anything else be accomplished. Even our bodies are organized groups of cells, tissues, organs, and systems. All good things come to pass through organization and planning.

We cannot fight evil by being passive, by procrastination, or by complacency. We must organize, form committees, and put up a united front for righteousness and against evil in every form it takes. Let us, as world citizens, as nations, and as church members no longer allow evil to exist in any form without a battle. Let our voices he heard. Let the power within us, our faith, be felt and allowed to grow, to mature, and to be felt in the world as the great force God intends.

It is my prayer that we all take our responsibilities more seriously, realizing that we *can make a difference* and improve ourselves by using the tools outlined in this book and in the Scriptures in a righteous manner. We can fight evil and embrace God's ways. We can truly learn to know and love Him and the paths He has outlined in the scriptures. We can become better and more productive individuals. We can be forgiven of our sins and achieve perfection. We can accomplish anything we set our minds to do. We must love God and serve Him.

9

REPENTANCE

What was the most stupendous, colossal, fantastic, remarkable, and awesome event in earth's history? It is not a tidal wave, cyclone, tornado, earthquake, volcano, war, or disease. These cataclysmic events have killed hundreds of millions of people around the world, yet they do not come close to the most important event of all time—*the atonement of Jesus Christ.* Although the events listed, except for the atonement, has changed the world in many ways, the atonement has given mankind hope like no other occurrence. If man takes advantage of the repentance associated with the atonement, he may again reside with his Father in heaven, free of sin, sickness, and pain, etc.

"Be ye therefore perfect, even as you're Father which is in Heavens is perfect" (Matthew 5:48). This scripture is given as a commandment, pure and simple. There is no room for argument or interpretation. Yet the Christian world at large considers it blasphemy to think that we could possibly become perfect like our Father in heaven.

As I have studied and meditated on sin and repentance, this scripture has stuck in my mind, and I have come back to it many times. How many of us in this world have obtained perfection? If we haven't, then we are living in a state of sin because we have not attained perfection as God has commanded. To repent of this sin, we must constantly strive to overcome our imperfections and be in a continuous state of complete repentance. To me, this scripture tells us that it is a journey, a commandment that lasts through our sojourn on earth and during the millennium as well. Since our perfection can be like our Father in heaven, it only exists when we have become like Him—all knowledgeable, all intelligent, all wise, all powerful, etc.

To me, sin is any thought or action which would keep me out of the celestial kingdom at the last judgement day. In other words, we must be spiritually clean every whit by complete repentance and obedience.

Perfection is being totally free from the actions related to the influence of any counterproductive trait or characteristic (total self-discipline) and the development and expansion of each of our productive traits, talents, and attributes to the same degree as our Savior. God and Jesus Christ are the exemplifiers of all perfection; therefore, if we have imperfections in the traits that make up our personalities, we have a comparison to show where we are with respect to perfection for any given trait.

It is important that we realize sin is not only doing things that are contrary to God's commandments, but it also exists in the imperfections of our personalities, which makes it possible for us to err—our lack of righteous judgment, lack of self-control, and lack of self-discipline. Sin, therefore, exists in us all until we have become completely Christlike. We cannot survive without God. He sustains us on a minute-to-minute basis with His awesome powers and maintains order in the universe and sustains all of His creations. When we fully understand and accept this, our trust and faith in Him will be magnified.

The true and total acceptance of God's love for us allows us to extend our love back to Him without fear of betrayal and with a sure knowledge that he will sustain us and help us in every way possible to regain His presence. If His love and power were withdrawn, we would be at the absolute mercy of Satan who would then destroy us and the opportunity to gain God's presence would be lost. Essentially, this means that the power for good, the power controlled by God is the controlling power in the universe and the power that maintains the balance between good and evil in each of us. If the power of evil should gain control of the world, the balance would be interrupted and there would be no power for good; we would then be totally

EXPANDING OUR LIGHT

overcome by the evil forces around us. Our agency would not exist, our growth would be halted, and we would have nothing but misery in our lives and would soon be destroyed. This is why we are so dependent on God. Without His power, we could not exist.

If sin includes the existence of imperfections within our personalities, which cannot be completely accomplished in this earth life, then part of repentance must be the perfecting of our productive traits, characteristics, and attributes extended to and through the millennium. Our repentance can only be complete when we have replaced all of our counterproductive and nonproductive traits with productive, righteous ones. To do this, we must rely on the sustaining strength and power of God on a minute-to-minute basis. Each day, we need to pray for an awareness of our imperfections and take the steps required to eliminate them. God will only sustain and strengthen us to the extent that we ask and allow Him to. Part of the perfection process is learning how to let God (through Christ) help us.

How many of us have the kind of relationship with God that will let Him sustain us and help us to cleanse and strengthen ourselves in every aspect of our lives? Whether we recognize it or not, we all need this very special relationship in order to survive this world. Those who reject it to the greatest extent are those who commit the greatest sins, the greatest crimes. We all need a close and loving relationship with God, the same as babies and children need it from their parents. If we were to withdraw our love and sustaining strength from our children, they would soon become disoriented and confused. They cannot survive long because of the harmful and damaging effects of that loss. There would be little difference if God severed His relationship with us. We would become disoriented and soon be at the mercy of Satan. A good example of this is when God withdrew His spirit from the Israelites many times, allowing other nations to conquer them. This withdrawal left them at the mercy of Satan to do with them as he would.

When we are not in a state of continual repentance, we are, in effect, telling God that we don't need Him and that we feel we are sufficient unto ourselves. The more we rely on our own strength and not God's, the more we severe our relationship with Him.

God has said (James 1:5–6; emphasis added), "If any of you lack wisdom let him ask of God who giveth to all men liberally and upbraideth not; and it shall be given him, *but let him ask in faith, nothing wavering;* for he that wavereth is like a wave of the sea driven with the wind and tossed."

God will give us His wisdom and strength if we are sincere and humble. We must let Him help us in our quest for repentance, and perfection, or our efforts will be in vain.

"Repentance is the process whereby a mortal soul - unclean and stained with the guilt of sin - is enabled to cast off the burden of guilt, wash away the filth of iniquity, through baptism and the atonement of Jesus Christ, and become clean every whit, entirely free from the bondage of sin" (D & C 58: 43-45; 64: 3-13; Isaiah 1:16-20; Ezekiel 18: 19-31; Ezekiel 33:7–20). "To gain forgiveness through repentance, a person must have a conviction of guilt, a Godly sorrow for sin and a contrite spirit. He, then, must desire to be relieved of the burden of sin, have a fixed determination to forsake his evil ways, be willing to confess his sins, and forgive those who have trespassed against him; he, must accept the cleansing power of the blood of Christ as such is offered through the waters of baptism and a conferral of the Holy Ghost" (*Articles of Faith*, pp. 109–116).

Repentance is essential to salvation; without it, no accountable person can be saved in the kingdom of God (D & C 29:29).

There are seven basic steps to repentance:

1. Recognition that we have sinned.
2. Have godly sorrow for the wrongs we have done.
3. Confession to God, and if the sin is major, to the proper authority.
4. Ask the forgiveness of God and the ones sinned against.
5. Make restitution to the ones sinned against to the greatest extent possible.
6. Refrain from ever doing them again.
7. Undergoing baptism by one having the authority to act in the name of Jesus Christ.
8. Receive the Holy Ghost by the laying on of hands by one having the authority.

If any of these steps are omitted, when memory permits, our repentance is not complete. Baptism is the washing away of the sins committed. If God could forgive us of our sins without baptism, there would be no need for it.

Here are some of God's commandments and scriptures concerning repentance:

> "Therefore I will judge ye, oh house of Israel, everyone according to his ways," saith the Lord God. "Repent, and turn yourself from all your transgressions; so iniquity will not be your ruin." (Ezekiel 18:30)

> From that time Jesus began to preach and to say, "Repent; for the kingdom of heaven is at hand." (I believe that what Jesus is referring to here is for us to repent before we die. (Matthew 4:17)

> Now that after John was put in prison, Jesus came unto Galilee preaching the gospel of the kingdom of God.
> And saying, "The time is fulfilled, and the kingdom of God is at hand; repent ye, and believe the Gospel." (Mark 1:14–15)

> Repent, and be baptized every one of you in the name of Jesus Christ for the remission of sins, and ye shall receive the gift of the Holy Ghost. (Acts 2:38)

> Repent ye, therefore and be converted, that your sins may be blotted out. (Acts 3:19)

> Therefore if that man repenteth not, and remaineth and died an enemy to God, the demands of Devine Justice do awaken his immortal soul to a lively sense of his own guilt, which doth cause him to shrink from the presence of the Lord, and doth fill his breast with guilt, and pain, and anguish, which is like an unquenchable fire, whose flame ascendeth up forever and ever. (Isaiah 2:38)

> And again I say unto you, is there one among you that doth make a mock of his brother, or that heapeth upon him persecutions?
> Wo unto such an one, for he is not prepared, and the time is at hand that he must repent or he cannot be saved!

Yea, even wo unto all ye workers of iniquity; repent, repent, for the Lord God hath spoken it. (Alma 5:30–32)

Wherefore teach it unto your children, that all men everywhere must repent, or they can in no wise inherit the kingdom of God, for no unclean thing can dwell there, or dwell in His presence. (D & C 6:57)

10

FORGIVENESS

It is human nature to be unforgiving to one another. Many of us will never make it to the celestial kingdom because of our unwillingness to forgive the trespasses of others. Frequently, I hear quoted the old cliché, "I don't get angry, I get even." How sad that we could jeopardize our own salvation and exaltation by letting the pain and anguish we have shouldered by not forgiving someone their trespasses, which doesn't hurt them but ourselves. Why carry the burden of unforgiveness, when with a little courage we can forgive?

Our Savoir is very explicit on this subject. We must forgive others or we won't be forgiven. How can we overcome the hurt and resentment, the feeling of needing to punish those who have offended us? These are primal emotions; they often control our actions in spite of all our efforts to forgive.

Forgiving others of their trespasses is not always easy. For instance, when someone offends us, and we are deeply hurt by it and we go through a period of suffering and angst. But when there seems to be no remorse on the offender's part, it becomes extremely difficult to forgive or even generate a desire to forgive. Here, we are dealt a triple whammy. First, we are hurt by the trespass itself; next, we are hurt by the lack of concern on the part of the offender; and last, we feel the pangs of guilt because we can't seem to forgive the offence. In most cases, we must do some soul searching, fasting, and praying before we can accomplish it. It becomes easier, if we regard it as a permanent encumbrance, it will remain with us until we make the choice to release it to Christ. If we treat forgiveness as a choice, it becomes easier to forgive.

Forgiveness never comes without the help of our Heavenly Father. We must learn how to turn our pain and anguish over to Him. This is not always easy and is rarely done on the first try. Our Father in heaven may test our patience, our faith, and our sincerity before heeding our prayers. If, after our first try, we haven't succeeded and we still feel the pain and anguish, many of us just give up. We may even start nurturing the pain and resentment, which often turns to hate and revenge. We must be persistent and sincere in our efforts to obtain our Lord's help. He will help us, but sometimes, we must prove our faith and sincerity in Him and in desiring His aid. If deep down in our hearts we are not sincere in our pleas for His guidance and our desire to forgive, He most assuredly will not help.

Many of us take a sick pleasure in holding on to our unforgiveness. It makes us feel superior to those whom we won't forgive.

It takes courage to ask someone to forgive our trespasses when we have brought pain into their lives. Many of us simply cannot bring ourselves to ask anyone for forgiveness. Which brings the least pain into our lives: to work up the courage to ask for forgiveness or go through life feeling guilt and pain for the suffering we have caused another? Procrastination is not an option. The righteous use of our agency is at stake, and we must act quickly. We have three choices: (1) we can procrastinate and put it off until later (this is justified only if we are in the process of fasting and prayer) (2) we can make the decision to ignore the whole thing and never ask for forgiveness thus going through life in a state of misery and guilt; or (3) we can do what is right and what needs to be done for our own salvation and maybe even the salvation of the individual against whom we have trespassed. *Just ask for their forgiveness and the ordeal will be over.*

Often, we do not have the courage to approach someone we have offended. Humility determines that we recognize our need to rely on God for everything in this life. Is it not within His power to help us obtain the courage we need? Do not be afraid to ask God to give us the courage and determination to seek forgiveness.

Many times, and for many trespasses, more courage is needed to forgive someone than to ask for forgiveness. This is especially true for some of the more serious sins such as rape and murder. Nevertheless, both forgiving someone else and asking others to forgive us are among the more essential things we must do to work out our salvation. Let us examine some of the principles of forgiveness. If we do not use the law of forgiveness, it may lead to our destruction.

The following basic principles of forgiveness are similar to the steps for repentance, of which they are a part:

1. We must recognize that we have sinned against or hurt someone.
2. Feel godly sorrow for what we have done.
3. Ask forgiveness of those sinned against and also ask the Lord for forgiveness.
4. Make restitution whenever it is necessary. For some things, restitution is next to impossible. Gossip, slander, adultery, murder, and rape are among the most difficult things for us to make restitution. It is far better to refrain from committing such sins than to try to take the steps of repentance and forgiveness to gain absolution.
5. Never do it again.
6. Confession to the proper authority, though not really a step of forgiveness, may be required if the sin is of a serious moral nature.

These six steps are essential in order to gain forgiveness. There is no other way, no shortcuts. Time will not erase, correct, or absolve us from the responsibility or the necessity of going through them.

If those of whom we seek forgiveness will not do so, we have, at least, taken the steps necessary for working out our own salvation; the problem, then lies in their hands.

The steps of forgiving others are equally difficult. They fall into two categories:

a. Those who have trespassed against us and have asked us for forgiveness.

b. Those who have trespassed against us and have not asked us for forgiveness.

For those who have asked, it is absolutely necessary that we do forgive. The Savoir has said:

> For if ye forgive men their trespasses, your heavenly Father will also forgive you:
> But if ye forgive not men their trespasses, neither, will your Father forgive your trespasses. (Matthew 6:14–15)

To be told we must forgive others their trespasses does not necessarily mean it will be easy to accomplish. Often, the trespasses against us are of a serious nature, actions that have literally changed our lives and put them in a chaotic state. What about the man or woman who steals a spouse? Or through viciousness, maligns or slanders us, tells vicious lies about us, or, in extreme cases, perhaps even murders a member of our family? We are bound to forgive them if they follow the steps of repentance and ask for our forgiveness. For some cases, however, restitution cannot be made. The murderer cannot bring back the dead or the philanderer may be unable to restore a stolen spouse. What then? We must still forgive; as the Lord says in Mormon 8:20, "Behold what the scripture says - man shall not smite, neither shall he judge; for judgment is mine, saith the Lord, and vengeance is mine also, and I will repay."

When we encounter a problem forgiving someone for their trespasses and identify a sin we have committed against another that we have not asked to be forgiven or if we sin against our Lord which has not been resolved, we should search deeply inside and ask, "Just how much would I like to be forgiven?" Then remember that if we desire forgiveness, we must forgive in return. As an example, my wife was railing at the children for something they were doing for the third or fourth time. They had promised not to do it again, but here they were, repeating the offence. I stepped in to try and stop her from killing them. "What's the matter?" I asked. She answered, *"The children keep doing the same things over and over again. They say they are sorry but they're not. Now I'm supposed to forgive them again? I'm tired of it! What am I supposed to do?"* I then asked *her how many times she had committed a sin more than once and asked our Lord to forgive her and He had. Could she do less for our children?*

I have often heard this saying, "I will forgive, but I won't forget." I believe in most cases this attitude does not show true forgiveness. It is true we cannot completely forget many of the things we experience in life, but to make that statement often implies that we really may not have forgiven. When our Savoir said he would forgive, He also stated that He would remember the sin no more. Literally, to forgive means absolution from payment of debt and not accusing them of the sin. The *New Webster's Dictionary* defines it thusly: "To cease to feel resentment against; to give up a claim on account of; to grant remission of an offence, debt, fine, or penalty; to pardon; to free from the consequences of an injurious act or crime." So, if someone cheats me in a business deal, I can forgive him and cease to carry a grudge. However, trust is another matter. Until he wins my trust by righteous actions, I will, probably, have no further business dealings with him. This does not mean that I haven't forgiven him, it's just that I have lost my faith and trust in him.

In a previous ward, we have a dear sweet lady who has had money owed to her for several years for babysitting. She has tried many times to get this money paid to her but to no avail. In relief society, she mentioned that this was having a very adverse effect on her. She was feeling anger, frustration, and even the beginning of hatred. She asked for suggestions from the class on how to handle the situation. We were dealing with approximately $125.00, so it is no small matter as she needs this money very much.

My wife came up with a solution that may work if one feels they can afford it. "Write her a letter and forgive her of the debt," she said. "That should help to get rid of those destructive feelings that are building up inside of you."

This lovely lady said she would give it another try or two before she was willing to go that far. This may be one method to consider for those who are indebted to us. Our Savoir used this method in one of His parables which is listed at the end of this chapter under the scriptural references.

Another thing we should never do is say we forgive when in our hearts we haven't. When someone comes to us to ask forgiveness, don't just say, "I forgive you," unless the incident was of minor importance to us and there is no question in our minds that we have forgiven. If the incident is of a serious nature, however, then with sincerity of heart tell them something like this: "I feel I must pray about this. I am having a difficult time dealing with my feelings on the matter. But I really appreciate your coming to me. May we talk about it later?" This may help.

On the other hand, there are some acts that perhaps should not be discussed, such as adultery or rape, but for which more time should be given to ponder and meditate. To ask for the time to pray and contemplate should not be unreasonable. In the end, our hearts must be purged of any unkind feelings or grudges. Hate, malice, grudges, and unkind feelings toward others are the poisons that destroy men's souls.

Sometimes, we may feel that the pain may never be erased from our hearts but, remember, what is necessary is ridding ourselves completely of the guile, the resentment, the need to retaliate, hate, dislike, rancor, and anger toward the offending party. This we must do if we ever expect the Lord to forgive us. It is far better to endure the pain than to harbor these destructive feelings in our heart. Remember, Satan is behind it all.

If we still have destructive feelings toward someone who has come to us asking forgiveness, we need to purge ourselves of them using the steps outlined.

Bishops, branch, and stake presidents have been ordained and set apart and have the power of discernment necessary to help us cope with any problem that comes our way. We should never hesitate to seek their help in coping with these serious problems.

Once we have purged ourselves of these destructive feelings, we must contact the one who has come to us for forgiveness and explain that through fasting, prayer, counseling, and with the help of the Lord, we have been able to rid ourselves of any bad feelings toward them and can truly forgive them. Be honest with them at all times. Our honesty is as important to them as it is to us. It is counterproductive to say we forgive while harboring ill feelings toward them.

There are those who have trespassed against us and have not asked for our forgiveness. This does not necessarily mean they are not sorry. Some may be, some may not. It all depends on the individual.

If they are trying to work out their salvation, they probably have Godly sorrow but don't know the steps they must take. Or they may know the steps but not have the courage to take them. These people fear man more than they fear God. This problem must be conquered before they can make the progress that is necessary to inherit the Celestial Kingdom.

Those who, out of vindictiveness and hate, deliberately sin against us and display no sorrow or remorse for what they have done and don't ask for forgiveness, perhaps, have a special place waiting for them in hell. For in sinning against man they have also sinned against God. Our only problem is that of coping with what they do or have done and trying to change their attitude toward us. What we must not do is allow our destructive characteristics and traits control us. We must continually purge ourselves of these elements and proceed to work out our own salvation. There is no way we can harbor negative, destructive feelings and still make it to the celestial kingdom. This means, as our Lord has commanded, we must forgive them; we cannot exact punishment against them unless their persistence in hurting us cannot be curbed. Then, in righteousness, we must do whatever is necessary to protect our families and ourselves.

The success or failure of forgiveness rests entirely within ourselves and in how much faith we have in God's ability to help us. The degree to which we are able to forgive is the degree that God will forgive us. If we will not forgive completely, He will not forgive us completely. Our success depends on our persistence in pursuing the steps outlined above. When we do succeed, our blessings will be far greater than we can imagine, however, maybe not in this life.

Some of us nurture our grudges, but we can never forgive anyone if we follow the pattern listed above. The best avenue to follow is to not dwell on the wrongs people do to us. What others say or do to us does not describe us but does describe them. We shouldn't even think about them, instead, we should use the method outlined in chapter 2 to improve our attitudes on forgiveness. It helps if we dwell on the good qualities of others. We must go out of our way to do things for those we are trying to forgive. It is not easy, but the forgivers will be blessed beyond their abilities to contain God's blessings when they succeed.

You may wish to try this therapy. First, choose someone who has brought pain into your life. Get out a pencil and paper and make a list of his or her good and positive qualities. Then, try consciously to forget bad or negative traits possessed by this person. Everyone has at least a few good qualities. In really trying to pick out the redeeming traits of that person, we will tend to erase the grudge we have against him or her. It will help us to forgive or at least start us on the path of forgiveness.

I have found that when I think or dwell on the wrongs someone has done to me, they tend to be magnified beyond what the original intentions may have been. This is Satan's plan to diminish the good and magnify the bad. If I can control my thoughts and turn to something that is spiritual in nature, I harbor less animosity. Controlling our thoughts is the secret to almost any success or failure.

It is difficult to overstress the importance of praying sincerely for help in all stages of the forgiveness process. Learn how to turn loose of the ill feelings, the pain, and the remorse and let our Lord shoulder the burden. If we really know that to dwell on any of these feelings is a choice, it becomes easier to forgive and forget. Remember it is a *choice* to be upset or be annoyed at real or imagined offenses aimed at us. God has promised us that if our hearts are right before Him and our faith is sufficient, He will take our burdens on himself so we no longer have to feel the guilt associated with the offense.

Here are some of the scriptural references that may help us understand the significance and importance of forgiveness:

> And forgive us our debts, as *we* forgive our debtors. (Matthew 6:12)

> And whosoever speaketh a word against the Son of man, it shall be forgiven him: but whosoever speaketh against the Holy Ghost, it shall not be forgiven him, neither in this world, neither in the world to come. (Matthew 12:32)

> Then came Peter to him, and said, Lord, how oft shall my brother sin against me, and I forgive him? till seven times?
> Jesus saith unto him, I say not unto thee, until seven times: but, until seventy times seven.

Therefore is the kingdom of heaven likened unto a certain king, which would take account of his servants.

And when he had begun to reckon, one was brought unto him, which owed him ten thousand talents.

But forasmuch as he had not to pay, his lord commanded him to be sold, and his wife, and children, and all that he had, and payment to be made.

The servant therefore fell down, and worshipped him, saying, Lord, have patience with me, and I will pay thee all.

Then the lord of that servant was moved with compassion, and loosed him, and forgave him the debt.

But the same servant went out, and found one of his fellow servants, which owed him an hundred pence: and he laid hands on him, and took him by the throat, saying, Pay me that thou owest.

And his fellow servant fell down at his feet, and besought him, saying, Have patience with me, and I will pay thee all.

And he would not: but went and cast him into prison, till he should pay the debt.

So when his fellow servants saw what was done, they were very sorry, and came and told unto their lord all that was done.

Then his lord, after that he had called him, said unto him, O thou wicked servant, I forgave thee all that debt, because thou desirest me:

Shouldest not thou also have had compassion on thy fellow servant, even as I had pity on thee?

And his lord was wroth, and delivered him to the tormenters, till he should pay all that was due unto him.

So likewise shall my heavenly Father do also unto you, if ye from your hearts forgive not everyone his brother their trespasses. (Matthew 18:21–35)

Wherefore, I say unto you, that ye ought to forgive one another; for he that forgiveth not his brother his trespasses standeth condemned before the Lord; for there remaineth in him the greater sin.

I, the Lord, will forgive whom I will forgive, but of you it is required to forgive all men. (D & C 64:9–10)

And again, verily I say unto you, if after thine enemy has come upon thee the first time, he repent and come unto thee praying thy forgiveness, thou shalt forgive him, and shalt hold it no more as a testimony against thine enemy –

And so on unto the second and third time; and as oft as thine enemy repenteth of the trespass wherewith he has trespassed against thee, thou shalt forgive him, until seventy times seven.

And if he trespass against thee and repent not the first time, nevertheless thou shalt forgive him.

And if he trespass against thee the second time, and repent not, nevertheless thou shalt forgive him.

And if he trespass against thee the third time, and repent not, thou shalt also forgive him.

But if he trespass against thee the fourth time thou shalt not forgive him, but shalt bring these testimonies before the Lord; and they shall not be blotted out until he repent and reward thee four-fold in all things wherewith he has trespassed against thee.

And if he do this, thou shalt forgive him with all thine heart; and if he do not this, I, the Lord, will avenge thee of thine enemy an hundred-fold;

And upon his children, and upon his children's children of all them that hate me, unto the third and fourth generation.

But if the children shall repent, or the children's children, and turn to the Lord their God, with all their hearts and with all their might, mind, and strength, and restore four-fold for all their trespasses wherewith they have trespassed, or wherewith their fathers have trespassed, or their father's fathers, then thine indignation shall be turned away;

And vengeance shall no more come upon them, saith the Lord thy God, and their trespass shall never be brought any more as a testimony before the Lord against them. Amen. (D & C 98:39–48)

11

BAPTISM AND THE BASIC ELEMENTS OF CHRIST'S CHURCH

There are six basic principles of the Gospel of Jesus Christ:

1. Faith in the Lord Jesus Christ.
2. Repentance.
3. Baptism by immersion by a proper authority for the remission of sins.
4. The laying on of hands for the gift of the Holy Ghost by a proper authority.
5. Obedience to God's laws and participation in his ordinances.
6. Enduring to the end.

Baptism is the portal of entry into the kingdom of God. Our sins cannot be remitted without it. But baptism is an empty ordinance without authority, faith, and repentance. Repentance alone will not get us into God's kingdom unless we must also have the faith that Christ can and will take upon himself the burden of our sins through baptism. Repentance also has direct benefits. If we quit smoking, for instance, we reap the health that is earned therein. If we repent and are baptized, forgiving and redeeming us for eternal life with God is part of His eternal mission. These basic principles have been established by God and are absolutely essential for our salvation. There is no way to bypass them. Every accountable human born into this world must pass through the portal of baptism or have this work done for him after he has passed on or he cannot live with our Father in heaven in the eternities to come.

> And the first fruits of repentance is baptism; and the baptism cometh by faith unto the fulfilling the commandments; and the fulfilling the commandments bringeth remission of sins;
>
> And the remission of sins bringeth meekness, and lowliness of heart; and because of meekness and lowliness of heart cometh the visitation of the Holy Ghost, which comforter, filleth with hope and perfect love, which love endureth by diligence unto prayer, until the end shall come, when all the saints shall dwell with God. (Moroni 8:25–26; emphasis added)

So, without true repentance, baptism has no effect and is as empty as repentance without faith. Without baptism, there is no forgiveness for transgressions. Sin can only be washed away in its waters. The covenants we make at this sacred ordinance are renewed each time we partake of the sacrament, which cleanses us from the sins we inadvertently commit in our everyday lives. This is the reason so much emphasis is placed on attending sacrament meeting. Without the sacrament, there would be no way to renew our covenants. Our sins would continue to build and our feeling of unworthiness would increase, making it even harder to attend and to repent. Satan plans his deceptions with great care and cunning. Watch for his traps; they are many and everywhere.

To gain a better understanding of the principle of baptism, I offer the following points for clarification and understanding:

- Baptism must be by total immersion, as performed for Jesus Christ by John the Baptist.
- Baptism is essential for the salvation and exaltation of all who are accountable, both the living and the dead.

- Baptism must be administered by one holding the proper authority, the holy priesthood of God, one to whom Christ has given the right to act in His name.
- John the Baptist demonstrated that baptism is done properly only by immersion, as he took Jesus Christ down into and under the water.

"And Jesus when he was baptized, went straight way out of the water;" (Matthew 3:16)

"Having authority given me of Jesus Christ, I baptize you in the name of the Father, and the Son, and of the Holy Ghost. Amen.
And then shall ye immerse them in the water, and come forth again out of the water. (The word baptize comes from the Greek word meaning, "To immerse.") (3 Nephi 11:25–26)

The scriptures are replete with verses which state the necessity for baptism before we can inherit the kingdom of God. There are those who believe and teach that baptism is not necessary in order to be saved. This is true only if we apply the narrowest possible meaning to the term, "salvation." In this context, being saved means only that we are saved from the grave and that we will be resurrected. The broad meaning of salvation encompasses the perfection process. We are saved from the grave by grace, but we are judged according to our repentance and our works, good or evil. In other words, to the degree we are committed to obeying God's commandments and accepting and participating in the ordinances He has placed here for our progression and growth toward perfection is the degree to which He will forgive us.

How, then, can we determine if one who has the authority to act in the name of Christ is performing our baptism? First, he must belong to a church which has the authority, then the person performing the ordination must hold the holy priesthood of God and be able to trace its conferral through a pedigree back to Christ. Man cannot assume this right. Nor can he receive it from another person unless that person has had it given to him by someone who possesses it and has the keys to perform it. Sound confusing? What this means is that the authority to act in the name of Christ must come from Him through those whom He has chosen by revelation and ordination or the ordinance will not be recognized. Even then, an ordination will have no effect unless the keys to ordain it are given by proper authority. If I have the authority to ordain someone to the office of elder in the Melchizedek Priesthood, I must still get permission from higher authority—the stake president—who holds the keys. The first presidency of the church, who are the anointed prophets of God have given the stake president these keys through ordination. They are then disseminated to others so necessary ordinations can be performed. God's kingdom here on earth then becomes a place of order, a place where all actions of priesthood holders are recognized and recorded. This prevents confusion and assures that persons having the authority and the keys perform all ordinances. Whether on earth or in heaven, God's kingdom is one of order and cannot function with any degree of confusion. Christ will not recognize any action, unless the authority to perform it has been given by one of His ordained disciples.

God, being a God of truth and order, cannot lie or will deceive us. What He says is truth and try, as man will, he cannot change the truth. As Paul wrote to the Ephesians 4:4–5: "There is one body and one spirit, even as ye are called in one hope of your calling. One Lord, one faith, one baptism" (emphasis added).

How many "Christian" faiths are there? How many baptisms are there?

> "Because strait is the gate, and narrow is the way, which leadeth unto life, and few there be that find it." (This implies that a search must be made to find the strait gate, and the narrow way.) (Matthew 7:14)

How many are deceived by Satan and chose the wrong baptism?

This, perceived by many Christians, is that the path seems to be very broad, not narrow, and it seems that anyone can find it. The common perception is that all we have to do is accept Christ as our personal Savoir and we are guaranteed a place with Him in the eternities. *"*Strait is the gate.*" Christ's teachings are very explicit: "follow my commandments." (They cannot be followed if we don't learn what they are and make them a part of our everyday lives. *Strait refers to the dictionary, meaning restricted, constricted, narrow, strict, rigid, exacting, narrow passage.)

> Beware of false prophets, which come to you in sheep's clothing, but inwardly they are ravening wolves.
> Ye shall know them by their fruits. Do men gather grapes of thorns? Or, figs of thistles?
> Even so, every good tree bringeth forth good fruit; but a corrupt tree bringeth forth evil fruit. (Matthew 7:15–17)

> That we henceforth be no more children, tossed to and fro, and carried about with every wind of doctrine, by the slight of man and cunning craftiness, whereby they lie in wait to deceive.
> But speaking truth in love, may grow up unto him in all things, which is the head, even Christ:
> This I say therefore, and testify in the Lord, that ye henceforth walk not as other Gentiles walk, in the vanity of their mind,
> Having the understanding darkened, being alienated from the life of God through the ignorance that is in them, because of the blindness of their heart; (Ephesians 4:14–18)

How then can we be sure of the one true faith, the one true church or body of Christ through which He accepts the one and only true baptism; the only Church to which He has given the authority to act in His name?

Let us go to the scriptures and find how Christ organized His church while He was on the earth. It existed as He had organized it until the death of the apostles, which He had personally chosen and ordained before His crucifixion, and those who were anointed after His death by living apostles. These were the ones who Christ Himself had given the authority to act in His name.

God cannot deceive us. When we are deceived, it is by our own blindness, the hardness of our hearts, or by the craftiness and designs of men. Often, we do not want to change or to listen because we are satisfied with our lives as they are; we just don't want to hear the truth. But to know the truth we must turn to God in prayer so it can be felt in our hearts.

God is not a changeable God. His church and His concepts were designed to be everlasting. We have received no revelation rescinding the following doctrine. It is not sufficient that a church possess only one or two but that they possess all of these points of doctrine. They are as unchangeable as God Himself.

Let us now examine the scriptures, which tell us of what Christ's church, or faith, should consist. No revelation has changed these scriptures:

1. Christ's church must claim divine authority—that power given by Christ to act in His name.

> And when he (Christ) was come into the temple, the chief priests and the elders of the people came unto him as he was teaching, and said, by what authority doest thou these things? And who gave thee this authority? (Matthew 21:23; parenthesis was added to clarify whom they were talking about.)
> (These chief Priests knew that proper authority was needed to preach the gospel. They knew it must come from God in the proper manner.)

> For as the Father has life in Himself; so hath he given to the Son to have life in himself;
> And hath given him authority to execute judgment also, because he is the Son of man. (John 5:26–27)
> (God the Father has given Christ the authority to act in His name.)

> Ye have not chosen me, but I have chosen you, and ordained you, that ye should go and bring forth fruit, and that your fruit should remain: that whatsoever ye shall ask of the Father in my name, he may give it you. (John 15:16)
> (Here Christ is giving His authority to the twelve - the power and authority to act; to perform ordinances in His name.)

> As they ministered to the Lord, and fasted, the Holy Ghost said, Separate me Barnabas and Saul for the work whereunto I have called them.
> And when they had fasted and prayed, and laid their hands on them, they sent them away. (Acts 13:2–3)
> (The authority to act in Christ's name is bestowed on Paul and Barnabas by ordination, the laying on of hands. This was done after the death of Christ.)
>
> And when they had ordained them elders in every church, and had prayed with fasting, they commended them to the Lord, on whom they believed. (Acts 14:23)
> (It is very evident that the apostles recognized the necessity of having the authority to act in Christ's name and that one is called to the ministry by praying, fasting and through the ordinance of laying on of hands by those having the power and authority to do so.)

No one can take these rights on himself or can he bestow them without first having them and the keys that make them functional. If this authority were not needed, Christ, who set the example in all things, would not have given it to His apostles by ordination, the laying on of hands. If it were not needed, His apostles would not have given it to others. God and Christ are the same yesterday, today, and forever. *Man cannot effectively change God's teachings.* God and Christ are the only ones who can change them by revelation and this they have not done.

There are only two churches that could possibly have the divine authority to act in the name of Christ, the Catholic Church and the Church of Jesus Christ of Latter-day Saints. No Protestant Church can have this authority because when they broke away from the Catholic Church, the authority, if possessed, would have been dissolved.

As we examine the remainder of the seventeen points identifying the true church, we must study the scriptural references, then, in all humility, faith, and sincerity, fast and pray to our Heavenly Father in the name of Jesus Christ and ask to know which of these two churches is the true church of Jesus Christ. Only then can the appropriate decision and action be made.

2. The true church of Jesus Christ must have a foundation of apostles and prophets.

> Now therefore ye are no more strangers and foreigners, but fellow citizens with the saints, and of the household of God:
> And are built upon the foundation of the apostles and prophets, Jesus Christ himself being the chief corner stone; (Ephesians 2:19–20)

Another scripture that tells of the absolute necessity of having a prophet to head Christ's church follows: Surely the Lord God will do *nothing,* but he revealeth his secrets unto his servants the prophets (Amos 3:7; emphasis added).

How, then, can Christ's church be governed without a prophet and apostles? If there are no apostles or prophet at the head of the church, it most assuredly is not Christ's for He will do *nothing* except through one of His prophets.

3. The true Church of Jesus Christ must have the same organization as the primitive church which He organized while He was still on the earth.

When Christ was on the earth, He organized and designed His church in a specific way. This is the way He wanted it. This is the way it functions best. There has been no revelation changing it from its original structure. He is the same yesterday, today, and forever. If He weren't, we could not rely on Him and "truth" would become meaningless. *But He is unchangeable.* He tells us what He wants, and we have our choice to obey Him or not. It is when we interject our various beliefs ahead of His desires that we get into trouble.

> And He gave some apostles; and some, prophets; and some evangelists; and some, pastors and teachers;
> For the perfecting of the saints, for the work of the ministry, for the edifying of the body of Christ:
> Till we all come in the unity of the faith, and of the knowledge of the Son of God, unto a perfect man, unto the

measure of the stature of the fullness of Christ: (Emphasis added)

That we henceforth be no more children, tossed to and fro, and carried about with every wind of doctrine, by the sleight of men, and cunning craftiness, whereby they lie in wait to deceive; (Ephesians 4:11–14)

How long does the scriptures say that we should have these apostles, prophets, evangelists, pastors, and teachers? "Till we all (the whole world) come in the unity of the faith, and the knowledge of the Son of God, unto a perfect man, unto the measure of the stature of the fullness of Christ:" Have we all came to a unity of the faith? Do we all belong to the same church? How many Christian faiths are there in the world today, perhaps many hundreds? This is not a unity of the faith, because each of these religions is preaching different doctrine. Was there ever in the history of the world when we so need a prophet, need the direct word from God to help solve our problems and bring a unity to the faith? *These prophets and these apostles are here on the earth today. They are giving us the word directly from God:* Listen to them and pray for enlightenment and you too can know for sure.)

4. <u>The true</u> church of Jesus Christ must bear His name.

> I will say to the north, Give up; and to the south, keep not back: bring my sons from far, and my daughters from the ends of the earth;
> *Even every one that is called by my name*: for I have created him for my glory, I have formed him; yea, I have made him. (Isaiah 43:6–7; emphasis added)

Who is talking here? Verse 3 says, "For I am the Lord thy God, The Holy one of Israel, Thy Savior: I gave Egypt for thy ransom, Ethiopia and Seba for thee. (It is Jesus Christ, our Savoir)

> [23] For the husband is the head of the wife, even as Christ is the head of the church: and he is the savior of the body.
> [30] For we are members of his body, of his flesh, and of his bones. (Ephesians 5:23, 30)

If Christ is the head of the church, then as quoted by Isaiah, the church must be called by His name. How many churches today bear His name?

5. The true church of Jesus Christ must have no paid ministry.

> I have raised him up in righteousness, and I will direct all his ways: he shall build my city, and he shall let go my captives, not for *price nor reward*, saith the Lord of hosts. (1 Isaiah 54:13; emphasis added)

> The elders which are among you I exhort, who am also an elder, and a witness of the sufferings of Christ, and also a partaker of the glory that shall be revealed:
> Feed the flock of God which is among you, taking the oversight thereof, not by constraint, but willingly; *not for filthy lucre*, but of a ready mind; (Emphasis added)
> Neither as being as lords over God's heritage, but being ensamples to the flock. (1 Peter 5:1–3)

Reason informs us that when there is a paid ministry, there are certain strings attached. If the congregation is displeased with his sermons, the minister can be fired. I personally have seen this happen several times. It places the minister under pressure to preach the things the congregation wants to hear, not *what the Lord wants them to hear*. This is the same situation that existed with the pagan priests who ministered to idols. They always told the people the things they wanted to hear. This is what made the worshiping of idols so popular. Are the churches today so much different? For fear of losing their position, pastors will do many things they know are wrong. They will always try to please their employer, to ensure their security. The congregation is also placed in a position to have their personal growth diminished. They do not have to visit the sick, the widows, the orphans, and the poor. In fact, they have hired someone else to assume their spiritual growth, thus displacing it from themselves.

6. The true church of Jesus Christ must baptize by immersion.

> Then cometh Jesus from Galilee to Jordan unto John, to be baptized of him.
> But John forbad him, saying, I have need to be baptized of thee, and comest thou to me?
> And Jesus answering said unto him, suffer it to be so now: for thus it becometh us to fulfil all righteousness. Then he suffered him.
> And Jesus, when he was baptized, went up straightway out of the water: and, lo, the heavens were opened unto him, and he saw the Spirit of God descending like a dove, and lighting upon him:
> And lo a voice from heaven, saying, This is my beloved Son, in whom I am well pleased. (Matthew 3:13–17)

Two things become apparent from these scriptures. First, baptism must be done by immersion. Christ could not have come up out of the water unless He had been down under the water. Second, baptism is an extremely important ordinance. Christ, who had no real need for baptism because of His perfection and lack of sin, was baptized anyway to set the example for all mankind. This importance is stressed even further by the Father's voice coming from heaven, praising Christ for what he had done. The complete Godhead is manifest here. Christ was present in His physical form, His Father was manifest by His voice from heaven, and the Holy Ghost, the third member of the Godhead, was present in the likeness of a dove. In spite of the evidence given in many places in the scriptures, there are those who still don't believe baptism is important or necessary for the salvation of mankind.)

7. The true church of Jesus Christ must bestow the gift of the Holy Ghost by the laying on of hands.

> Now when the apostles, which were at Jerusalem, heard that Samaria had received the word of God, they sent unto them Peter and John:
> Who, when they were come down, prayed for them, that they might receive the Holy Ghost:

> (For as yet he was fallen upon none of them: only they were baptized in the name of the Lord Jesus.)
>
> Then laid they their hands on them, and they received the Holy Ghost.
>
> And when Simon saw that through laying on of the apostles' hands the Holy Ghost was given, he offered them money,
>
> saying, Give me also this power, that on whomsoever I lay hands, he may receive the Holy Ghost.
>
> But Peter said unto him, Thy money perish with thee, because thou has thought that the gift of God may be purchased with money. (Acts 8:14–20)

8. The church of Jesus Christ must practice divine healing.

> And he ordained twelve, that they should be with him, and that he might send them forth to preach,
>
> And to have power to heal sicknesses, and to cast out devils: (Mark 3:14–15)
>
> (Also, notice they had to be ordained before they could preach.)

None of Christ's apostles, disciples, or followers took on these tasks in and of themselves but were first given the authority to do so through the laying on of hands. This does not mean that we cannot pray for health and through faith receive it, but calling on the powers of God through His holy priesthood to not only perform healing but all manner of miracles, is an entirely different matter.

9. The church of Jesus Christ must teach that God and Jesus Christ are separate and distinct beings.

These are personal Gods to whom we can go, to help us with our individual problems; Gods in whose image we are created.

> God, who at sundry times and in divers manners spake in time past unto the fathers by the prophets,
>
> Hath in these last days spoken unto us by his Son, whom he hath appointed heir of all things, by whom also he made the worlds;

> Who being the brightness of his glory, and the express image of his person, and upholding all things by the word of his power, when he had by himself purged our sins, sat down on the right hand of the Majesty on high; (*By this we see that Christ looks like His Father - in His express image.*) (Hebrews 1:1–3)
>
> And God said, Let us make man in *our* image, after *our* likeness: and let them have dominion over the fish of the sea, and over the fowl of the air, and over the cattle, and over all the earth, and over every creeping thing that creepeth upon the earth. (Italics added)
> So God created man in his own image, in the image of God created he him, male and female created he them. (Christ was a distinct being before and after His resurrection. He was the express image of His Father, who then must be a separate righteous being from His Father, whose glory and power exceeds our finite understanding. We in our mortal state resemble God and Christ in our physical features. In righteousness, power, glory, justice, and mercy etc., we fall far short of being like Him. Thus God and Christ become very personal to us, Deities to whom we can and should turn for our every need. Deities, on whom we can rely absolutely, without fear of betrayal, without fear of punishment when we obey all their laws, and commandments and stay in a state of repentance. We can have an absolute knowledge that they cannot lie or mislead us in any way that only truth can come from them.) (Genesis 1:26–27)

10. The church of Jesus Christ will believe in the divinity of Jesus Christ.

    > Jesus saith unto him, I am the way, the truth, and the life: no man cometh unto the Father, but by me. (John 14:6)

    All of Christ's teachings point to the fact that He is divine, that His existence on this earth was, first, to break the bonds of death through the resurrection and second, to redeem His children by taking upon Himself their sins if they so desire and providing they obey His commandments. I testify that Christ is the living Son of the living God. That only through the grace of His redemptive powers, continual repentance, by obedience to His laws and commandments, and by embracing all His teachings and ordinances, can we live with Him again.

11. The church of Jesus Christ must have leaders called by God.

> [1] For every high priest taken from among men is ordained for men in things pertaining to God, that he may offer both gifts and sacrifices for sins:
> [4] And no man taketh this honor unto himself, but he that is called of God, as was Aaron. (Hebrews 5:1, 4)

> And take thou unto thee Aaron thy brother, and his sons with him, from among the children of Israel, that he may minister unto me in the priest's office, even Aaron, Nadab and Abihu, Eleazar and Ithamar, Aaron's sons. (Exodus 28:1)

> And thou shalt put upon Aaron the holy garments, and anoint him, and sanctify him; that he may minister unto me in the priest's office. (Exodus 40:13)

By these scriptures, we see that God called Aaron through His prophet, Moses, by anointing (ordination) and sanctifying. God is the same yesterday, today, and forever, His method of doing things never changes. Through the centuries, man has changed the way God has wanted things done. This does not mean that God accepts the changes. This is only Satan's way to pollute God's teachings and to discredit Him in the eyes of man.

12. The true church of Jesus Christ must claim divine revelation from God.

> Surely the Lord God will do nothing, but he revealeth his secret unto his servants the prophets. (Amos 3:7)

> But he answered and said, It is written, Man shall not live by bread alone, but by every word that proceedeth out of the mouth of God. (Matthew 4:4)

> When Jesus came into the coasts of Caesarea Philippi, he asked his disciples, saying, Whom do men say that I the Son of man am?
> And they said, Some say that thou are John the Baptist: some, Elias; and others, Jeremias, or one of the prophets.
> He saith unto them, But whom say ye that I am?
> And Simon Peter answered and said, Thou art the Christ, the Son of the living God.
> And Jesus answered and said unto him, Blessed art thou, Simon Barjona: for flesh and blood hath not revealed it unto thee, but my Father, which is in heaven.
> And I say also unto thee, That thou art Peter, and upon this rock (Revelation) I will build my church; and the gates of hell shall not prevail against it. (To clarify the meaning of rock, the word, revelation, was added in parenthesis) (Matthew 16:13–18)

The church of Jesus Christ does have revelation from God through His contemporary prophets.

13. The true church of Jesus Christ must be a missionary church.

> And Jesus came and spake unto them, saying, all power is given unto me in heaven and in earth.
> Go ye therefore, and teach all nations, baptizing them in the name of the Father, and of the Son, and of the Holy Ghost.
> Teaching them to observe all things whatsoever I have commanded you: and, lo, I am with you alway, even unto the end of the world Amen. (Matthew 28:18–20)

14. The true church of Jesus Christ must be a restored church.

> Repent ye therefore, and be converted, that your sins may be blotted out, when the times *of refreshing* shall come from the presence of the Lord;

> And he shall send Jesus Christ, which before was preached unto you:
>
> Whom the heaven must receive until the times *of restitution* of all things, which God hath spoken by the mouth of all his holy prophets since the world began.
>
> For Moses truly said unto the fathers, A prophet shall the Lord your God raise up unto you of your brethren, like unto me; him shall ye hear in all things whatsoever he shall say unto you.
>
> And it shall come to pass, that every soul, which will not hear that prophet, shall be destroyed from among the people.

Yea, and all the prophets from Samuel and those that follow after, as many as have spoken, have likewise foretold of these days. (Acts 3:19–24; italics added for emphasis)

The following comes from the Bible dictionary:

> Restitution; Restoration: These terms denote a return of something once present, but which has been taken away or lost. It means re-establishment of the Gospel of Jesus Christ on the earth in the last days, with the powers, ordinances, doctrines, offices, and all things, as they have existed in former ages.

To have a restoration there must first have been an apostasy—a falling away—a time when the word of God was not given through prophets. Paul's second letter to the Thessalonians states that before Christ comes the second time there must first be a falling away.

> Now we beseech you, brethren, by the coming of our Lord Jesus Christ, and by our gathering together unto him,
>
> That ye be not soon shaken in mind, or be troubled, neither by spirit, nor by word, nor by letter as from us, as that the day of Christ is at hand.
>
> Let no man deceive you by any means: for that day shall not come, except there come a *falling away* first, and that man of sin be revealed, the son of perdition; (2 Thessalonians 2:1–3; emphasis added)

I testify to you that this restitution has been accomplished, that the church of Jesus Christ is on the earth today, and that Christ ministers it through His living prophets.

> And I saw another angel fly in the midst of heaven, having the everlasting gospel to preach unto them that dwell on the earth, and to every nation, and kindred, and tongue and people. (Revelations 14:6)

If the gospel were already here, why would there be an angel flying in the midst of heaven with the everlasting gospel to preach to us here on the earth? The gospel is here. It is being taught to the world. Listen to the Spirit of God and He will testify to you, and you too can know within your heart that I speak the truth.

15. The true church of Jesus Christ must practice baptism for the dead.

> Then cometh the end, when he shall have delivered up the kingdom to God, even the Father; when he shall have put down all rule and all authority and power.
> For He must reign, till he hath put all enemies under his feet.
> The last enemy that shall be destroyed is death.
> (Notice the subject is the resurrection)
> For he hath put all things under his feet. But when he saith all things are put under him, it is manifest that he is excepted, which did put all things under him.
> And when all things shall be subdued unto him, then shall the Son also himself be subject unto him that put all things under him, that God may be all in all.
> Else what shall they do which are baptized for the dead, if the dead rise not at all? Why are they then baptized for the dead? (1 Corinthians 15:24–26)

The people in Corinth were practicing baptism for the dead but were teaching that there was no resurrection, and Paul is chiding them for not believing in the resurrection. From this scripture, it is evident that baptism for the dead was in common practice at that time.

The scriptures are replete with the teachings that baptism is an absolute prerequisite for one to enter the kingdom of God. He could not be a just God if He were to deny the privilege of baptism to all who had died, without a knowledge of the gospel. The opportunity of hearing the gospel in the spirit world (prison) and having this ordinance performed for them by proxy (here on earth) must be guaranteed if He is a just God.

> But sanctify the Lord God in your hearts: and be ready always to give an answer to every man that asketh you a reason of the hope that is in you with meekness and fear:
> Having a good conscience; that, whereas they speak evil of you, as of evildoers, they may be ashamed that falsely accuse your good conversation in Christ.
> For it is better, if the will of God be so that ye suffer for well doing, than for evil doing.
> For Christ also hath once suffered for sins, the just for the unjust, that he might bring us to God, being put to death in the flesh, but quickened by the Spirit:
> By which also he went and preached unto the spirits in prison; (Emphasis added)
> Which sometime were disobedient, when once the longsuffering of God waited in the days of Noah, while the ark was a preparing, wherein few, that is, eight souls were saved by water.
> The like figure whereunto even baptism doth also not save us (not flesh, but the answer of a good conscience toward God,) by the resurrection of Jesus Christ: (1 Peter 3:15–21)

Verse 19 informs us that Christ preached to the spirits in prison. What did He preach to these spirits? He preached the same thing to the spirits in prison as He preached to the living, the Gospel of Jesus Christ. What is the Gospel of Jesus Christ? First, faith in the Lord Jesus Christ, second is repentance, third is baptism by immersion for the remission of sin, and fourth, the laying on of hands for the gift of the Holy Ghost. Obedience to His laws and commandments is another of these basic principles. Would He teach another gospel to them? Certainly not! If He did teach baptism, which is an extremely important principle of the gospel, how then did He propose to get these spirits baptized? It could only be done by proxy by someone living, standing in for those who had died. This is the baptism for the dead to which Paul referred in his letter to the Corinthians. If Christ did not teach the necessity for baptism in the spirit prison, then it is not necessary for our salvation, since we must all die. Christ has then lied to us. *However, God or Christ cannot lie to us.* If so, the Scriptures would have no meaning or value and they could not be trusted.

> Jesus answered, verily, verily, I say unto thee, Except a man be born of water and of the Spirit, he cannot enter into the kingdom of God. (John 3:5)

16. The body of the church of Jesus Christ must be called *saints*.

> Now therefore ye are no more strangers and foreigners, but fellow citizens with the *saints*, and of the household of God; (Ephesians 2:19; emphasis added)

> Then Ananias answered, Lord, I have heard by many of this man, how much evil he hath done to thy *saints* at Jerusalem: (Acts 9:13; emphasis added)

> To all that be in Rome, beloved of God, called to be *saints*: Grace to you and peace from God our Father, and the Lord Jesus Christ. (Romans 1:7; emphasis added)

> Unto the church of God which is at Corinth, to them that are sanctified in Christ Jesus, called to be *saints*, with all that in every place call upon the name of Jesus Christ our Lord, both theirs and ours: (1 Corinthians 1:2; emphasis added)

> Paul and Timotheus, the servants of Jesus Christ, to all the *saints* in Christ Jesus which are at Philippi, with the bishops and deacons: (Philippians 1:1; emphasis added)

There are many more references to saints in the scriptures and they all refer to the body of the Church of Jesus Christ. He intends that His people be called saints!

17. The church of Jesus Christ will have additional scripture, which is not had in the Bible, that will testify as a second witness to the divinity and mission of Jesus Christ.

> The word of the Lord came again unto me, saying,
>
> Moreover, thou son of man, take thee one stick, and write upon it, For Judah, and for the children of Israel his companions: then take another stick, and write upon it, For Joseph, the stick of Ephraim, and for all the house of Israel his companions:
>
> And join them one to another into one stick; and they shall become one in thine hand.
>
> And when the children of thy people shall speak unto thee, saying, Wilt thou not shew us what thou meanest by these?
>
> Say unto them, Thus saith the Lord God; Behold, I will take the stick of Joseph, which is in the hand of Ephraim, and the tribes of Israel his fellows, and will put them with him, even with the stick of Judah, and they shall be one in mine hand.
>
> And the sticks whereon thou writest shall be in thine hand before their eyes. (Ezekiel 37:15–20)

The following scripture is referring to the coming forth of the Book of Mormon, which is the stick of Joseph buried in the earth. The Book of Mormon is a history of God's dealings with the inhabitants of the American continent who were descendants of the tribe of Joseph.

> [4] And thou shalt be brought down, and shalt speak out of the ground, and thy speech shall be low out of the dust, and thy voice shall be, as of one that hath a familiar spirit, out of the ground, and thy speech shall whisper out of the dust.
>
> [11] And the vision of all is become unto you as the words of a book that is sealed, which men deliver to one that is learned, saying, Read this, I pray thee: and he saith, I cannot; for it is sealed:

> [12] And the book is delivered to him that is not learned, saying, Read this, I pray thee: and he saith, I am not learned.
>
> [13] Wherefore the Lord said, Forasmuch as this people draw near me with their mouth, and with their lips do honor me, but have removed their heart far from me, and their fear toward me is taught by the precept of men:
>
> [14] Therefore, behold, I will proceed to do a marvelous work among this people, even a marvelous work and a wonder: for the wisdom of their wise men shall perish, and the understanding of their prudent men shall be hid.
>
> [18] And in that day shall the deaf hear the words of the book, and the eyes of the blind shall see out of obscurity, and out of darkness.
>
> [19] The meek also shall increase their joy in the Lord, and the poor among men shall rejoice in the Holy One of Israel.
>
> [20] For the terrible one is brought to nought, and the scorner is consumed, and all that watch for iniquity are cut off:
>
> [21] That make a man an offender for a word, and lay a snare for him that reproveth in the gate, and turn aside the just for a thing of nought. (Isaiah 29:4, 11–14, 15–21)

The gold plates from which the Book of Mormon was translated were sealed and were hid in the ground. The latter-day prophet, Joseph Smith, was directed by God through an angel to get these plates and translate them. The prophet had only a third-grade education but, nevertheless, under the direction of the Lord, he translated the Book of Mormon and proceeded to do *a marvelous work and a wonder* by re-establishing the Church of Jesus Christ on the earth.

> And I saw another angel fly in the midst of heaven, having the everlasting gospel to preach unto them that dwell on the earth, and to every nation, and kindred, and tongue, and people. (Revelations 14:6)

If the earth already had the true and everlasting gospel, it would not have been necessary for an angel of the Lord to deliver it here.

I testify to you that the everlasting gospel is again here on the earth, brought by an angel of the Lord and delivered to Joseph Smith, Jr. in all its purity and simplicity. I believe it is unaffected by the teachings of man, unpolluted, and undefiled. Jesus Christ is the head, and he delivers His counsel to His servants, the prophets, as He did in the days of the ancient apostles.

His message today is the same as it was then. Repent of your sins. Be baptized in the name of the Father and of the Son and of the Holy Ghost for the remission of your sins. Receive the gift of the Holy Ghost by the laying on of hands all by one having the authority to act in the name of Jesus Christ. And learn obedience to all of His laws, ordinances, and commandments.

Baptism, even with all of its ramifications, is not hard to understand. However, there is, a tremendous responsibility attached to accepting it and in making a total commitment to embrace the complete Gospel of Jesus Christ.

This commitment should never be contemplated if the reasons for desiring it are anything but total love for our Savior and the embracing of all the concepts of the gospel.

To be baptized because our intended mate is a member and won't marry outside of the Church may be the wrong reason.

Believing that baptism is all that is necessary for salvation is also a misconception. Our activity and support of all the uplifting programs and activities of the church are an absolute requirement for working out our salvation and growing toward perfection. To be baptized, then, only to become totally or even partially unsupportive or inactive is worse than not being baptized at all. Our spiritual growth depends on our interaction with our fellow saints. A man alone on an island can progress very little. Isolation breeds ignorance, and man cannot be saved in ignorance.

To know the truth of the gospel and not be willing to make all of the commitments and changes in our lifestyles is, in effect, telling our Savior that the required sacrifices are too great and they are unwilling to change themselves to meet the necessary standards and qualifications in order to live with Him again. Are they not telling Christ that they have no need of Him and His redemptive powers?

EXPANDING OUR LIGHT

The promises we make at baptism are the most important commitments we will ever make in our lives. They have eternal consequences.

I have used many references in the body of this chapter and will not use them again in the scriptural references that follow. Please enjoy.

> He that believeth and is baptized shall be saved; but he that believeth not shall be damned. (Mark 16:16)

> Then Peter said unto them, repent, and be baptized every one of you in the name of Jesus Christ for the remission of sins, and ye shall receive the gift of the Holy Ghost. (Acts 2:38)

> And the Lord said unto him: I give unto you power that ye shall baptize this people when I am again ascended into heaven.
>
> And again the Lord called others, and said unto them likewise; and gave unto them power to baptize. And he said unto them: On this wise shall ye baptize; and there shall be no disputations among you.
>
> Verily I say unto you, that whoso repenteth of his sins through your words, and desireth to be baptized in my name, on this wise shall ye baptize them - Behold, ye shall go down and stand in the water, and in my name shall ye baptize them.
>
> And now behold, these are the words which ye shall say, calling them by name, saying:
>
> Having authority given me of Jesus Christ, I baptize you in the name of the Father, and of the Son, and of the Holy Ghost. Amen
>
> And then shall ye immerse them in the water, and come forth again out of the water. (3 Nephi 11:21–26)

> Behold I say unto you that this thing shall ye teach - repentance and baptism unto those who are accountable and capable of committing sin; yea, teach parents that they must repent and be baptized, and humble themselves as their little child, and they shall all be saved with their little children.

And their little children need no repentance, neither baptism. Behold, baptism is unto repentance to the fulfilling the commandments unto the remission of sins.

But little children are alive in Christ, even from the foundation of the world; if not so, God is a partial God, and also a changeable God, and a respecter to persons; for how many little children have died without baptism!

Wherefore, if little children could not be saved without baptism, these must have gone to an endless hell.

Behold I say unto you, that he that supposeth that little children need baptism is in the gall of bitterness and in the bonds of iniquity; for he hath neither faith, hope, nor charity; wherefore, should he be cut off while in the thought, he must go down to hell. (Moroni 8:10–14)

And their children shall be baptized for the remission of sins when eight years old, and receive the laying on of hands. (D & C 68:27)

(Sixteen of 17 points of the true gospel were taken from the pamphlet "The Church as organized by Jesus Christ." Printed in the USA by Deseret Press.)

12

OBEDIENCE

Due to the deceptions and lies of man under Satan's control, it is not always easy to determine to which force or power we are responding. Fasting and prayer will help us find the right answer. The road to perfection is not easy. Those who teach that it is easy and all we must do to be saved is accept Christ as our personal Savoir are not teaching the gospel as Christ did when He was on earth. One of His great teachings is that we are to be judged according to our works and the degree of our repentance. We must read and study the scriptures for ourselves, then in all humility, fast, pray, and meditate on what we have read and ask our Father in heaven to reveal to us the truth; and He will. To accept only the teachings of man, without question, without verifying the truth through the scriptures, and without asking God for conformation is to place us in a position to be deceived. The truth is that *we alone* are responsible for accepting or rejecting whatever teachings are presented to us. We cannot hold anyone else responsible; we alone are accountable for what we believe and what we become. God gave us our agency to make these choices and, when we make wrong selections, we cannot foist the responsibility on to anyone else. The truth is here to be had. We must search for and find it for ourselves, not let others do it for us with the probability of being led astray.

Knowingly disobeying God's laws and commandments is rebellion. The same type of rebellion exhibited by Satan when God did not accept his plan for the salvation of mankind. At some time, we all rebel against God's laws and commandments to one degree or another. Rebellion is one of the greatest causes for our earthly problems. In the pre-existence, we did not rebel to the extent that Satan did or we would have been cast out with him. But some of us weren't as valiant as we should have been. Neither are we as valiant here as we should be, otherwise our progression would be much more rapid. Part of obedience, then, is overcoming the desire to rebel what Satan puts in our hearts. I'm not referring to complete open rebellion against God but rather the little, and sometimes big, indiscretions we commit against his laws and commandments on a day-to-day basis.

Those who are obedient to the laws and commandments of God generally fall within four categories:

1. Those who obey willingly with love, who embrace the concepts behind the commandments, and expecting no reward. They obey because they understand and cherish the laws of love and God's commandments.
2. Those who obey willingly but do it out of a sense of duty and responsibility, not out of love.
3. Those who obey willingly but do it for the rewards and blessings gained through obedience. They fail to comprehend the need to love the concepts behind the laws and commandments.
4. Those who obey the laws and commandments when it is convenient. They often do so reluctantly and also because of the fear of punishment. They disobey if they feel they won't be caught or that their punishment may be slight. Their obedience fills the minimum requirements, and they do not hesitate to rebel against any commandment they do not esteem. Their tunnel vision prevents them from weighing the eternal consequences of their infractions. To them, the pleasure and fun of the moment far outweighs any eternal or long-term rewards. *Satan's deceptions are many and varied.*

Sometimes, depending on the commandment involved, we may all fall into one or more of the categories listed above. It is most difficult to embrace category 1 for all commandments every

EXPANDING OUR LIGHT

waking minute of every day. Our mood swings, angers, prejudices, attitudes, and appetites prevent this. But we need to set our goal on choosing this first category. Strive with humble, prayerful hearts to achieve this state of perfection for all of God's laws, ordinances, and commandments during each waking hour.

Many of our attitudes toward the commandments determine our obedience to them. The more positive our attitude and the more faith we have can help in our quest. I was watching an ad on television the other day where a lady threw a stick into a lake and told her dog to retrieve it. There was no hesitation on the dog's part—no questioning, no doubts, just pure obedience. He didn't stop to decide if this was one of the commands he would or would not obey. There was complete compliance, absolute trust. He didn't stop to reason if the water was too cold or how the command would affect his health or wellbeing. The dog didn't decide to retrieve the stick only part way, he brought it all the way back to his mistress. May we all be as submissive to God's commandments as was the dog to its owner!

Obedience is doing what we are commanded to do because we recognize the authority and wisdom of those giving the orders or making the request. To obey blindly the orders of man may lead to misery and pain. His orders cannot always be trusted because whoever gave them is prone to make mistakes which may lead to a lack of growth and progress.

Obeying God's laws and commandments blindly will not lead us astray. However, to continue to follow in blindness without attempting to understand the reasons for them may slow our growth and progress. God does not require us to do unrighteous things in our pursuit of perfection. *We can always put our faith in obedience to His commandments* but placing the same faith in man may result in disaster. We should always carefully weigh the effects of placing implicit faith in anyone regardless of how enticing their programs or goals may appear. Man's motivations are rarely righteous; more often they are selfish or greedy. Satan dresses his wares in silver and gold and with his smooth oily tongue entices the unwary, the gullible, and the innocent into the web of his clutching fingers.

I am immediately reminded of the horror of the Jonestown incident in which Satan influenced the leader to cause hundreds of deaths, some willingly, others by forced ingestion of cyanide.

There are many other instances in which man, in his innocence or gullibility, has succumbed to the wiles of greedy, grasping men under the influence of Satan only to find later that they had been duped, often losing their life savings. Even worse, they may lose faith in all organized religion and stop their quest for the truth. We should all beware of organizations that promise much but deliver only partial truths and, ultimately, slavery. It is not my intention to encourage the serving and worship of our Deity in blindness. To do so precludes getting to know them better and to love them through study, prayer, and righteous activity.

We should all study the material God has made available to us, and with our reasoning powers, faith, and wisdom, attempt to understand His purposes. Through study and prayer, even the most difficult issues are opened to our hearts and minds, the mysteries become understandable, and knowledge of the divine purpose for which God placed man on earth becomes evident.

Once we accept this purpose, we should follow the law of obedience to which Bruce R. McConkie referred in Mormon Doctrine as the, "The first law of Heaven." When obeying man's laws and commandments, there is seldom an apparent reward for obedience. But when caught being disobedient, there is almost always a punishment attached; and true justice is seldom used in the execution of this punishment. There are always blessings associated with obedience to God's commandments as well as just punishment for disobedience in the absence of repentance.

We can have absolute faith that we will not be judged differently from any other person who has ever lived on this planet. God plays no favorites; He is no respecter of persons. We may question that He treated Moses differently than us, but this is not so. God may have blessed Moses more, but Moses obeyed God's commandments to a much greater extent than do most of us. He earned the blessings he received by obeying the laws upon which they were predicated, just as we earn our blessings. If our intelligence and valiancy are equal to Moses's, we will receive the same spiritual riches enjoyed by him. Our intelligence, wisdom, and knowledge of the gospel plan plays a big part in the blessings we receive. Also, our desire to search for the truth brings the same rewards.

Obedience falls into two specific categories. First, obeying the urgings and whisperings of Satan and those under his control, both people and his host of evil spirits. This obedience leads to physical, mental, and spiritual destruction and ultimate slavery. Second, obeying the still small voice of God and all His commandments leads to perfection and eternal life with Him. Obedience to the powers of darkness gradually leads us out of the light and knowledge of God into everlasting darkness and destruction. The more we learn about obedience, the more likely we are to obey.

At some time in our lives, it becomes necessary for us to stand back and examine our attitude toward each of God's laws and commandments and question our motives for obedience or disobedience. Only then can we assess our position with respect to God and His plan for eternal progression, happiness, and salvation.

Another big stumbling block, and there are many, to our obedience is our appetites for various things: sex, worldly collectables, food, money, power, etc. When we allow these appetites to control us instead of controlling them, we are in deep trouble. The degree of our control over our appetites determines the degree of our obedience to them. Our attitudes and thoughts are the keys to self-discipline, which is the key to obedience, and obedience is the first law of heaven.

As I was driving down the highway recently, I discovered myself exceeding the speed limit most of the time, constantly looking in the rearview mirror and scanning the highway ahead fearful of being caught by the highway patrol. I suddenly realized that the stress I was placing myself under would abate if I slowed down to the speed limit. I did so and ceased looking over my shoulder for the patrolman. I then began to compare that situation with obedience to God's laws and commandments. We do not have to worry and feel guilty (stress) when we are within the limits of obedience. The big difference is that when we disobey God's laws, the "Patrolman" always knows, and punishment is eminent unless we repent and then stay within the limits of God's laws from then on. Obedience brings peace, serenity, and happiness plus the blessings associated with it. Disobedience brings stress, misery, unhappiness, guilt, and eventual punishment. Which is the best route to take? The choice is ours.

DR. LAUREN J. BALL

There are many references in the scriptures relating to obedience to God's commandments. Please enjoy the selections I have included and study others that will increase your knowledge and faith on the subject.

> Now therefore, if ye will obey my voice indeed, and keep my covenant, then ye shall be a peculiar treasure unto me above all people: for all the earth is mine:
> And ye shall be unto me a kingdom of priests, and an holy nation… (Exodus 18:5–6)

> Ye shall therefore keep my statutes and my judgments, and shall not commit any of these abominations; neither any of your own nation, nor any stranger that sojourneth among you: (Leviticus 18:26)

> But he answered and said, It is written, Man shall not live by bread alone, but by every word that proceedeth out of the mouth of God. (Matthew 4:4)

> And Samuel said, Hath the Lord as great delight in burnt offerings and sacrifices, as in obeying the voice of the Lord? Behold, to obey is better than sacrifice, and to hearken than the fat of rams.

> For rebellion is as the sin of witchcraft, and stubbornness is as iniquity and idolatry. Because thou hast rejected the word of the Lord, he hath also rejected thee from being king. (1 Samuel 15:22–23)

> If they obey and serve him, they shall spend their days in prosperity, and their years in pleasures.
> But if they obey not, they shall perish by the sword, and they shall die without knowledge. (Job 36:11–12)

> Let us hear the conclusion of the whole matter: Fear God, and keep his commandments: for this is the whole duty of man.
> For God shall bring every work into judgment, with every secret thing, whether it be good, or whether it be evil. (Ecclesiastes 12:13–14)

EXPANDING OUR LIGHT

But this thing commanded I them, saying, Obey my voice, and I will be your God, and ye shall be my people: and walk ye in all the ways that I have commanded you, that it may be well unto you.

But they hearkened not, nor inclined their ear, but walked in the counsels and in the imagination of their evil heart, and went backward, and not forward. (Jeremiah 7:23–24)

And the kingdom and dominion, and the greatness of the kingdom under the whole heaven, shall be given to the people of the saints of the most High, whose kingdom is an ever-lasting kingdom, and all dominions shall serve and obey him. (Daniel 7:27)

And they that are far off shall come and build in the temple of the Lord, and ye shall know that the Lord of hosts hath sent me unto you. And this shall come to pass, if ye will diligently obey the voice of the Lord your God. (Zechariah 6:15)

And when they had brought them, they set them before the council: and the high priest asked them,

Saying, Did not we straitly command you that ye should not teach this name? And, behold, ye have filled Jerusalem with your doctrine, and intend to bring this man's blood upon us.

Then Peter and the other apostles answered and said, we ought to obey God rather than men. (Acts 25:27–29)

There hath no temptation taken you but such as is common to man: but God is faithful, who will not suffer you to be tempted above that ye are able; but will with the temptation also make a way to escape, that ye may be able to bear it. (1 Corinthians 10:13)

[13] Wherefore gird up the loins of your mind, be sober, and hope to the end for the grace that is to be brought unto you at the revelation of Jesus Christ;

[14] As obedient children, not fashioning yourselves according to the former lusts in your ignorance:

[17] And if ye call on the Father, who without respect of persons judgeth according to every man's work, pass the time of your sojourning here in fear: (1 Peter 1:131–14, 17)

And it come to pass that I, Nephi, said unto my father: I will go and do the things which the Lord hath commanded, for I know that the Lord giveth no commandments unto the children of men, save he shall prepare a way for them that they may accomplish the thing which he commandeth them. (1 Nephi 3:7)

Behold, I, the Lord, command; and he that will not obey shall be cut off in mine own due time, after I have commanded, and the commandment is broken. (D & C 56:3)

Verily I say unto you, that I, the Lord, will chasten them and will do whatsoever I list, if they do not repent and observe all things whatsoever, I have said unto them. (D & C 98:21)

13

COMMANDMENTS AND BEATITUDES

COMMANDMENTS

As the Lord's commandments are studied, we should take note that they deal with many of the character traits listed in chapter 2. This is no coincidence. They are these Christlike traits we must perfect and these satanic traits we must overcome before we can expect to live with our Father throughout the eternities. These traits must be dealt with in the perfection process, which is finalized during the millennium. Before we can live with God again, we must be cleansed every whit.

None of us should be complacent about, or satisfied, with our progress toward perfection in this life. Complacency and being satisfied with whom and what we are will probably be harmful to our growth. They are offshoots of and just as destructive as procrastination. "For behold, if ye have procrastinated the day of your repentance even until death, behold, ye have become subjected to the spirit of the devil, and he doth seal you his; therefore, the Spirit of the Lord hath withdrawn from you, and hath no place in you, and the devil hath all power over you; and this is the final state of the wicked" (Alma 34:35).

Humility is a vital component in studying this or any other book. Humility and honesty are necessary as we analyze each of our character traits regarding our growth. This is always essential as we pursue eternal life or try to attain any goal. By just glancing at the list in chapter 2 and refusing to act, we are in essence procrastinating the day of our repentance. We are saying, "I can't be bothered," "I just don't have the time," or "I'll look at it more seriously some other time." We are approaching it without humility and without a true desire to know the will of our Father in heaven. God has commanded us, either directly or indirectly, to perfect or bring under control each of the traits listed. To know if these commandments are true, all we have to do is pray and listen for the answer.

Throughout the scriptures, the Lord informs us to be obedient to His commandments. Most of us have only a vague understanding of this and a lack of appreciation for the rewards of obedience and punishments of disobedience.

The commandments listed in this book have been copied from the scriptures. They are arranged by subject matter and include scriptures from the Bible, Book of Mormon, Doctrine and Covenants, and the Pearl of Great Price.

It is difficult to comprehend the tremendous value of obedience to God's commandments. In Abraham 3:23–25, the Lord said,

> And God saw these souls that they were good, and he stood in the midst of them, and he said: These I will make my rulers; for he stood among those that were spirits, and he saw that they were good; and he said unto me: Abraham, thou art one of them; thou wast chosen before thou wast born.
>
> And there stood one among them that was like unto God, and said unto those who were with him: We will go down, for there is space there, and we will take of these materials, and we will make an earth whereon these may dwell;
>
> And we will prove them herewith, to see if they will do all things whatsoever the Lord their God shall command them; (emphasis added)

I believe that learning to obey God's commandments is the most important reason He placed us here on earth. The consequences for obedience or disobedience are of an eternal nature, being good or evil, depending on the degree of our repentance for those commandments disobeyed.

Wherever I travelled in the so-called "Christian" countries, one of the beliefs I hear most quoted by Christians at large is that it is not necessary to obey the commandments in order to be saved. Many teach that all that is required is for us to accept Christ as our personal Savoir and we are saved by grace. If we place the narrowest possible meaning on being saved just being resurrected and attaining the lowest degree of glory, then this is true. (See how Satan deceives?) However, included in the plan of salvation is a righteous judgment. We will all be judged according our works whether they are good or evil and whether or not we have sincerely taken all the steps of repentance and have been baptized. This judgment will be recognized as just and merciful by each of us and will be totally acceptable to us no matter which mansion or to which glory or kingdom we are assigned. The degree of our achievement, progression, or condemnation (because of the judgment) will be a direct result of the way we have lived on this earth. In other words, the degree to which we obey all of God's commandments and repent of our sins shall determine where we will go. Salvation has a much broader meaning than just being saved from the grave. It encompasses the whole perfection process. Two absolutes in this world are: we will all die and we will all be judged.

From the scriptures, it is obvious that we will not all be assigned to the same place. The following are some of the many scriptures that inform us of where we may be going:

> There are also celestial bodies, and bodies terrestrial: but the glory of the celestial is one, and glory of the terrestrial is another.
> There is one glory of the sun, and another glory of the moon, and another glory of the stars: for one star differeth from another star in glory.
> So also is the resurrection of the dead. It is sown in corruption; it is raised in incorruption: (1 Corinthians 15:40–42)

> In my Father's house are many mansions: if it were not so, I would have told you. I go to prepare a place for you. (John 14:2)

Those who inherit the highest degree of glory, the celestial glory, and the greatest blessings are those who love Christ the most, those who obey His commandments to the greatest extent, and those who are committed to living and imparting the gospel because of a love for God and His great plan of salvation. To be just and merciful, this plan must include obedience to God's laws and commandments. It must also include repentance when through weakness we break the laws and disobey Him. To be valid, repentance must come from a humble heart—be thorough and sincere.

The scriptures are records of God's dealings with man through His prophets. They include His revealed laws and commandments by which we all are to be judged. They were not given to hinder our growth or cause pain and frustration but to encourage us to become more perfect, to help us express our love and compassion for our fellow man, and to grow spiritually. Our Father in heaven wants us to live with Him again, but he will not force us. The scriptures show us the way to accomplish this. Don't get caught up in the fun, games, pleasures, and other distractions from the straight and narrow path to God's kingdom.

We were given our agency, the freedom to choose between the forces of good and evil and one of God's greatest gifts to man. The righteous are those who love and embrace the power of good and who love their fellow man and God enough to obey His commandments. They progress each day toward complete obedience and perfection. They do their utmost to remain in a constant state of repentance and obey all of God's laws.

The scriptures were not written for just a few or just for the Jews or Christians but also for the whole world. They were written first, to give us knowledge of God and to let us know that He exists, that He, through His son, Jesus Christ, is the creator of this world and all that it contains. They also let us know that Christ is the Redeemer, the one responsible for our salvation and exaltation. Secondly, they were written as a guide for our growth toward perfection.

The laws and commandments in the scriptures were written for and apply to every accountable, man, woman, and child ever born on this earth. No one is excluded from obedience because of gender, race, religion, or for any other reason. These laws are universal, eternal, and immutable. They apply equally to each of us, whether we are a great religious leader, a poor peasant, a king, or a pauper. God will hold us responsible for obeying them to the degree that we have had access to them, and whether or not we wish to accept them.

Each of us is a child of God and will be judged according to our works to the degree of our commitment, repentance, obedience to His will, and according to the knowledge and availability we have of His word. It is necessary to obey His laws and commandments in order to achieve perfection, to attain the highest possible degree of progression, and to achieve the eternal world of God.

As mentioned before, obedience to God's commandments is not stifling or retarding but, instead, allows the greatest possible freedom from undesirable traits (which are built on disobedience). It also gives us freedom from the bondage of sin, which in effect is the habit of disobedience. Obedience keeps an individual alive and free, while disobedience causes spiritual and even physical death and enslavement.

Those of us who believe that only a few of the commandments pertains us and who use every easy excuse for not obeying God's laws are only deluding themselves. If we would only look deep into the reasons for being here and ask ourselves who we are, why we are here, where we are going after we leave here, and if our ultimate place in the eternities could be affected by obedience or disobedience to God's laws, we would certainly change our ways.

> Obedience is the first Law of Heaven, the cornerstone upon which all righteousness and progression rests. It exists in compliance with divine law, and in conformity to the mind and will of Deity, in complete subjection to God and His commandments. To obey Gospel Law is to yield to obedience to the Lord, to execute the command of and be ruled by Him whose we are. (Mormon Doctrine, Bruce R. McConkie)

If our desire is to regain the presence of God and reside with Him throughout the eternities, it is absolutely necessary to obey all His commandments, beginning with the Ten Commandments, which follow.

The Ten Commandments were given to Moses for the children of Israel. Many believe the Ten Commandments were done away with when Christ came, but Jesus Himself said:

> Think not that I have come to destroy the law, or the prophets: I am come not to destroy, but to fulfill.
>
> For verily I say unto you, Till heaven and earth pass, one jot or one tittle shall in no wise pass from the law, till all be fulfilled.
>
> Whosoever therefore shall break one of the least commandments, and shall teach men so, he shall be called the least in the kingdom of heaven: but whosoever shall do and teach them, the same shall be called great in the kingdom of heaven. (Matthew 5:17–19)

It is true that Christ gave us the beatitudes to help us follow Him more closely. They are part of the celestial law of love and they help us in the process of perfection. However, most of us find it difficult to lead the life they embody and, therefore, must look to some of His other more explicit commandments, such as The Ten Commandments, which are more easily followed and understood.

> And God spoke all these words, saying,
>
> I am the Lord thy God, which have brought thee out of the land of Egypt, out of the house of bondage.
>
> Thou shalt have no other Gods before me.
>
> Thou shalt not make unto thee any graven image, or any likeness of anything that is in Heaven above, or that is in the earth beneath, or that is in the water under the earth:
>
> Thou shalt not bow down thyself to them, nor serve them: for I the Lord thy God am a jealous God, visiting the iniquity of the fathers upon the children unto the third and fourth generations of them that hate me;
>
> And showing mercy unto thousands of them that love me, and keep my commandments.

EXPANDING OUR LIGHT

Thou shalt not take the name of the Lord thy God in vain; for the Lord will not hold him guiltless that taketh his name in vain.

Remember the Sabbath day, to keep it Holy.

Six days shalt thou labor, and do all thy work:

But the seventh day is the Sabbath of the Lord thy God: in it thou shalt not do any work, thou, nor thy son, nor thy daughter, nor thy manservant, nor thy maidservant, nor thy cattle, nor thy stranger that is within thy gates:

For in six days the Lord made the heaven and the earth, the sea, and all that in them is, and rested the seventh day: wherefore the Lord blessed the Sabbath day, and hallowed it.

Honor thy father and thy mother: that thy days may be long upon the land which the Lord thy God giveth thee.

Thou shalt not kill.

Thou shalt not commit adultery.

Thou shalt not steal.

Thou shalt not bear false witness against thy neighbor.

Thou shalt not covet thy neighbor's house, thou shalt not covet thy neighbor's wife, nor his manservant, nor his maidservant, nor his ox, nor his ass, nor any thing that is thy neighbor's. (Exodus 20:1–17)

Ye have heard that it hath been said, Thou shalt love thy neighbor, and hate thine enemy.

But I say unto you, Love your enemies, bless them that curse you, do good to them that hate you, and pray for them which despitefully use you, and persecute you;

That ye may be the children of your Father, which is in heaven: for he maketh his sun to rise on the evil and on the good, and sendeth rain on the just and on the unjust.

For if ye love them which love you, what reward have ye? do not even the publicans the same?

And if ye salute your brethren only, what do ye more than others? do not even the publicans so?

Be ye therefore perfect, even as your Father, which is in heaven, is perfect. (Matthew 5:43–48)

Judge not, that ye be not judged.

For with what judgment ye judge, ye shall be judged: and with what measure ye mete, it shall be measured to you again. (Matthew 7:1–2)

[3] And said, Verily I say unto you, Except ye be converted, and become as little children, ye shall not enter into the kingdom of heaven. (Little children are trusting, have faith, are teachable, are innocent, loving, and are free of guile.)

[4] Whosoever therefore shall humble himself as a little child, the same is greatest in the kingdom of heaven.

[21] Then came Peter to him, and said, Lord, how oft shall my brother sin against me and I forgive him?

[22] Jesus saith unto him, I say not unto thee, Until seven times: but, Until seventy times seven. (Matthew 18:3–4, 21–22; read verses 23 through 35)

[32] And this is my doctrine, and it is the doctrine which the Father hath given unto me; and I bear record of the Father, and the Father beareth record of me, and the Holy Ghost beareth record of the Father and me; and I bear record that the Father commandeth all men, everywhere, to repent and believe in me.

[33] And whoso believeth in me, and is baptized, the same shall be saved; and they are they who shall inherit the kingdom of God.

[34] And whoso believeth not in me, and is not baptized, shall be damned.

[38] And again I say unto you, ye must repent, and be baptized in my name, and become as a little child, or ye can in nowise inherit the kingdom of God.

[39] Verily, verily, I say unto you, that this is my doctrine, and whoso buildeth upon this buildeth upon my rock, and the gates of hell shall not prevail against them.

[40] And whoso shall declare more or less than this, and establish it for my doctrine, the same cometh of evil, and is not built upon my rock; but he buildeth upon a sandy foundation, and the gates of hell stand open to receive such when the floods come and the winds beat upon them. (3 Nephi 11:32–34, 38–40)

EXPANDING OUR LIGHT

²³ Therefore, if ye shall come unto me, or shall desire to come unto me, and rememberest that thy brother hath aught against thee-

²⁴ Go thy way unto thy brother, and first be reconciled to thy brother, and then come unto me with full purpose of heart, and I will receive you.

³⁴ But verily, verily, I say unto you, swear not at all; neither by heaven, for it is God's throne;

³⁵ Nor by the earth, for it is his footstool;

³⁶ Neither shalt thou swear by thy head, because thou canst not make one hair black or white;

⁴⁸ Therefore I would that ye should be perfect even as your Father who is in heaven is perfect. (Matthew 12:23–24, 34–36, 48)

Therefore I would that ye should be perfect even as I, or your Father who is in heaven is perfect. (3 Nephi 12:48)

¹ Verily, verily, I say that I would that ye should do alms unto the poor; but take heed that ye do not your alms before men to be seen of them; otherwise ye have no reward of your Father who is in heaven.

² Therefore, when ye shall do your alms do not; sound a trumpet before you, as will hypocrites do in the synagogues and in the streets, that they may have glory of men. Verily I say unto you, they have their reward.

¹⁹ Lay not up for yourselves treasures upon earth, where moth and rust doth corrupt, and thieves break through and steal;

²⁰ But lay up for yourselves treasures in heaven, where neither moth nor rust doth corrupt, and where thieves do not break through nor steal.

²¹ For where your treasure is, there will your heart be also. (3 Nephi 13:1–2, 19–21)

Give not that which is holy unto the dogs, neither cast ye your pearls before swine, lest they trample them under their feet, and turn again and rend you.

Ask, and it shall be given unto you; seek, and ye shall find; knock, and it shall be opened unto you.

For everyone that asketh, receiveth; and he that seeketh, findeth; and to him that knocketh, it shall be opened. (3 Nephi 14:6–8)

There are many more commandments pertaining to this subject throughout the scriptures. To just choose these to obey would be doing us and God a great disservice and would surely keep us from the perfection and salvation required of us by our Savoir. Search the scriptures for the other commandments, study them, and meditate upon them, and the Lord will reveal to them His secrets.

THE BEATITUDES

The Ten Commandments have often been called the law of duty and responsibility. The Lord has also said that those who have to be commanded in all things are slothful servants. If you had many people working for you, who would you appreciate the most: those who had to be told everything to do or those who would accomplish the same things on their own out of love and gratitude? I imagine the Savoir feels much the same about us. If we do all things in righteousness and with love and gratitude for God's bounty, we should need no commandments because we would be living the law of love.

This is the difference between the Ten Commandments and the Beatitudes. The Ten Commandments are the laws of duty and responsibility and they comprise the terrestrial law. The Beatitudes comprise the celestial law or the law of love. This law is of doing the right thing because we love doing it, not because we have the duty or responsibility of doing it. The law of love needs no commandments because those who practice it are dedicated to and love doing what is right and embrace all that is good and righteous. These are the true Christians.

Listed below are the Beatitudes. They are but a few of the traits that the Savoir would have us cultivate and perfect as we work out our salvation and exaltation. Just reading them will do no good. Even memorizing them will do no good. We must examine each one and define its purpose and meaning and with diligent effort perfect it and make it a part of our lives. Some of these beatitudes I have defined in later chapters, some I haven't. It is my prayer that we will all carefully examine and embrace the concepts they represent. To do so will enrich our lives immeasurably and help us to live our lives, as the Savior would have us do.

> And seeing the multitude, he went up into a mountain: and when he was set, his disciples came unto him:
> And he opened his mouth, and taught them, saying,
> Blessed are the poor in spirit: for theirs is the kingdom of heaven.
> Blessed are they that mourn: for they shall be comforted.
> Blessed are the meek: for they shall inherit the earth.
> Blessed are they which do hunger and thirst after righteousness: for they shall be filled.
> Blessed are the merciful: for they shall obtain mercy.
> Blessed are the pure in heart: for they shall see God.
> Blessed are the peacemakers: for they shall be called the children of God.
> Blessed are they which are persecuted for righteousness' sake: for theirs is the kingdom of heaven.
> Blessed are ye, when men shall revile you, and persecute you, and shall say all manner of evil against you falsely, for my sake.
> Rejoice, and be exceeding glad: for great is your reward in heaven: for so persecuted they the prophets which were before you.
> Let your light so shine before men, that they may see your good works, and glorify your Father which is in heaven. (Matthew 5:1–16)

14

LOVE AND CHARITY

LOVE

The law of love is celestial. It is the highest, most profound, and all-encompassing of God's laws. If we want to insure ourselves of a place in His kingdom, we should embrace and practice all of the concepts this law entails to the full extent of our capabilities. Every law and commandment the Lord has given to us has its roots in this basic eternal principle.

To love is to be able to trust, be loyal to, be charitable toward, be kind to, have compassion for, ignore faults, endure hardships for, cry over, be patient with, and be considerate of another. It is unbiased, forgiving, enduring and tolerant. In fact, it is the base from which all productive, righteous characteristics and traits flow, just as hate and fear are the bases from which all destructive, unrighteous traits arise.

Albert Schweitzer felt that love of life was the "holy grail" of life.

When we are afraid to love or be loved because we might be rejected or betrayed, we are, in a sense, protecting ourselves from the pain associated with it. At the same time, we are denying ourselves the joy and happiness that comes from being vulnerable to love. Allowing us to be open to love is not always easy in a society, which often takes advantage of our openness. The rewards are far greater when we can freely give and accept love. Secluding ourselves in our own self-pity and the paranoid fears associated with love halts our progress and spiritual growth, thus diminishing our joy and happiness.

One of Satan's worst creations is the association between love and sex, diminishing the meaning of love to the level of a basic emotion. Love is then equated with the pleasure sex brings us. Love is a very special spiritual gift given to as we can accept it. The act of procreation is also supposed to be sacred, but we have diminished it to the extent that it is no longer sacred. It should be accepted as a beautiful gift and used as a special act of the creation of life.

Had our Savoir succumbed to fear and refused to be vulnerable to the pain of giving and receiving love, there could have been no sacrifice that allows us the privilege of repenting and we would all have been lost to Satan. There would be no hope for us. Satan does not make it easy for us to open up, to be susceptible. He places stumbling blocks in our path; he pushes all our buttons and uses every devious device at his command to stop us from progressing and loving. By allowing ourselves to love unselfishly or receive love without fear of betrayal, we thwart his efforts. This law of love must be studied and sincerely practiced before we can realize the blessings associated with it. We should learn to love one another as the Savoir loves us—a free, wholehearted, and no-strings-attached type of love. This love must be infinitely greater than that which we now give to our children, parents, or mates. It must be given unselfishly and with true charity in our hearts.

The greatest manifestation or indication of love is the willingness to sacrifice. The degree of our ability to sacrifice is a measure of our love for others.

I'm reminded of the air disaster in Washington DC a few years back where a steel worker saved many lives. A plane had crashed in the Potomac river in freezing water. He dove in the frigid waters of the river time after time to bring others safely to shore until exhaustion and the freezing water overtook him. He gave his life so that others, whom he did not know, could live. This is a sacrifice that depicts a love for all humanity, a love that we would all be wise to emulate. Our unwillingness to sacrifice is a measure of our selfishness and greed. These two traits are among the greatest destroyers of all love relationships, especially marriage.

As my wife and I were coming from my Trinidad office one day, we chanced to see a single railroad vehicle slowly moving south.

She asked me what it was. There appeared to be an instrument on the back of the vehicle between the rails. I surmised that it was a device that measured the distance between the tracks and that a certain tolerance was required and when exceeded, the road crew would have to be called in to make a correction.

I began thinking about the tolerance limitations of love. We all place restrictions on the love we have for others and also attempt to set limitations on the love others have for us. Throughout our married lives, we tend to test these limitations often resulting in disaster, perhaps even dissolving a marriage. What we are really doing is testing the degree of love they have for us and testing their ability to tolerate our idiosyncrasies and our shortcomings, making them prove they love us in spite of all we do to them.

In the early years of marriage, this love tolerance is likely to be quite broad; but as time elapses, we become less tolerant. Little things we thought were cute now become irritating. If we don't broaden the base of this tolerance, we soon find the marriage in jeopardy. If the relationship lasts beyond this period of adjustment, the boundaries again begin to broaden. We get used to the little irritations and we stop demanding the changes that seemed so important a short time before. This is the first sign of true maturity. Our own desires become less important, selfishness goes by the wayside, and we are more inclined to give of ourselves, more willing to sacrifice. As our maturity grows, our tolerance broadens and our love increases.

The limits we place on our love for others are another important factor in relationships. I will love my mate if he/she loves me, doesn't hurt me too deeply, is faithful, remains slim and trim, keeps a clean house, is generous, is pleasant to be around, doesn't nag, etc. This kind of love is conditional; it depends on the actions of others. If we place conditions on our love, we also tend to limit the sacrifices we are willing to make to maintain and grow our love.

What if Christ's love for us was as conditional as the love we give others. Maybe he wouldn't love us if we didn't pray every night or if we yelled at our spouses or children. He might say you have done too much evil, so I don't love you anymore. You are now Satan's, to do with as he pleases. However, His love for us is unconditional. He may give more blessings to those who pray every night or don't beat their wives, etc., but this is no indication that His love for the disobedient is less than for the obedient. He suffered for all who sin, and to ensure that His suffering was not in vain, we must all repent and remain in that condition by partaking the sacrament every Sunday possible. The magnitude of His love for us is beyond our comprehension. How could He possibly love us so much that he assumed all of our sins? His suffering was so great that He bled from every pore. He willingly sacrificed his life for us in a horribly painful way so that we might have the opportunity to gain salvation and exaltation. Now that's love.

It is far too easy to place conditions, limitations, and tolerances on the love we have for others. How narrow is the love tolerance we have for our enemies? How narrow is the love tolerance we have for casual acquaintances or even for those we dearly love? It is not easy to broaden these tolerances, but it is necessary. The "I love you if" syndrome must be removed if we expect to inherit the highest kingdom of God. Again, this is a journey we must work on a step at a time mostly in this life.

It is essential that we set certain priorities at the beginning of a marriage union, especially those that magnify love. These priorities must be nurtured and held fast during and beyond the lifetime of those involved. The first item of importance in this list of priorities is our interaction with God. Placed at the center of our lives, He will bless our relationships beyond our abilities to contain them.

The second priority is the marriage relationship itself. This priority should make the union more important than the individual's needs. The marriage, then, has a much greater chance of surviving and growing and maturing as well. The spouse ranks third in value to the survival of this bond. If we place ourselves next, we emphasize our own needs as being more important than those of our mate and marriage. This is a manifestation of selfishness which cannot help but create resentment and anger, thus jeopardizing the relationship. When children enter the family, whether ours, yours, or mine, the father goes to the bottom of the list. By using this order of values, we take all the selfishness out of the marriage union giving it a much greater chance of survival.

I have found that most selfish people are not aware of their problem and, hence, are unwilling to look closely at themselves and admit they need help. One of the great principles of growth is our ability to look within ourselves and see the imperfections such as selfishness, greed etc., and be willing to take the steps necessary to eliminate them from our personalities. By so doing, we enhance our capacity to love those around us. We are even able to see the good qualities in our enemies and, subsequently, we are able to develop a love for them. When we do this, we are obeying the commandment "to love our enemies."

There are many different types of love and many degrees of each kind. The love we have for our parents is entirely different from the one we feel for our spouses and children, which is different from the feelings we have for a neighbor or a best friend. There is also romantic love, true love, and, perhaps the most important, self-love but not self-adoration. Until we can learn to truly love ourselves in spite of our frailties, it is very difficult to love others. I'm not discussing a hyper self-worship that is destructive to our growth but rather a high self-esteem, feeling good about ourselves, enjoying the kind of individuals we are. A person who loves himself has forgiven the imperfections in his personality and the things he has done wrong throughout his life and always encompassing the law of repentance.

Perhaps the intensity of love for a particular person is based on the degree of trust we have in them, the ability to feel free from possible betrayal. When betrayal does take place by a loved and trusted friend or lover, our ability to love and trust anyone decreases. Faith is also very important—faith that our love will be reciprocated and treated with tenderness, kindness, and nurtured so it can grow and bloom with the radiance God intended. This radiance is our personal circle of love. Love is the very fabric that binds humanity together and is the base for all productive, righteous relationships.

Hate, fear, greed, selfishness, and envy are the great destroyers of this fabric. To one degree or another, we all abuse the loved ones in our lives. Having this love abused and betrayed throughout our lives often prevents us from extending unconditional love to those around us. It is absolutely necessary that we make every effort to overcome this fear of giving our love without reservation. We may be hurt from time to time in the process, but the rewards will far outweigh the pain involved.

Project ourselves into a world where there is no fear of having our love betrayed and no fear of having to betray someone else's love, a world in which there is implicit faith and trust in everyone. Just imagine the joy and happiness therein? In such an environment, Satan could have little or no power over us whatsoever. We humans have a habit of giving our love to a chosen few and withdrawing it from everyone else. We do this for many reasons: we don't like the way they look, the way they talk, their race, or other inconsequential reasons. We may be prejudiced, bigoted, hateful, and, usually, unwilling to change.

How do we extend our love to the rapists, the murderers, the thieves, and in general, those who take advantage of and literally try to destroy the rest of us? These are the dregs of humanity, the cancer of society! The key is to not confuse the individual with the act. How would the Savoir treat these individuals? I firmly believe He would love them and teach them the gospel when He could. He would call them to repentance, just as He did the Sadducees, Scribes, and Pharisees. He did not embrace their ways but rebuked their actions and called for them to change their ways.

Loving our enemies does not necessarily mean that we throw our arms around them or hug and kiss them, but rather that we treat them nicely, perhaps, teach them the gospel, and if possible, call them to repentance. They may not respond, especially if they are deep into the bondage of sin, but this does not alleviate our responsibility of trying. It is not easy to look past the sins and love some individuals, but this is what we are required to do. We should never be judgmental of a person's worthiness or receptivity to receive the gospel; that is for God to decide. And when we are judgmental, we may be jeopardizing their opportunity for embracing the gospel, thus depriving them of salvation and exaltation.

Others we have difficulty loving are those to whom we have extended love in the past, but having it betrayed, rebuked, or rejected. The reasons are immaterial, but just having to deal with the emotional upheaval and strain can be overwhelming. There are angers and fears that must be dealt with. At times, the rejection alone can be too much to bear. For these situations we should all turn to God in prayer to help us forgive and gain the peace and serenity necessary for our mental, spiritual, and emotional well-being. There are some things we cannot possibly do alone; this is one of them. In fact, for most things, we cannot do without God's help. That is why we are commanded to have a prayer in our hearts at all times. Often it becomes necessary to rely on the compassion of a friend or professionals such as our bishop, branch president, or a therapist.

Christ, of course, exemplifies the greatest love possible. His sacrifice included not only His willingness to die for us and seal His mission with His own blood, but also, if we repent, take on our collective sins. It is impossible for us to comprehend this kind of love, this willingness for Christ to sacrifice his life and take on our multitude of sins. All the pain associated with this exceeds our understanding. Our love for Him and our love for one another can never come close to the depth of His love for us. However, we are to try with all our hearts to love as He loves.

Studying the scriptures below may help us gain a greater appreciation for the necessity of loving unconditionally without bias and prejudice.

> Master, which is the greatest commandment in the law?
> Jesus said unto him, Thou shalt love the Lord thy God with all thy heart and with all thy soul and with all thy mind.
> This is the first and great commandment.
> And the second is like unto it, thou shalt love thy neighbor as thyself.
> On these two commandments hang all the law and prophets. (Matthew 22:36–40)

> A new commandment I give unto you that you love one another; as I have loved you, that ye also love one another. (John 13:34)

> If ye love me keep my commandments. (John 14:15)

> But behold, the Lord hath redeemed my soul from hell; I have beheld his glory, and I am encircled about eternally in the arms of His love. (2 Nephi 1:15)

> Wherefore, ye must press forward with a steadfastness in Christ, having a perfect brightness of hope, and a love of God and all men, wherefore, if ye shall press forward, feasting upon the words of Christ, and endure to the end, behold, thus saith the Father, ye shall have Eternal Life. (2 Nephi 31:20)

And gave unto them commandments that they should love and serve Him, the only living and true God and He should be the only being whom they should worship. (D & C 20:19)

Love, being the most precious principle and the greatest commandment from God, should elicit our most intense efforts in its development so that we can become perfect as Christ.

CHARITY

Charity is the pure love of Christ. A love that embraces all righteousness, all goodness, all perfection, and all humanity. A love that is so encompassing that we mortals cannot begin to comprehend it. And yet, we are commanded to be charitable, and the Lord gives us no commandment we cannot obey. Perhaps the perfection of charity, like other traits, should be considered a journey that lasts throughout this life and on through the millennium to be improved a little each day. He also gives no commandment unless He provides a way for us to obey. I like the scripture in Alma, which gives us a better understanding of our Savior's teachings on charity.

> And now behold, my beloved brethren, I say unto you, do not suppose that this is all; for after ye have done all these things, if ye turn away the needy, and the naked, and visit not the sick and afflicted, and impart of your substance, if you have, to those who stand in need - I say unto you, if you do not any of these things, behold, your prayer is vain, and availeth you nothing, and ye are as hypocrites who do deny the faith.
> Therefore, if you do not remember to be charitable, ye are as dross, which the refiners do cast out, (it being of no worth) and is trodden under foot of men. (Alma 34:28–29)

This emphasizes the point that it's not just the giving but also the spirit of giving that is important. If we give grudgingly, there is no charity in our hearts. Essentially, this indicates we have selfish hearts in which charity cannot exist. Other traits that oppose charity are greed, hate, avarice, anger, and pride, etc.

The development of charity, then, means the eradication of many destructive traits, the reforming of our attitudes, rethinking of our priorities, and allowing sweetness of service to permeate our souls. Doing these things will bring the true joy of charity into our hearts and help us become more like our Savoir.

The following scriptures will help us put into perspective, the inclusion of charity into our daily lives:

> Though I speak with the tongues of men and of angels, and have not charity, I am become as sounding brass, or a tinkling cymbal.
>
> And though I have the gift of prophecy, and understand all mysteries, and all knowledge; and though I have all faith, so that I could remove mountains, and have not charity, I am nothing.
>
> And though I bestow all my goods to feed the poor, and though I give my body to be burned, and have not charity, it profiteth me nothing.
>
> Charity suffereth long, and is kind; charity envieth not; charity vaunteth not itself, is not puffed up.
>
> Doth not behave itself unseemly, seeketh not her own, is not easily provoked, thinketh no evil;
>
> Rejoiceth not in iniquity, but rejoiceth in the truth;
>
> Beareth all things, believeth all things, hopeth all things, endureth all things.
>
> Charity never faileth: but whether there be prophecies, they shall fail; whether there be tongues, they shall cease; whether there be knowledge, it shall vanish away.
>
> For we know in part, and we prophesy in part.
>
> But when that which is perfect is come, then that which is in part shall be done away.
>
> When I was a child, I spake as a child, I understood as a child, I thought as a child: but when I became a man, I put away childish things.
>
> For now we see through a glass, darkly; but then face to face: now I know in part; but then shall I know even as also I am known.

And now abideth faith, hope, charity, these three; but the greatest of these is charity. (1 Corinthians 13:1–13)

Lie not one to another, seeing that ye have put off the old man with his deeds;

And have put on the new man, which is renewed in knowledge after the image of him that created him:

Where there is neither Greek nor Jew, circumcision nor uncircumcision, Barbarian, Scythian, bond nor free: but Christ is all, and in all.

Put on therefore, as the elect of God, holy and beloved, bowels of mercies, kindness, humbleness of mind, meekness, longsuffering;

Forbearing one another, and forgiving one another, if any man have a quarrel against any: even as Christ forgave you, so also do ye.

And above all these things put on charity, which is the bond of perfectness. (Colossians 3:9–14)

Now the end of the commandment is charity out of a pure heart, and of a good conscience, and of faith unfeigned: (1 Timothy 1:5)

But Charity is the pure love of Christ, and it endureth forever; and whoso is found possessed of it at the last it shall be well with him. (Moroni 7:47)

15

MEEKNESS AND HUMILITY

MEEKNESS

The *New Webster's Dictionary* defines the meaning of meekness as follows: soft, pliant, supple; mild of temper; gentle; not easily provoked or irritated; submissive; lacking courage.

I agree with most of it but lacking courage and being submissive I cannot accept.

A meek person may appear to lack courage, when in fact it takes more courage for non-action that it would to act. Most of the saints thrown to the lions in Rome displayed a great amount of courage when they avoided taking action against the Romans who brought abuse and even death upon them. These saints were meek but not lacking in courage. Many of the prophets were meek but extremely courageous as they warned the people many times to repent and were often killed for their trouble. Were they meek? Yes! Were they courageous? Yes!

The strength of meekness lies in the self-discipline required to bring all of our counterproductive traits under control, the courage to go against convention, when we know we are right. This is not a display of cowardice but is a manifestation of meekness also strength. Often, we are ridiculed and reviled for our stand on truth and right. As the second coming nears, Satan will marshal his forces and increase his terrible onslaught against the righteous, especially the Church of Jesus Christ of Latter-day Saints, by concentrating on their weaknesses. He will twist the right into looking wrong. He will attempt to make righteousness unacceptable in the eyes of those who deride and persecute the godly. There are those who would blame God and turn from him when the going getting gets rough. How could God let or cause these things to happen?

Remember the saints, while crossing the plains, they went through hardships that we can only imagine. They lost loved ones and endured coldness that would turn most people from believing in a God who would let these things happen, and yet they knew it was a test of their faith and they never wavered. Many of them were our ancestors, to whom we owe a great debt of gratitude.

The trials and tribulations that are coming just before the second coming of Jesus Christ will be just as bad, if not a lot worse, and will really be a great trial of our faith. With these expectations, it would behoove each of us to prepare for the worst of it, especially the young among us, who will be the most susceptible to hardships. As parents, the preparation and teaching of our offspring about the coming disasters is imperative.

To be committed and remain steadfast in our stand against evil may not be acceptable to the world, but it is certainly acceptable to Christ and the body of his church. Complete commitment to Him and unconditional love for him, would certainly show a great display of courage and meekness, particularly in the face of the great adversities to come. Let us, therefore, rely on the strengths of meekness and shun the image that the world may put on its possession. Let us embrace its concepts and develop and perfect it in our lives, as the saints of old have done before us.

Prophet Joseph Smith displayed great courage and meekness when he turned himself over to the authorities, knowing that he was going to his death. As He put it, "I am going like a lamb to the slaughter." In the face of impossible odds, odds that could not be overcome by the strength of man, he brought forth the gospel in these latter days. His implicit trust in our Lord is a constant reminder that we must all humble ourselves in meekness and faith. Out of necessity, we should commit our hearts and minds to the obedience required to gain salvation and exaltation.

Daniel, who was thrown into the lion's den, required an enormous amount of meekness, humility, and faith. They all go together like Moses when he parted the Red Sea and Joshua when he stopped the sun in the sky for a day. The same is required of us to be as steadfast as all of the great prophets. Can we, as ordinary members of the Church of Jesus Christ of Latter-day Saints, expect to reach the same heights of perfection as them without expending the same effort, faith, humility, and meekness? For every blessing received, it is absolutely necessary to obey the law upon which it is predicated. The blessings these great prophets received required obedience, and to get those same blessings it is necessary that we obey the same laws. If we are of the opinion that we can coast to the celestial kingdom, we need to reexamine the scriptures more closely.

The celestial kingdom is like a very high mountain, uphill all the way. At the bottom of the hill is the telestial kingdom and somewhere, perhaps three quarters of the way up, we find the terrestrial kingdom. At the top we find the celestial kingdom. Along the way, we find skateboards. These coasting devices have names such as procrastination, pride, bigotry, prejudice, hate, anger, etc. It is easy to step on one, either accidentally or on purpose, and coast downhill. Unfortunately, the only way to get off is by repentance, which we must acquire with a humble and contrite spirit. When pride, anger, and other destructive traits get in our way, it becomes nearly impossible to get to the top. Through continuous prayer and by meekness and humility, we can repent and get off the skateboard. Often, we will ride to the bottom of the mountain where we must start over again. If the desire is great enough, we will.

Other skateboards are drugs, alcohol, tobacco, illicit sex, pornography, gaming, and anything else that appears to be exciting, gratifying, and satisfying but which delivers nothing but bondage, misery, and slavery. Many appear to be having such a good time coasting down that they don't even realize where they're headed until it is too late. They like to justify their downhill ride in many ways: "What I'm doing is not so bad, there are many others that are doing much worse!", "Just a little ride never hurt anyone!", "I can quit (get off) anytime I want!", and "I'm not hurting anyone!"

EXPANDING OUR LIGHT

It takes courage, meekness, humility, knowledge, and obedience to stay off the skateboards of life; it also takes dedication and commitment. It takes faith and, sometimes, all the courage and effort we can muster to stay off of them. If we can, though, the rewards are eternal. If we can't, the punishments may also be eternal. Regardless of what or who influences us, the choices we make are ours. We ultimately make the decisions ourselves that determine the heights we attain on the mountain of trials, tribulations, refining fire, and the joy of exaltation.

The following scriptures unite charity, which is the pure love of Christ, to meekness and emphasizes the importance of meekness:

> And again, behold I say unto you that he cannot have faith and hope, save he shall be meek, and lowly of heart.
>
> If so, his faith and hope is vain, for none is acceptable before God, save the meek and lowly in heart; and if a man be meek and lowly in heart, and confesses by the power of the Holy Ghost that Jesus is the Christ, he must needs have charity; for if he have not charity he is nothing; wherefore he must needs have charity.
>
> And charity suffereth long, and is kind, and envieth not, and is not puffed up, seeketh not her own, is not easily provoked, thinketh no evil, and rejoiceth not in iniquity but rejoiceth in the truth, beareth all things, believeth all things, hopeth all things, endureth all things.
>
> Wherefore, my beloved brethren, if ye have not charity, ye are nothing, for charity never faileth. Wherefore, cleave unto charity, which is the greatest of all, for all things must fail
>
> But charity is the pure love of Christ, and it endureth forever; and whoso is found possessed of it at the last day, it shall be well with him.
>
> Wherefore, my beloved brethren, pray unto the Father with all the energy of heart, that ye may be filled with this love, which he hath bestowed upon all who are true followers of his Son, Jesus Christ; that ye may become the sons of God; that when he shall appear we shall be like him, for we shall see him as he is; that we may have this hope; that we may be purified even as he is pure. Amen. (Moroni 7:43–48)

Blessed are the meek: for they shall inherit the earth. (Matthew 5:5)

The meek also shall increase their joy in the Lord, and the poor among men shall rejoice in the Holy One of Israel. (Isaiah 29:19)

Teach them to never be weary of good works, but to be meek and lowly in heart; for such shall find rest to their souls. (Alma 37:34)

Learn of me, and listen to my words; walk in the meekness of my Spirit, and you shall have peace in me. (D & C 19:23)

No power or influence can or ought to be maintained by virtue of the priesthood, only by persuasion, by long-suffering, by gentleness and meekness, and by love unfeigned: (D & C 121:41)

HUMILITY

The scriptures are replete with admonitions to be humble. In order to be humble, we must have an accurate definition of humility to guide us as we attempt to incorporate it into the perfection process. In my opinion, the definition in the *New Webster's Dictionary* is incomplete. The scriptural references to humility almost always exclude deity. *Webster's* definition is given below. Following that I have given my own amplification, which does include the biblical references to deity.

Webster's definition: Not proud or arrogant; modest; meek; submissive; low in rank or conditions. To render humble; to bring down the pride or vanity of; to reduce the power, status, or independence of; to abase.

To this I add the following: Our recognition of and actions related to our total dependence on God for anything and everything in this life. That with His power and through His Son Jesus Christ and the Holy Ghost, He has created and controls all things in the universe as He sees fit.

The recognition that everything in His creation is subject to His will and desires. That He has a personal love for each of us, and that He wants us to perfect our bodies, minds, and spirits. We must also recognize that it is by repentance and obedience to His laws, commandments, and participating in His ordinances that we may enjoy all the benefits of His love and caring.

The recognition that God considers us all to be spiritually equal in value and that separation does exist is because of our individual thoughts and deeds and that the blessings we do receive are because of obedience to law. We all are equal regardless of who we are or our station is in life. None of us are greater or lesser than anyone else in the world.

The recognition that each of us has faults and imperfections which need attention and that these imperfections are to humble us make us aware that we are, indeed, unable to become perfect and attain salvation and exaltation without the aid of our Father in heaven.

To humble us before God not only means that we recognize Him but also that we love, obey, and serve Him. To be humble in our various stations in life may be very difficult because we must treat everyone equally. It is not right to place ourselves above others, regardless of our position, race, intelligence, or for any other reason.

Each of us has equal value in God's eyes, but he does not treat each of us the same. As mentioned above, the difference lies in our thoughts and deeds. God blesses each of us according to our obedience, repentance, righteousness and what is needed to promote our individual need for spiritual growth. When needed, God may chastise one more than another because of the need for repentance or spiritual growth.

> There is a law, irrevocably decreed in heaven before the foundations of this world, upon which all blessings are predicated –
> And when we obtain any blessing from God, it is by obedience to that law upon which it is predicated. (D & C 130:20–21)

The humbler we are, the more blessings we receive. The more we grow toward perfection, the less adversity God needs to place in our path to guide us in the right direction. When there is more adversity placed in our path, we need to examine ourselves for a lack of humility, faith, tolerance, or other traits that may be slowing our progress.

It is difficult to give God all the recognition due Him. The majority of us reject His teachings to some extent. We may not read the scriptures, or pray, or repent as we should, or show charity, or love our fellow man. In some way, we all fall short of allowing Him to always be part of our lives so that we may receive a full measure of His blessings.

The following are things we may not do that show a lack of humility toward God: We may fail to pray as individuals, as families, or groups. We don't carry a prayer in our hearts at all times. When we do pray, they are often vain repetitions, lack of substance, sincerity, enthusiasm, and faith. We may pray with no emotion, and, more often than not, our prayers fail to recognize that God is instrumental in helping us in every aspect of our lives. We may fail to search and study the scriptures for their true meaning. We may not meditate on what we do read. We may deny the personal revelation and inspiration coming from God in regard to the meaning and impact intended by Him. When we study the scriptures, we often rely on the interpretation given by others rather than by relying on the Holy Spirit of God. Therein lies one of the greatest downfalls of man.

Deceits pass from generation to generation in the form of false assumptions, bias, beliefs, attitudes, and misinformation for the evil purpose of deliberately leading congregations and whole churches astray. One example is the pastor who tells members of his congregation that they will be damned for even looking into another faith or questioning interpretations that have been given to them. A closed mind is one of the deadliest weapons Satan uses to destroy us.

Another fault some of us have is accepting certain scriptures as being true, while rejecting others because we believe they don't pertain to us or have any value. There are those who teach "that to be saved all we need to do is accept Christ as our personal Savoir." They totally ignore the scriptures that tell us "faith without works is dead," "we will be judged by our works," or "baptism isn't necessary to inherit the Kingdom of God." In humility, we should study and accept all of the scriptures and not just parts of them until we all come to a unity of the faith and acceptance of the complete plan of salvation and happiness, as given to us by Jesus Christ.

As parents, we like to have our children come to us for the solutions to their various problems. We enjoy knowing what they are doing. We need for them to tell us of their comings, their goings, and their doings. We want them to do the things we have prompted them to do, not what someone else has taught them. Is our Father in heaven so much different and uncaring that He has no concern for us? He wants our comings and goings to be in conformance with His teachings and laws. D & C 109:9 says, "That your incomings may be in the name of the Lord, that your outgoings may be in the name of the Lord, that all your salutations may be in the name of the Lord, with uplifted hands unto the Most High." This is the total acceptance of God into every aspect of His teachings. Our life is a noble and righteous goal well worth achieving.

We often fail to be righteous. Our righteousness only meets the standards we set for it at any given moment. Often, we put it on and take it off, much as we would a garment. We often meet an occasion with the degree of righteousness we feel is called for at the time. I have seen instances where righteousness was worn like a badge especially when members of the individual's church or congregation were present, but when they were with their peers it was shed like unwanted apparel. Most of us are guilty of doing this at times. This is one big reason why many people do not like organized religion. The members present one face on Sunday and another for the rest of the week. This is bigotry! The destructive trait of hypocrisy is alive and well in the world today. This is one trait we should do well to eliminate.

Accepting and practicing prejudice and bias in all of their ugly forms is one of the greatest evils in the world today. Prejudice and pride show a lack of humility unsurpassed by all of the other destructive traits. Man attempts to show his superiority over others by elevating his race, religion, knowledge, his wisdom, looks, position, etc. above theirs. God is no respecter of persons because of these things. He is a respecter of obedience and righteousness. He is a respecter of love, compassion, charity, humility, and all other righteous traits. If He is no respecter of people because of these things, then what right do we have to place ourselves above someone else because of them?

One of the saddest things I have heard is a mother or father making statements to their children that reflects an attitude of superiority over others. When one of my daughters was sixteen, she went out with a very nice gentleman who was nineteen and who respected her chastity, defending references to it vehemently in front of others. She overheard a conversation between a mother, who is a very lovely lady whom I admire, and her daughter, fifteen, who was a classmate in seminary. She made the statement that she was glad her daughter was not like my daughter, going out with someone much older than she. With statements like this, it is not hard to understand why this young lady felt she was better than my daughter, who was very hurt by this statement and seriously considered staying out of the Sunday school class in which they both participated. Thankfully, she prayed about it and decided to stay in.

As parents, we must be on guard every moment of our lives to watch what we say and do. We must be humble and not say things that would perpetuate prejudices or biases to our children, which they may pass on to their children, thus affecting generations to come. It is not hard to teach bigotry to our offspring. We can do it daily by our speech and our actions. We need to be very careful of the things we say and do that teach prejudices and biases to our children.

He's nothing but a Jew or a black or a white. How often we hear these statements day in and day out? How often do we hear or tell ethnic jokes? Our willingness to listen to or pass them on is a measure of our humility. Are they uplifting? Are they things that are part of our Savior's personality? Certainly not! Why then are we so prone to listen to or tell them? They are satanic and have no place in the lives of righteous people. The big question is, do we have the humility, agency, and courage to stop telling these jokes and discourage our associates from doing so?

There are many other aspects of humility that could be discussed in this chapter, but the message I wish to convey is that we should become more aware of the need for humility as a tool to enrich our lives. We truly need to draw closer to our Heavenly Father and recognize all the influences and blessings he bestows on His children here on earth. We need to recognize that we are, in fact, no better or

EXPANDING OUR LIGHT

worse than any of His other children, and base all of our actions on these truths.

Here are some of the available scriptures which may help inspire and motivate us to become as humble as Christ encourages us to become:

> If my people, which are called by my name, shall humble themselves, and pray, and seek my face, and turn from their wicked ways; then will I hear from heaven, and will forgive their sin, and will heal their land. (2 Chronicles 7:14)

> Before destruction the heart of man is haughty, and before honor is humility. (Proverbs 18:12)

> For thus saith the high and lofty One that inhabiteth eternity, whose name is Holy; I dwell in the high and holy place, with him also that is of a contrite and humble spirit, to revive the spirit of the humble, and to revive the heart of the contrite ones. (Isaiah 57:15)

> He hath shewed thee, O man, what is good; and what doth the LORD require of thee, but to do justly, and love mercy, and to walk humbly with thy God? (Micah 6:8)

> Whosoever therefore shall humble himself as this little child, the same is greatest in the kingdom of heaven. (Matthew 18:4)

> And whosoever shall exalt himself shall be abased; and he that shall humble himself shall be exalted. (Matthew 23:12)

> Let this mind be in you, which was also in Christ Jesus:
> Who, being in the form of God, thought it not robbery to be equal with God:
> But made himself of no reputation, and took upon him the form of a servant, and was made in the likeness of men:

And being found in fashion as a man, he humbled himself, and became obedient unto death, even the death of the cross.

Wherefore God also hath highly exalted him, and given him a name which is above every name:

That at the name of Jesus every knee should bow, of things in heaven, and things in earth, and things under the earth.

And that every tongue should confess that Jesus Christ is Lord, to the glory of God the Father. (Philippians 2:5–11)

But he giveth more grace. Wherefore he saith, God resisteth the proud, but giveth grace unto the humble.

Submit yourselves therefore to God. Resist the devil, and he will flee from you.

Draw nigh to God, and he will draw nigh to you. Cleanse your hands, ye sinners; and purify your hearts, ye double minded.

Be afflicted, and mourn, and weep: let your laughter be turned to mourning, and your joy to heaviness.

Humble yourselves in the sight of the Lord, and he shall lift you up.

Speak not evil one of another, brethren. He that speaketh evil of his brother, and judgeth his brother, speaketh evil of the law, and judgeth the law: but if thou judge the law, thou are not a doer of the law, but a judge.

There is one lawgiver, who is able to save and to destroy: who art thou that judgest another? (James 5:6–12)

And whoso knocketh, to him will he open; and the wise, and the learned, and they that are rich, who are puffed up because of their learning, and their wisdom, and their riches - yea, they are they whom he despiseth; and save they shall cast these things away, and consider themselves fools before God, and come down in the depths of Humility, he will not open unto them. (2 Nephi 9:42)

Have ye walked, keeping yourselves blameless before God? Could ye say, if ye were called to die at this time, within yourselves, that ye have been sufficiently humble? That your garments have been cleansed and made white

EXPANDING OUR LIGHT

through the blood of Christ, who will come to redeem his people from their sins:

Behold, are ye stripped of pride? I say unto you, if ye are not ye are not prepared to meet God. Behold ye must prepare quickly; for the kingdom of heaven is soon at hand, and such an one hath not eternal life.

Behold, I say, is there one among you who is not stripped of envy? I say unto you that such an one is not prepared; and I would that he should prepare quickly, for the hour is close at hand, and he knoweth not when the time shall come; for such an one is not found guiltless.

And again I say unto you, is there one among you that doth make a mock of his brother, or that heapeth upon him persecutions?

Wo unto such an one, for he is not prepared, and the time is at hand that he must repent or he cannot be saved!

Yea, even wo unto all ye workers of iniquity; repent, repent, for the Lord God hath spoken it! (Alma 5:27–32)

And they were lifted up in pride, even to the persecution of many of their brethren. Now this was a great evil, which did cause the more humble part of the people to suffer great persecutions, and to wade through much affliction.

Nevertheless they did fast and pray oft, and did wax stronger and stronger in their humility, and firmer and firmer in the faith of Christ, unto the filling their souls with joy and consolation, yea, even to the purifying and the sanctification of their hearts, which sanctification cometh because of their yielding their hearts unto God. (Helaman 3:34–35)

And no one can assist in this work except he shall be humble and full of love, having faith, hope, and charity, being temperate in all things, whatsoever shall be entrusted to his care. (D & C 12:8)

LISTEN to the voice of Jesus Christ, your redeemer, the Great I AM, whose arm of mercy hath atoned for your sins;

Who will gather his people even as a hen gathereth her chickens under her wings, even as many as will hearken to my voice and humble themselves before me, and call upon me in mighty prayer.

Behold, verily, verily, I say unto you, that at this time your sins are forgiven you, therefore ye receive these things; but remember to sin no more, lest perils shall come upon you. (D & C 29:1–3)

16

JUSTICE AND MERCY

JUSTICE

Justice is meting out the correct punishment to one who breaks or disobeys a law. The murderer should not be slapped on the hand nor should death be the punishment for stealing a loaf of bread. Down through the ages, man has not been known for righteous judgment. Some people have served years for stealing a crust of bread and others have murdered without paying the penalty. There is little equitable judgment anywhere in the world today. Man has proven to be an inequitable administrator of justice.

Justice should be equally applied to and by us all without regard to differences such as life, station, race, or religion. God's justice to his children will be equitably and righteously applied to everyone. He has no favorites! Each of us will get exactly what we have earned according to the laws of justice and mercy. The law of mercy can and will have no effect unless the law of repentance has been observed according to God's teachings and commandments. If we expect the law of mercy to apply without studying, understanding, and embracing the complete law of repentance first, we will be greatly disappointed. Punishment for a broken law must be and will be exacted. Justice cannot be robbed. All of our sins must be paid for; there are no exceptions. If we repent as outlined in the scriptures, then Christ will atone for them. If we do not repent, then we alone must pay for them. This is the law! It will not and cannot be changed.

Even though our memory has been blocked, we all agreed to accept the plan of salvation before coming to earth. This plan allows us to use our agency to work out our salvation. Therefore, this law binds every mortal born on earth. There are no exceptions! It doesn't matter if we believe it or not or if we choose not to accept the plan here on earth. It is still God's law, and everyone will be justly judged according to the laws they have been given. These laws were setup and agreed upon before this world was created. In the end, justice will be satisfied. The scriptures tell us that if we have truly repented, we will not repeat the sin. So, if we ask God to forgive us of all of our sins, even those we have forgotten, He will do so, as long as we don't repeat them.

How can we, as mere mortals, be expected to mete out righteous judgment to our fellow man? For most things, we are not expected to judge. "Judge not, and ye shall not be judged: condemn not, and ye shall not be condemned: forgive, and ye shall be forgiven" (Luke 6:37).

There are times, however, when we are required to make judgments. How should we judge? We are told to do so in righteousness. This means prayerfully, studiously, and meditatively.

When we hear gossip and make a judgment of another based on what we hear, we are in jeopardy of God's judgment. When we make an unrighteous judgment and act on it, allowing it to affect our love for someone, we are not demonstrating forgiveness or compassion. If we do not forgive, we cannot be forgiven. Judgment, forgiveness, and repentance are closely allied. The laws pertaining to them should be carefully and prayerfully studied so we do not inadvertently fall into the insidious traps Satan sets for us. When we consider forgiveness for those like Hitler, Stalin, and others who have committed terrible sins against humanity, we must first consider if they have personally done something against us, if not, it is not up to us to forgive. Forgiveness in these cases is God's responsibility, not ours.

Here are some of the profound scriptures God has made available for our enlightenment:

> And I charged your judges at that time, saying, Hear the causes between your brethren, and judge righteously

between every man and his brother, and the stranger that is with him.

Ye shall not respect persons in judgment; but ye shall hear the small as well as the great; ye shall not be afraid of the face of man; for the judgment is God's: and the cause that is too hard for you, bring it unto me, and I will hear it. (Deuteronomy 1:16–17)

The proverbs of Solomon the son of David, king of Israel;
To know wisdom and instruction; to perceive the words of understanding;
To receive the instruction of wisdom, justice, and judgment, and equity; (Proverbs 1:1–3)

Thus saith the Lord, keep ye judgment, and do justice: for my salvation is near to come, and my righteousness to be revealed. (Isaiah 56:1)
He hath shewed thee, O man, what is good; and what doth the Lord require of thee, but to do justly, and to love mercy, and to walk humbly with thy God? (Micah 6:8)

And the word of the Lord came unto Zechariah, saying,
Thus speaketh the Lord of hosts, saying, Execute true judgment, and shew mercy and compassions every man to his brother:
And oppress not the widow, nor the fatherless, the stranger, nor the poor; and let none of you imagine evil against his brother in your heart. (Zechariah 7:8–10)

These are the things that ye shall do; Speak ye every man the truth to his neighbor execute the judgment of truth and peace in your gates: (Zechariah 8:16)

Who shall give account to him that is ready to judge the quick and the dead.
For this cause was the gospel preached also to them that are dead, that they might be judged according to men in the flesh, but live according to God in the spirit.
But the end of all things is at hand: be ye therefore sober, and watch unto prayer.

And above all things have fervent charity among yourselves: For charity shall cover the multitude of sins. (1 Peter 4:5–8)

Behold, will ye reject these words? Will ye reject the words of the prophets; and will ye reject all the words which have been spoken concerning Christ, after so many have spoken concerning him; and deny the good word of Christ, and the power of God, and the gift of the Holy Ghost, and quench the Holy Spirit, and make a mock of the great plan of redemption, which hath been laid for you?

Know ye not that if ye will do these things, that the power of the redemption and the resurrection, which is in Christ, will bring you to stand with shame and awful guilt before the bar of God?

And according to the power of justice, for justice cannot be denied, ye must go away into that lake of fire and brimstone, whose flames are unquenchable, and whose smoke ascendeth up forever and ever, which lake of fire and brimstone is endless torment.

O then, my beloved brethren, repent ye, and enter in at the strait gate, and continue in the way, which is narrow, until ye shall obtain eternal life. (Jacob 6:8–11)

Therefore if that man repenteth not, and remaineth and dieth an enemy to God, the demands of divine justice do awaken his immortal soul to a lively sense of his own guilt, which doth cause him to shrink from the presence of the Lord, and doth fill his breast with guilt, and pain, and anguish, which is like an unquenchable fire, whose flame ascendeth up for-ever and ever.

And now I say unto you, that mercy hath no claim on that man; therefore his final doom is to endure a never-ending torment. (Mosiah 2:38–39)

And now, it came to pass that after Abinadi had spoken these words he stretched forth his hand and said: The time shall come when all shall see the salvation of the Lord; when every nation, kindred, tongue, and people shall see eye to eye and shall confess before God that his judgments are just. (Mosiah 16:1)

Therefore God gave unto them commandments, after having made known unto them the plan of redemption, that they should not do evil, the penalty thereof being a second death, which was an everlasting death as to things pertaining unto righteousness; for on such the plan of redemption could have no power, for the works of justice could not be destroyed, according to the supreme goodness of God.

But God did call on men, in the name of his Son, (this being the plan of redemption which was laid) saying: If ye will repent, and harden not your hearts, then will I have mercy upon you, through mine Only Begotten Son;

Therefore, whosoever repenteth, and hardened not his heart, he shall have claim on mercy through mine Only Begotten Son, unto a remission of his sins; and these shall enter into my rest.

And whosoever will harden his heart and will do iniquity, behold, I swear in my wrath that he shall not enter into my rest. (Alma 12:32–35)

I say unto thee, my son, that the plan of restoration is requisite with the justice of God; for it is requisite that all things should be restored to their proper order. Be-hold, it is requisite and just, according to the power and resurrection of Christ, that the soul of man should be restored to its body, and that every part of the body should be restored to itself.

And it is requisite with the justice of God that men should be judged according to their works; and if their works were good in this life, and the desires of their hearts were good, that they should also, at the last day, be restored unto that which is good.

And if their works are evil they shall be restored unto them for evil. Therefore, all things shall be restored to their proper order, every thing to its natural frame - mortality raised to immortality, corruption to incorruption - raised to endless happiness to inherit the kingdom of God, or to endless misery to inherit the kingdom of the devil, the one on one hand, the other on the other –

The one raised to happiness according to his desires of happiness, or good according to his desires of good;

and the other to evil according to his desires of evil; for as he has desired to do evil all the day long even so shall he have his reward of evil when the night cometh.

And so it is on the other hand. If he hath repented of his sins, and desired righteousness until the end of his days, even so he shall be rewarded unto righteousness. (Alma 41:2–6)

Thus, none shall be exempted from the justice and the laws of God, that all things may be done in order and in solemnity before him, according to truth and righteousness. (D & C 107:84)

MERCY

Webster's dictionary defines mercy:

1. a - Compassion or forbearance shown especially to an offender or to one subject to one's power. b - Imprisonment rather than death imposed as a penalty for first degree murder.
2. a - A blessing that is an act of divine favor or compassion. b - A fortunate circumstance.
3. b - Compassionate treatment of those in distress.

Mercy implies compassion that forbears punishing even when justice demands it or that extends help even to the lowliest or most humble.

Kindness, consideration, and humility are also intrinsic units of mercy. These are traits we need to develop before we can show true mercy toward anyone.

Mercy shows two faces: one of giving and one of receiving. However, we cannot show mercy to God but only receive it as a blessing. We cannot demand it or buy it except with complete obedience to His commandments and repentance. We can only be merciful to others and pray that we are worthy to receive it from God. To obtain mercy, we must be obedient to His laws; we must try to emulate the Savior to the best of our ability and pray for His forgiveness when we go astray.

Since mercy is a blessing from God, we must follow and obey the law to which it is bound before we can obtain it. D & C 130:20, 21 says, "There is a law irrevocably decreed in heaven before the foundations of this world, upon which all blessings are predicated - and when we obtain any blessing from God, it is by obedience to that law upon which it is predicated."

So, when we want mercy from God, we must obey the law necessary to receive it. What is that law? The Savoir summed it up when he stated in Matthew 5:7, "Blessed are the merciful, for they shall obtain mercy."

We cannot obtain mercy from God unless we are merciful to those who need our mercy. We must realize that the whole plan of salvation is based on the mercy of Christ, in His willingness to forgive us of our sins. This satisfies the law of justice because Christ has paid for our debt, if we will but repent and endure to the end. If we do not repent, then we must suffer for the sins we commit. How important it is, then, that we learn how to forgive others their trespasses against us, thus showing mercy to them? Developing the trait of mercy is the key that opens the door to receive mercy from God, allowing us to live with Him again in the eternities to come. Our salvation depends on it.

It is not given for us to understand how Christ can take on our sins in His act of mercy toward us. The fact that He has done this is a matter of record, and we must accept it by faith. Many of the scriptures on mercy have been introduced in the discussion of justice since they go hand in hand. However, the following will help to clarify the subject even more:

> For he shall have judgment without mercy, that hath shewed no mercy; and mercy rejoiceth against judgment.
> What doth it profit, my brethren, though a man say he hath faith, and have not works? can faith save him?
> If a brother or sister be naked, and destitute of daily food,
> And one of you say unto them, Depart in peace, be ye warmed and filled; notwithstanding ye give them not those things which are needful to the body; what doth it profit?

DR. LAUREN J. BALL

Even so faith, if it hath not works, is dead. (James 2:13–17)

And behold, this is the whole meaning of the law, every whit pointing to that great and last sacrifice; and that great and last sacrifice will be the Son of God, yea, infinite and eternal.
And thus he shall bring salvation to all those who shall believe on his name; this being the intent of this last sacrifice, to bring about the bowels of mercy, which overpowereth justice, and bringeth about means unto men that they may have faith unto repentance.
And thus mercy can satisfy the demands of justice, and encircles them in the arms of safety, while he that exercises no faith unto repentance is exposed to the whole law of the demands of justice; therefore only unto him that has faith unto repentance is brought about the great eternal plan of redemption.
Therefore may God grant unto you, my brethren, that ye may begin to exercise your faith unto repentance, that ye begin to call upon his holy name, that he would have mercy upon you;
Yea, cry unto him for mercy; for he is mighty to save. (Alma 34:14–18)

The poor is hated even of his neighbor: but the rich hath many friends.
He that despiseth his neighbor sinneth: but he that hath mercy on the poor, happy is he.
Do they not err that devise evil? but mercy and truth shall be to them that devise good. (Proverbs 14:20–22)

By mercy and truth iniquity is purged: and by the fear of the Lord men depart from evil. (Proverbs 16:6)

Blessed are the merciful: for they shall obtain mercy. (Mathew 5:7)

But now I tell it unto you, and ye are blessed, not because of your iniquity, neither your hearts of un-belief; for verily some of you are guilty before me, but I will be merciful unto your weakness. (D & C 38:14)

17

HONESTY AND INTEGRITY

HONESTY

Honesty is one of the most revered of all personality traits. Employers and people in all walks of life seek those who are honest and forthright in their dealings with others. We can always trust those who are honest. We can depend on them to keep their word and be true to their duties and responsibilities. They do not cheat or use people in an unrighteous manner. In most instances, they will not betray our trust or our love.

Therefore, we can have confidence in them, and they will not be disloyal to a confidence.

Honesty is being truthful in all our dealings with others, using no deceit, being forthright, and living our lives so we have nothing to hide.

Honesty begins within our minds. Said Shakespeare, "To thine own self be true." In other words, being honest with ourselves makes it easier to be honest with others.

Honesty is really an attitude or state of mind that needs to be nurtured and cultivated from childhood. If it is not learned and embraced, then it is very difficult to incorporate it later in our lives.

The rewards for its development compensates more than the time and difficulty expended in its cultivation. Honesty is an integral part of repentance.

We must always be completely honest with God when we confess our sins, when we seek His forgiveness, or in any of the steps of repentance. Our motives must be honest when we approach baptism or when we ask anything of our Lord and Savior. It will then be easier to be honest with others and ourselves.

Honesty is not just a black-and-white issue. There is probably no one who is completely honest. Conversely, there is probably no one who is totally dishonest. Most of us fall somewhere in between because of our thinking, attitudes, experiences, etc. That is why we can never, completely, place our trust in man. Deity, having infinite honesty, can always be trusted.

Those who are truly on the road to perfection will honestly evaluate themselves to determine where they stand, with respect to God-like honesty and sincerely make the effort necessary, to perfect this most cherished character trait. They may even ask others to evaluate them to make the rating more viable. Others do not always share the opinion we have of our own personalities. The way others see us or the way we view ourselves may not reflect our true personalities. Repeatedly, we project ourselves the way we want others to view us. We hide from them the things we do not want them to know. We magnify the good points and play down the bad points; in other words, we are not being completely honest with everyone. We do not need to completely expose our past to them either. There are many things that would be detrimental to us and to others if our pasts were to be totally revealed. By and large, our privacy is important to us and should be kept private. But when we have committed serious moral indiscretions, we need to confess, not to the public, but to one who is in authority, and clear the matter up with our Lord. Part of the reward of true repentance is that God will no longer remember our sins.

The big question is how to incorporate the "honesty" trait into our daily lives? How do we become perfect in our honesty? Becoming aware of and admitting that we are not completely honest in everything that we do is a good step in the right direction. Then, on a continuing basis, we must analyze the deceits and dishonesties we practice on others with whom we come in daily contact. "What a tangled web we weave, when at first we practice, to deceive," said Shakespeare.

Once we become aware of the little things we do and say, each day, that are dishonest, untruthful, and deceitful, we can start eliminating them from our repertory.

Dishonesty stems from not wanting to be responsible to others for our actions. When we do something wrong, we often try to hide it from others. We become afraid. We fear that our loved ones and others will care less for us if they know. We fear that their opinion of us will diminish. We often try to place the blame on others. So, we lie, we deceive, and we shy away from being responsible for our actions, and we become dishonest.

Honesty takes effort, both to develop and to practice. Satan would have us all be dishonest. When we understand that dishonesty leads to spiritual destruction and comes from the promptings of Satan, we will stand a better chance of casting it from our lives.

Here are some of scriptures to help motivate us to be as honest as our Heavenly Father would like us to be:

> But that on the good ground are they, which in an honest and good heart, having heard the word, keep it, and bring forth fruit with patience. (Luke 8:15)

> Wherefore, brethren, look ye out among you seven men of honest report, full of the Holy Ghost and wisdom, whom we may appoint over this business. (Acts 6:3)

> Recompense to no man evil for evil. Provide things honest in the sight of all men. (Romans 12:17)

> Let us walk honestly, as in the day; not in rioting and drunkenness, not in chambering and wantonness, not in strife and envying.
> But put ye on the Lord Jesus Christ, and make not provision for the flesh, to fulfill the lusts thereof. (Romans 13:13–14)

DR. LAUREN J. BALL

But have renounced the hidden things of dishonesty, not walking in craftiness, nor handling the word of God deceitfully; but by manifestation of the truth commending ourselves to every man's conscience in the sight of God. (2 Corinthians 4:2)

Finally, brethren, whatsoever things are true, whatsoever things are honest, whatsoever things are just, whatsoever things are pure, whatsoever things are lovely, whatsoever things are of good report; if there be any virtue, and if there be any praise, think on these things. (Philippians 4:8)

That ye may walk honestly toward them that are without, and that ye may have lack of nothing. (1 Thessalonians 4:12)

I exhort therefore, that, first of all, supplications, prayers, intercessions, and giving of thanks, be made for all men;
For Kings, and for all that are in authority; that we may lead a quiet and peaceable life in all godliness and honesty. (1 Timothy 2:1–2)

And they were among the people of Nephi, and also numbered among the people who were of the church of God. And they were also distinguished for their zeal towards God, and also towards men; for they were perfectly honest and upright in all things; and they were firm in the faith of Christ, even unto the end. (Alma 27:27)

And let every man deal honestly, and be alike among this people, and receive alike, that ye may be one, even as I have commanded you. (D & C 51:9)

EXPANDING OUR LIGHT

INTEGRITY

The *Webster's Collegiate Dictionary* defines integrity as:

1. Adherence to moral and ethical principles; soundness of moral character; honesty.
2. A sound, unimpaired or, perfect condition as in, 'the integrity of a ship's hull.

Bruce R. McConkie in *Mormon Doctrine* states, "The complete development of man's moral character in conformity with principles of justice and uprightness is termed integrity. A man of integrity is sound, incorruptible, and particularly strict about fulfilling the trusts reposed in him by others. Those who conform their conduct to the terms of those gospel covenants and promises, which they have made, exhibit the highest manifestation of integrity. Integrity goes hand in hand with uprightness and righteousness, and the Lord loves those who have integrity of heart."

Like honesty, integrity is one of the most sought-after character traits in the industrial world. Men and women of integrity are more often placed in positions of responsibility and leadership because they can be trusted to carry out assigned duties and trusted to be fair in their relationship with others.

Integrity in all aspects of our living should be pursued with intensity and determination. When we have developed this character trait, we will have gone a long way on the road to perfection. May God bless us in our sincere efforts to master integrity in our everyday life.

Enjoy these scriptures and search out others to help you in your quest for the perfection of integrity.

> And if thou wilt walk before me, as David thy father walked, in integrity of heart, and in uprightness, to do according to all that I have commanded thee, and wilt keep my statutes and my judgments:
> Then I will establish the throne of thy kingdom upon Israel for ever, as I promised to David thy father, saying, There shall not fail thee a man upon the throne of Israel. (Kings 9:4–5)

The integrity of the upright shall guide them: but the perverseness of transgressors shall destroy them. (Proverbs 11:3)

[15] And again, verily I say unto you, blessed is my servant Hyrum Smith; for I, the Lord, love him because of the integrity of his heart, and because he loveth that which is right before me, saith the Lord.
[20] And again, verily I say unto you my servant George Miller is without guile; he may be trusted because of the integrity of his heart; and for the love which he has to my testimony I, the Lord, love him. (D & C 124:15, 20)

18

COMPASSION AND KINDNESS

COMPASSION

The *New Webster's Dictionary* defines compassion as: "A sympathetic emotion created by the misfortunes of another, accompanied by a desire to help; pity; mercy."

Compassion should be given a high priority on our list of righteous traits in need of perfecting. It is through this trait that we can show an extended love for our fellow man and live a more perfect and harmonious life of service.

> And behold, I tell you these things that ye may learn wisdom; that ye may learn that when ye are in the service of your fellow beings ye are only in the service of your God. (Alma 2:17)

Although service is not compassion, it is certainly the prime mover in many cases. It was compassion that prompted the outburst of aid to Ethiopia during the 1985 famine. It was compassion that saved baby Moses. History is replete with outpourings of compassion in times of great need. The hymn from the LDS hymnal,

"The Poor Wayfaring Man of Grief," epitomizes the actions and blessings resulting from a compassionate nature. The development of compassion presupposes a love for our fellow man. Without love compassion cannot exist. Without tenderness it dies. Without compassion charity is dead. To become like our Savior, we should develop these traits to the greatest extent possible in this life. Christ is our salvation and exaltation through compassion and kindness.

One of Christ's ultimate teachings was "feed the poor and hungry and clothe the naked." They will always be with us, and we have the responsibility to care for them. God says that unless we have charity, we can in no wise enter into the kingdom of God. Doing this is not a natural trait for most of us. It *is* one which must be developed and nurtured. To be compassionate for the wrong reasons or with a selfish heart brings fewer blessings than if we develop a true compassionate nature, one that delights in helping others. They, who desire to be seen by others as they perform their compassionate deeds will receive their rewards in the praises they get from the public. But for those whose deeds are done in secret, I'm sure the Lord will bless openly.

Just being compassionate to those we love or to our friends and neighbors, is not God's way. Though blessings are received for the act, it is not the same as helping those we don't know. The whole human family deserves compassion. We are all part of this great family, and there are times when each of us needs compassion, even from strangers, to help us along the way.

Here are some powerful scriptures on the subject:

> If thine enemy be hungry, give him bread to eat; and if he be thirsty, give him water to drink: (Proverbs 25:21)

> Is it not to deal thy bread to the hungry, and that thou bring the poor that are cast out to thy house? When thou seest the naked, that thou cover him; and that thou hide not thyself from thine own flesh? (Isaiah 58:7)

> To him that is afflicted pity should be shewed from his friend; but he forsaketh the fear of the almighty. (Job 6:14)

Thus speaketh the Lord of hosts, saying, Execute true judgment, and shew mercy and compassions every man to his brother:

And oppress not the widow, nor the fatherless, the stranger, nor the poor; and let none of you imagine evil against his brother in your heart. (Zechariah 7:9–10)

Therefore is the Kingdom of heaven likened unto a certain king, which would take account of his servants.
And when he had begun to reckon, one was brought unto him, which owed him ten thousand talents.
But forasmuch as he had not to pay, his lord commanded him to be sold, and his wife, and children, and all that he had, and payment to be made.
The servant therefore fell down, and worshipped him, saying, Lord, have patience with me, and I will pay thee all.
Then the lord of that servant was moved with compassion, and loosed him, and forgave him the debt. (Matthew 18:23–27)

And there came a leper to him, beseeching him, and kneeling down to him, and saying unto him, If thou wilt, thou canst make me clean.
And Jesus moved with compassion, put forth his hand, and touched him, and saith unto him, I will; be thou clean. (Mark 1:40–41)

Having ascended into heaven, having the bowels of mercy; being filled with compassion towards the children of men; standing betwixt them and justice; having broken the bands of death, taken upon himself their iniquity and their transgressions, having redeemed them, and satisfied the demands of justice. (Mosiah 15:9)

And he shall go forth, suffering pains and afflictions and temptations of every kind; and this that the word might be fulfilled which saith he will take upon him the pains and the sickness of his people.

And he will take upon him death, that he may loose the bands of death which bind his people; and he will take upon him their infirmities, that his bowels may be filled with mercy, according to the flesh, that he may know according to the flesh how to succor his people according to their infirmities. (Alma 7:11–12)

And remember in all things the poor and the needy, the sick and the afflicted, for he that doeth not these things, the same is not my disciple. (D & C 52:40)

KINDNESS

Like compassion, kindness has its roots in love. It is being "sympathetic, friendly, gentle, tender-hearted, generous, cordial, loving, affectionate, etc." according to *Webster's New World Dictionary*.

Most of us have little trouble demonstrating these traits to those we love. We may have more difficulty in demonstrating them to others. Judging from my travels to many countries, I find that people from all nationalities are basically kind. They are unafraid to lend a helping hand to someone in need. However, there are a few in every society who do not fit into this general mold. By nature, these few are selfish and greedy not only with their finances but with their time and resources as well. Kindness comes from a giving and loving personality, from someone who cares about his or her fellow man. They have compassion for the human race and extend themselves in kindness to make the world a better place in which to live.

Developing kindness as a personality trait is really quite easy if we put our minds to it. We can cultivate it, even when it is totally alien to our makeup, simply by forcing ourselves to help someone in need. The gratification we get from acts like this is normally enough to generate the desire to continue. It can readily become a most enjoyable habit, one that is extremely satisfying and emotionally rewarding.

Christ is the greatest exemplifier of this much-desired personality trait. His acts of kindness were not only done for those in His time but are acts that will last down through the eternities. He set the example by performing them with no desire for recompense and no earthly reward. Each of us needs to evaluate ourselves on this trait and develop it as much as possible.

Here are some scriptures to help inspire us to help and to show everyday acts of kindness to all of those with whom we come in contact:

> Now therefore, I pray you, swear unto me by the Lord, since I have shewed you kindness, that ye will also shew kindness unto my father's house, and give me a true token. (Joshua 2:12)

> Have mercy upon me, O God, according to thy lovingkindness: according unto the multitude of thy tender mercies blot out my transgressions. (Psalm 51:1)

> And be ye kind one to another, tenderhearted, forgiving one another, even as God for Christ's sake hath forgiven you. (Ephesians 4:32)

> Whereby are given unto us exceeding great and precious promises: that by these ye might be partakers of the divine nature, having escaped the corruption that is in the world through lust.
> And besides this, giving all diligence, add to your faith virtue; and to virtue knowledge;
> And to knowledge temperance; and to temperance patience; and to patience godliness;
> And to godliness brotherly kindness; and to brotherly kindness charity.

> For if these things be in you, and abound, they make you that ye shall neither be barren nor unfruitful in the knowledge of our Lord Jesus Christ. (2 Peter 1:4–8)

> In a little wrath I hid my face from thee for a moment, but with everlasting kindness will I have mercy on thee, saith the Lord thy Redeemer. (3 Nephi 22:8)

19

LOYALTY

Loyalty is the state of being true to the vows, commitments, and obligations both real and implied which have been made to God, individuals, groups, or organizations. It should only be demonstrated under righteous circumstance and for righteous purposes. When we are supportive of or condone anyone in their unrighteous endeavors, we are not being loyal but rather are assuming partial or equal guilt with those who have committed an unrighteous act. To be loyal, we should not deny others the opportunity of repentance. When the question of loyalty arises, we should always ask ourselves, "Is this productive, nonproductive, or counterproductive to our growth toward perfection?" We cannot go wrong if we are true to productivity and to God's commandments. It is not hard to determine where our loyalty should lie when viewed in this context.

Are we being loyal to friends or relatives who have committed a serious crime by keeping silent? No! We are not only helping to bring about their damnation but ours as well. In our attempt to be loyal to them, we are being disloyal to God and to ourselves. When viewed from a righteous standpoint, we can only help them when we give them the opportunity for repentance, which we cannot do if we shield them from God's law or from whatever other justice is being denied. Thus, by shielding them, we are denying Christ by not allowing them the opportunity of exercising His redemptive powers. Our encouragement to those who have committed a serious infraction should always be toward repentance. If they refuse, then, we must make sure they understand that our responsibility lies in doing what is right in the eyes of God and the law.

Our first obligation and loyalty must always be to God and to righteousness. When we fully understand this principle, we will also understand where and when our loyalty to others ends. When others commit petty transgressions, we should always pray for guidance before acting.

Loyalty to our country is also important but not more important than loyalty to God. The 12th Article of Faith states, "We believe in being subject to kings, presidents, rulers, and magistrates, in obeying, honoring, and sustaining the law." This we should do but not at the expense of being disloyal to God. When a choice comes between God and state, there should be no question of our loyalty, unless interceded by direct revelation from God through the proper channels indicates otherwise.

In 1968, while I was serving in Vietnam, my family was staying with my wife's father in Casa Grande, Arizona. Our son David, aged eight, fell head over heels in love with a young girl that he wished very much to impress. Being short of funds, he went to the local Safeway Store and stole as many toys and games as he could and hid them in his jacket. That night, Geri discovered his hoard. When questioned, he claimed that a friend had given it to him.

"What would happen if I checked with your friend's mother?" she asked.

David bluffed it out, but the next morning confessed that he had taken the toys. All morning, Geri prayed about how to handle the situation. After lunch, she went to see the store manager. When she had apprised him of the problem, he asked her what she wanted him to do.

"I want him to realize that he cannot do this sort of thing. I want him to have to pay for these items, and I want him never to do anything like this again!" The manager promised to be very cooperative.

She didn't realize it then, but so would the Lord. As they pulled into the parking lot, two boys came out of the market and following about ten feet behind were two store employees. The boys were grabbed by the arms and marched back into the building. About one minute later, a police car arrived, red light flashing. Two policemen rushed in and joined the group of people who had gathered around the front of the information area. David's eyes got as big as saucers.

"What do you think those boys did?" Geri asked. David had no idea and didn't want to find out.

His mother insisted that they go into the grocery store, and a reluctant son followed. They watched as the officers placed handcuffs on the youngsters and marched them to the waiting police car. The manager then turned to David, who was peeking out from behind his mother.

"Did you want to see me?" he asked Geri. It seemed that his voice was unusually gruff.

"My son needs to talk to you," she answered and pushed David forward. He looked scared; he was almost shaking but was able to open the sack he was carrying, showing the stolen items.

"I took these," his voice quavered. The manager gave them a cursory glance.

"Did you see those boys that the policemen took out of here?"

David nodded his head.

"Do you want me to get them back to take you away too?"

This time the head shook no.

"Well, come into my office and let me think about this," commanded the man. He added up the price of the items. "With tax, they come to $5.43. Do you have that much money?"

No, shook the head.

"I have this much," David said drawing out a dollar bill and some loose change, $1.47.

"That's not enough. Let me tell you what I want you to do. I want you to get a job and earn the money to pay me. I want your money, not your mother's—yours. After you have paid me, you must never again come back into my store alone. I do not let thieves come in here. Do you understand?"

Up and down went the head. David reached for the sack, but his mother stopped him.

"Son, we do not profit by sin. Not only must you give up your money, but you do not get anything to show for its passing."

David went home that evening and got a neighbor to allow him to cut and weed her lawn. He earned $5.00 and was able to pay his debt that night.

When we see someone on the edge of wrongdoing and remain silent, we are actually denying the offenders the opportunity of repenting and working out their salvation. Sometimes, it may hurt and be difficult for us to do what is necessary to help them get back on the correct path. For the laws of justice and mercy to be effective, we must do what is right, even if it hurts us and those involved.

Loyalty also includes the support of others in their righteous endeavors. To sit back and watch others struggle to accomplish something we should also be in involved with, knowing that we should help, is not productive to our growth. Whenever possible, our loyalty and responsibility is to help others reach their righteous goals. This forms a beautiful bond between the parties and helps those involved work out their salvation.

In the Pearl of Great Price, The Book of Moses informs us that Satan's pre-existent plan was to force man to be righteous so that not one soul would be lost.

This plan would take away man's agency and make of him a slave. Christ's plan was to give man his agency, to teach him the right way, then, let him choose for himself which path he would take. Every man who has been born or will be born on this earth, to one degree or another, chose Christ's plan. In so doing, we have the obligation to follow and remain loyal to His plan. Our growth will then be sufficient to allow us to live with God in the celestial kingdom. Our first loyalty must always be to God and His complete gospel plan in preference to loyalty to anything or anyone else. It includes all of His teachings, laws, commandments, and ordinances. It commits us to continually strive toward the perfection He has commanded of us which is necessary for our salvation and exaltation.

History is replete with examples of loyalty and misplaced loyalty: Nathan Hale, who regretted that he had but one life to give to his country; Benedict Arnold who became a traitor to his country; and Prophet Eli in the Old Testament placed loyalty to his sons above that of God and, as a result, both he and his sons suffered death.

We all have the agency to choose our priorities of loyalty. Instead of meditating and praying about our order of priorities, many of us wait for a crisis to develop before making a decision, and thus often make the wrong choice. When we thoughtfully and prayerfully arrange our list of loyalty priorities in support of righteousness, our decisions will automatically be the right ones. We won't even have to stop and think about it.

There are some instances in which there may be a conflict and doing the right thing is difficult and painful. Nevertheless, the right decision must be made, and the Lord will bless all parties concerned.

The following scriptures may help to inspire us all to be more loyal to righteousness and to set a priority of loyalties that will help us make the right decisions when unpredicted situations and events arise:

> And the Lord said, Shall I hide from Abraham that thing which I do;
> Seeing that Abraham shall surely become a great and mighty nation, and all the nations of the earth shall be blessed in him?
> For I know him, that he will command his children and his household after him, and they shall keep the way of the Lord, to do justice and judgment; that the Lord may bring upon Abraham that which he has spoken of him. (Genesis 18:17–19)

> And he said, Lay not thine hand upon the lad, neither do thou any thing unto him: for now I know that thou fearest God, seeing thou hast not withheld thy son, thine only son from me. (Genesis 22:12)

> Now therefore fear the Lord, and serve him in sincerity and in truth: and put away the gods, which your fathers served on the other side of the flood, and in Egypt; and serve ye the Lord.
> And if it seem evil unto you to serve the Lord, choose you this day whom ye will serve; whether the gods which your fathers served that were on the other side of the flood, or the gods of the Amorites, in whose land ye dwell: but as for me and my house, we will serve the Lord. (Joshua 24:14–15)

> And Ruth said, Entreat me not to leave thee, or to return from following after thee: for whither thou goest,

EXPANDING OUR LIGHT

I will go; and where thou lodgest, I will lodge: thy people shall be my people, and thy God My God:

Where thou diest, will I die, and there will I be buried: The Lord do so to me, and more also, if ought but death, part thee and me. (Ruth 1:16–17)

No man can serve two masters: for either he will hate the one, and love the other; or else he will hold to the one, and despise the other. Ye cannot serve God and mammon. (Matthew 6:24)

For I am not ashamed of the gospel of Christ: for it is the power of God unto salvation to every one that believeth; to the Jew first, and also to the Greek. (Romans 1:16)

Wherefore, we would to God that we could persuade all men not to rebel against God, to provoke him to anger, but that all men would believe in Christ, and view His death, and suffer His cross and bear the shame of the world; wherefore I, Jacob, take it upon me to fulfill the commandment of my brother Nephi. (Jacob 1:8)

Now I say unto you, if this be the desire of your hearts, what have you against being baptized in the name of the Lord, as a witness before him that ye have entered into a covenant with him, that ye will serve him and keep his commandments, that he may pour out his Spirit more abundantly upon you? (Mosiah 18:10)

And Moroni was a strong and a mighty man; he was a man of perfect understanding; yea, a man that did not delight in bloodshed; a man whose soul did joy in the liberty and freedom of his country, and his brethren from bondage and slavery;

Yea, a man whose heart did swell with thanksgiving to his God, for the many privileges and blessings which he bestowed upon his people; a man who did labor exceedingly for the welfare and safety of his people.

Yea, and he was a man who was firm in the faith of Christ, and he had sworn with an oath to defend his people, his rights, and his country, and his religion, even to the loss of his blood. (Alma 48:11–13)

We believe that all men are bound to sustain and uphold the respective governments in which they reside, while protected in their inherent and inalienable rights by the laws of such governments; and that sedition and rebellion are unbecoming every citizen thus protected, and should be punished accordingly; and that all governments have a right to enact such laws as in their own judgments are best calculated to insure the public interest; at the same time, however, holding sacred the freedom of conscience.

We believe that every man should be honored in his station, rulers and magistrates as such, being placed for the protection of the innocent and the punishment of the guilty; and that to the laws all men show respect and deference, as without them peace and harmony would be supplanted by anarchy and terror; human laws being instituted for the express purpose of regulating our interests as individuals and nations, between man and man; and the divine laws given of heaven, prescribing rules on spiritual concerns, for faith and worship, both to be answered by man to his Maker.

We believe that rulers, states, and governments have a right, and are bound to enact laws for the protection of all citizens in the free exercise of their religious belief; but we do not believe that they have a right in justice to deprive citizens of this privilege, or proscribe them in their opinions, so long as a regard and reverence are shown to the laws and such religious opinions do not justify sedition nor conspiracy.

We believe that the commission of crime should be punished according to the nature of the offense; that murder, treason, robbery, theft, and the breach of the general peace, in all respects, should be punished according to their criminality and their tendency to evil among men, by the laws of that government in which the offense is committed; and for the public peace and tranquility, all men should step forward and use their ability in bringing offenders against good laws to punishment. (D & C 134:5–8)

20

PRAYER AND MEDITATION

PRAYER

Prayer, supplication, and meditation are among the greatest powers on earth. The very act of prayer is an indication of faith, an acknowledgment of the existence of God and Jesus Christ, in whose name we perform all activities related to our physical world, and to the gospel and salvation. The more we have learned to pray with true sincerity and faith, the more our prayers will be answered. Prayer is so important that many of our prophets have admonished us to pray continually, pray every morning, every noon, and every night. Pray for health, pray for our herds, our crops, wisdom, knowledge, and for understanding.

Those of us who pray have our special times and places to approach God. My wife, Geri, besides family prayer, prays when she does the dishes, paints, or does other repetitious chores that require little concentration. For her, this seems to be the best time to pray and to receive answers as well. Perhaps her success can be attributed to the receptivity of her mind during these periods. My greatest success occurs when I'm out driving or walking alone. During these periods,

I can meditate and pray without interruption and, like Geri, I receive the answers to many questions and problems while so doing.

Another good time for prayer is during the sacrament ordinance. Several years ago, one of our prophets informed us that we could get closer to God during this period than at any other time, excluding the temple. Both are good times and places to come "clean" before God, ask forgiveness for the indiscretions we have committed, and a time for deep reflection and meditation. These should be periods for self-analysis, goal setting, and deciding which areas of our lives are most in need of improvement. The temple and sacrament are quiet, sacred places and times that should be enjoyed and spent in communication with our Father in Heaven.

Most people, including me, do not pray often enough nor with enough emotion, sincerity, and desire. Our prophets and church leaders spend a great deal of time on their knees and encourage us to do the same. Few of us spend time on our knees as did Enos in the *Book of Mormon*, who prayed mightily all day long and on into the night to gain a confirmation of the remission of his sins and attain a positive knowledge of God's forgiveness (Enos 1:4–5). We all need to develop this kind of determination, commitment, and faith through prayer and thanksgiving.

Whether or not our prayers are answered depends on several things. First, our Father in heaven treats us very much like we treat our own children when favors are requested. We tend to withhold the requested item until it is earned. This is as it should be because God does the same for us. When repentant and obedient, we probably deserve the requests we make in our prayers. Then, if our faith is sufficient, if our prayers are sincere and from the heart, if the request is righteous and for our own good or for the good of another, God may grant it.

God knows what is best for us all, so not everything we request is freely given. Consequently, He may say no, even when we are worthy of receiving a sought-after blessing. This can either build or destroy faith, depending on our attitude. If we recognize that God knows what is best for us, then, if He withholds a blessing, we can accept His decision in good faith. It is when we continue to petition God after we have received a no that we get into trouble. If we continually pester Him, we just may get the thing for which we asked, even when God knows that it is not in our best interest. Then, we must go through the painful process of learning by the experience. After the trial is over, we may not be in such a hurry to pester Him again when He has said no.

An example of a person pursuing a request after God has said no was that of prophet Joseph Smith and Martin Harris, where parts of the translation of the Book of Mormon were lost. Joseph, at Martins insistence, kept on asking for the transcript so he could show it to his wife. He was told no several times. Finally, to teach Joseph and all of us a lesson, God relented and allowed the transcript to be taken, only to have it lost to the world. The lesson learned is to stop pestering when a no has been received. God knows best!

An experience in my life taught me and my wife how essential it is that we rely on the answers God gives and have the faith that things will turn out right.

Geri and I had only been married for a short time when we decided we needed another car. I was in the process of being transferred from Fort Huachuca, Arizona, to Fort Bliss, Texas, and we felt that our old Buick was on its last legs. We had decided to purchase a "new" used car in either Tucson or Phoenix and had prayed the night before and again the following morning that we would find the car we should buy. Having searched the Tucson market without finding one suitable to our needs, we decided to go on into Phoenix and see what we could find. The day was as hot as midsummer days can be in Arizona. We were suffering from the heat and frustrated because we had not found the car we wanted in Tucson. The baby, who was just a few weeks old, was hot and fussy, so we decided to leave him with his great-grandmother in Coolidge. She reluctantly agreed to watch him but asked that we be back before 2:00 PM so she could attend her Relief Society meeting.

The time was a little after 11:00 AM, and I was getting a strong impression that we should not buy a car at this time. Phoenix was still about an hour's drive away and time was running out, so we decided to go into Florence, just ten miles away, to get the car inspected to expedite the title transfer. When we arrived, we found the inspection mechanic had left for lunch a few minutes earlier and wouldn't be back for over an hour.

By this time, the heat and our frustration had reached a peak. We called the café where the inspector ate lunch, but he was not there. Geri was very distraught by this time. She felt there must be something more I could do to get things moving, but I felt that I had done everything that could be done. Geri went off in a huff with the heat and frustration bearing down on her. She crossed the street to a variety store and wandered around for a few minutes and also came to realize that we should not buy a car at this time. She came back with a box of Cracker Jacks, a peace offering, and said, "Let's go home." I agreed. We went back to Coolidge, got our child, and returned to Fort Huachuca.

As it turned out, had we bought a car, we would have been in *big* trouble with the payments. Upon arriving at Fort Bliss, we found the housing to be very expensive. Had we bought it, we would surely have lost the car. God, in His wisdom, had known what our monetary situation would be in Fort Bliss. By heeding His promptings, we saved ourselves a lot of misery. Our old Buick did survive the trip and gave us transportation for another two years. It's not always easy to hear when God speaks to us, especially when aggravating circumstance overwhelms us. We can't hear the music for the noise. So, we don't hear the still small voice and we often get into trouble that could be prevented if we would just be calm, patient, and learn to listen to the still small voice.

Other important considerations that affect answers to our prayers are vain repetitions, our emotional state, attitudes, love, and the intensity of our desire, enthusiasm, anger, greed, and our goals. These are some of the many traits that influence the answers to our prayers. Each of us may possess different components that block the answers coming from God. Let us briefly discuss some of these traits to gain a greater understanding of the necessity of approaching our Heavenly Father in the proper manner and in true humility, learning to rely on His wisdom, power, justice, and mercy without equivocation.

Vain repetitions. It is very difficult to pray day after day and not repeat our prayers. I believe vanity is the problem, not necessarily repetition. *Webster's New World Dictionary* defines vanity as: 1. Having no real value or significance, worthless, empty, idle, hollow, etc. 2. Without force or effect, futile, fruitless, unprofitable, unavailing, etc. 3.

Having or showing an excessively high regard for one's self, looks, possessions, abilities, etc.; indulging in or resulting from personal vanity; conceited. 4. [Archaic: Lacking in sense; foolish.]

From this definition, we can understand why our Savior dislikes vain repetitions. It is an enemy to humility. If our prayers are idle, hollow, empty, and have no force, I believe God will not look upon them with any degree of interest. If we approach Him under the influence of any of the counterproductive traits, it is unlikely that He will heed us.

Before our prayers will be answered, all destructive traits should be absent. The Lord has given us the Lord's prayer as an example, but to repeat it day after day with no feeling would be vain. To repeat it with feeling, determination, and commitment would be much more acceptable to Him. To repeat our own prayers with feeling, hope, and faith would probably be acceptable to God if the subject was righteous and included, not only us, but others also.

Emotional state. Experience has shown that we are more apt to gain solace, comfort, and receive answers to our prayers when we are in the depths of despair, when some crisis exists, when our emotions are deep and sincere, and our concern for others is at a peak; and if we are deserving, God is then more likely to respond to our needs. He wants to help us, and He will, if we learn to approach Him in humility. Seldom will we receive His help when we are unworthy, unrepentant, or undeserving, unless we are seeking His guidance to return to His presence.

The first step in making ourselves worthy is sincere daily repentance. Our supplications must be with true feeling and emotion and never faked. We should be hopeful, have faith, and pray only for that which is necessary for our sustenance, health, and other's ailments, and what is needful for our salvation and survival. God will hear our prayers and give us the challenges we need for growth and progress. Although He always knows what is best for us, He wants us to ask for it. It not only builds our faith but also helps us realize how much we must depend on Him for every needful thing.

Attitudes. The traits of humility, meekness, expectation, faith, and hope are among the most important attitudes we must demonstrate when approaching God in prayer. The realization that He is involved in every aspect of our lives is essential when we kneel before Him. If we pray not expecting to receive an answer, why pray unless we are just praying to give thanks for everything He has given us? This expectation is called hope, which must be followed by faith. When we kneel before God and feel deserving of His blessings, our expectations have a greater chance of being realized, except when they are harmful to our growth and progress.

Other attitudes that are equally important are service, love, and charity. If we strive to develop these positive attitudes and traits our Father in Heaven will be more likely to hear and answer our prayers.

Love. Love is so important that we must give its development top priority in our lives. The magnitude of God's love for us is mostly incomprehensible. It is difficult for us to understand how He is able to love us all equally even when we are disobedient and rebellious. To develop and elevate our love to the same level as God's love for us, especially when we have great evils perpetrated against us, is beyond our comprehension. It is easy to love those who are sweet, kind, and loving. The true test comes when we are required to love our enemies. Here, we must rely on God's power and wisdom to help us to create the desire first and then take the necessary actions to help us love them. As we develop this love, through prayer, our efforts will be much more effective. This is only possible if we continue to express and increase our love for others. We cannot hoard our love as a miser and expect it to grow. We cannot ignore it; we must develop and nurture it, give it, and accept it freely from others, and our prayers will take on a new meaning and be more acceptable to God. The growth of love and charity should be considered a journey throughout this life and all during the millennium.

Desire. If our desires are righteous and intense, God is more likely to hear our prayers. If we offer up an apathetic supplication, we have little hope of having it answered, but generating a false intensity is vain. Creating a genuine intense desire for something good, righteous, and needful for our growth and progress is not easy. If we are involved in conquering a destructive trait and approach God in a lackadaisical manner with no depth or feeling in our desire, He will see our insincerity. Therefore, He may not grant the strength or challenges we need to overcome it. On the other hand, if we, because of our intensity, sincerity, and persistence, know that we are really serious about our endeavor, He will be more likely to help us conquer the trait. God can look into our hearts and see when we're sincere. If our petition is truly our desire, He will give accordingly.

When we pray day after day for the same blessings and form no plan of action to gain them, He knows we are not really serious. Most of us are comfortable with our lifestyle and are not likely to change unless something drastic forces us to. If we pray and expect God to do it all, we are sure to be disappointed. How true the old saying is, "Pray as if everything depends on God, then act as if everything depends on us." God will help us only when we put forth the effort required to obtain the blessings we seek. "God will only help those who will help themselves." If we were God, would we answer the pleas of those who constantly asked us to help the needy, and the widows, especially when we had the means to give assistance ourselves? Now, if we asked God for help in finding ways to give aid and sustenance, He would be most happy to give us ideas and strength for this accomplishment.

When we pray, we should look into our hearts and determine if our desires are sincere and if what we seek is needful. Let us not pray for God to help the widows, the needy, the orphans etc., but let us pray that we can, with His great love for His children, find ways to help them ourselves. Not for our own glory but in secret, with a sincere desire to help, and with charity in our hearts. God will then provide the ways and means to make the plans we formulate come true.

Enthusiasm. I firmly believe that God answers our prayers with the same enthusiasm we use when we approach Him. If they lack vigor, how can we expect Him to be enthusiastic about answering? When we pray with sincere intensity and strive to accomplish that for which we have prayed with the same zeal, I believe that God will help us with that same enthusiasm and there is nothing we cannot accomplish. If we could just learn to approach our whole lives with enthusiasm, it would soon become second nature to pray in the same manner and, indeed, our prayers would not be vain.

Anger. When we are angry, hurt, or resentful, we are deeply in need of communicating with our Father in Heaven. However, it is counterproductive when we approach Him with these negative emotions. If we are angry and pray for the strength to overcome the anger and we are sincere, God will hear us and help, if we listen. We need to take a few moments and meditate. Think of other things, think of God and His great mercy and His tolerance for our own deficiencies and aberrations. Realize that it is Satan who is precipitating these negative feelings. Then, when we have calmed down and when humility and peace reigns, we can approach our Heavenly Father, and He will be more likely to hear our pleas.

Anger is one of the most violent of our emotions and can be extremely destructive to our relationship with others. It is a learned response to negative stimuli in our early childhood. It is a mask to hide our true emotions and vulnerabilities. We use it to protect ourselves from being hurt. We also use it to bend others to our will or way of thinking. It is used to blackmail, coerce, and to force others into submission. Anger is a satanic weapon used to control and dominate others.

Anger will be discussed at length in a later chapter. As suggested above, we must meditate for a while and try to see the other side of the picture or put ourselves in the place of our opposition when anger is present. Then after we have calmed down, it will be easier to call upon our Father in Heaven.

Greed. Greed is a real enemy to prayer. God knows our true personalities, and if we are greedy and selfish, we are unlikely to receive anything we ask for except the strength to overcome our greed and to be forgiven. If we continually seek for money or power, if gaining worldly goods is our primary goal in life, we are indeed in the bondage of sin. Our prayers are then likely to fall on deaf ears unless we are asking for help to overcome this destructive trait. If we are seeking after wealth for righteous purposes and with the intent of helping others, then God may hear our prayers and bless us accordingly. Giving is the secret to overcoming greed. With joy, we should give of our love, time, substance, and talents. Always be willing to help those who are less fortunate than we. God will then answer our prayers in every way He can. When we get involved in helping others, our own problems diminish and melt away and we become healthier and happier.

Goals. Our goals set the theme for many of our prayers. God will help us when we set our goals on righteous things, which are eternal in nature such as perfecting our bodies, minds, emotions, and spirits. To set them on attaining worldly acquisitions and possessions may not elicit a favorable response. Setting and accomplishing goals through prayer is essential to our salvation and exultation. However, they must be in harmony with God's plans for our eternal progress toward perfection. Our greatest accomplishments are the result of setting and attaining goals. We should set daily goals that will stretch the limitations of our capabilities for that day. Do the same thing on a weekly and monthly basis. Setting righteous long- and short-term goals will not only bring us closer to God but will also challenge our abilities and talents as well. Goals are the meat of accomplishment. Without them, we ride aimlessly on a sea of procrastination, waiting for fate to deal us a better hand, waiting for our ship to come in, and waiting for someone to drop that great deal in our laps. Goals will help us buy that ship, and we can deal ourselves whatever hand it takes to make us prosperous in the eyes of God. All we must do is learn to set and achieve those goals that are oriented toward spiritual growth and progress.

Several months after my wife and I were married and while living at Fort Huachuca, Arizona, we had occasion to move from a ranch apartment about 20 miles from the post to a trailer much closer to work. It was nearing the end of the month, and as most military families, we were dead broke, partly because the apartment in which we were living was costing us too much money and partly because our old Buick was a gas-guzzler. The gas gauge on this old Buick registered almost empty and when the indicator reached empty, there just wasn't any gas left. Prior to the move, we had prayed that there would be enough gasoline to make the move. We then proceeded to make three trips, moving all of our household goods with full confidence that we would have enough fuel. The last two trips were made with the indicator right on empty. In effect, we travelled at least one hundred miles with the gauge on empty. After the move, we decided to haul some full garbage cans to the dump still believing that the Lord had heard our prayers. Our friend, who had helped with the move, lost his faith as we started for the dump and said, "Pull into the nearest gas station. My faith has just run out." Our faith had never faltered, and the Lord blessed us accordingly. There have been many faith-building situations in my life. I know that when I am living in harmony with God's will and in a repentant state, the prayers I offer in humility are almost always answered.

God admonishes us many times in the scriptures to pray. Here are some scriptures that will help us understand the importance He places on sincere and humble prayer:

> Moreover as for me, God forbid that I should sin against the Lord in ceasing to pray for you: but I will teach you the good and the right way:
> Only fear the Lord, and serve him in truth with all your heart: for consider how great things he hath done for you. (1 Samuel 12:23–24)

> As for me, I will call upon God; and the Lord shall save me.
> Evening, and morning, and at noon, will I pray, and cry aloud: and he shall hear my voice. (Psalms 55:16–17)

> The Lord is far from the wicked: but he heareth the prayer of the righteous. (Proverbs 15:29)

> But I say unto you, Love your enemies, bless them that curse you, do good to them that hate you, and pray for them which despitefully use you, and persecute you:
> That ye may be the children of your Father, which is in heaven: for he maketh his sun to rise on the evil and on the good, and sendeth rain on the just and on the unjust. (Matthew 5:44–45)

> And when thou prayest, thou shalt not be as the hypocrites are: for they love to pray standing in the synagogues and in the corners of the streets, that they may be seen of men. Verily I say unto you, They have their reward.

But thou, when thou prayest, enter into thy closet, and when thou hast shut thy door, pray to thy Father which is in secret; and thy Father which seeth in secret shall reward thee openly.

But when ye pray, use not vain repetitions, as the heathen do: for they think that they shall be heard for their much speaking.

Be not ye therefore like unto them: for your Father knoweth what things ye have need of, before ye ask him. (Matthew 6:5–8)

Ask, and it shall be given you; seek, and ye shall find; knock, and it shall be opened unto you:

For every one that asketh receiveth; and he that seeketh findeth; and to him that knocketh it shall be opened. (Matthew 7:7–8)

And all things, whatsoever ye shall ask in prayer, believing, ye shall receive. (Matthew 21:22)

Therefore I say unto you, What things soever ye desire, when ye pray, believe that ye receive them, and ye shall have them.

And when ye stand praying, forgive, if ye have ought against any: that your Father also which is in heaven may forgive you your trespasses.

But if ye do not forgive, neither will your Father, which is in heaven, forgive your trespasses. (Mark 11:24–26)

And when he was at the place, he said unto them, Pray that ye enter not into temptation. (Luke 22:40)

And it came to pass, that, as he was praying in a certain place, when he ceased, one of his disciples said unto him, Lord, teach us to pray, as John also taught his disciples.

And he said unto them, when ye pray, say, Our Father which art in heaven, Hollowed be thy name. Thy kingdom come, Thy will be done, as in heaven, so in earth.

Give us this day our daily bread.

And forgive us our sins; for we also forgive everyone that is indebted to us. And lead us not into temptation; but deliver us from evil. (Luke 11:1–4)

Watch ye therefore, and pray always, that ye may be accounted worthy to escape all these things that shall come to pass, and to stand before the Son of man. (Luke 21:36)

And whatsoever ye shall ask in my name, that will I do, that the Father may be glorified in the Son.
If ye shall ask any thing in my name, I will do it. (John 14:13–14)

Likewise the Spirit also helpeth our infirmities: for we know not what we should pray for as we ought: but the Spirit itself maketh intercession for us with groaning's which cannot be uttered. (Romans 8:26)

If any of you lack wisdom, let him ask of God, that giveth to all men liberally, and upbraideth not; and it shall be given him.
But let him ask in faith, nothing wavering. For he that wavereth is like a wave of the sea driven with the wind and tossed. (James 1:5–6)

Ye ask, and receive not, because ye ask amiss, that ye may consume it upon your lusts. (James 4:3)

Likewise, ye husbands, dwell with them according to knowledge, giving honor unto the wife, as unto the weaker vessel, and as being heirs together of the grace of life; that your prayers be not hindered. (1 Peter 3:7)
Do ye not remember the things which the Lord hath said?--If ye will not harden your hearts, and ask me in faith, believing that ye shall receive, with diligence in keeping my commandments, surely these things shall be made known unto you. (1 Nephi 15:11)

Yea, I know that God will give liberally to him that asketh, Yea, my God will give me, if I ask not amiss;

therefore I will lift up my voice unto thee; yea, I will cry unto thee, my God, the rock of my righteousness. Behold, my voice shall forever ascend up unto thee, my rock and mine everlasting God. Amen. (2 Nephi 4:35)

But behold, I say unto you that ye must pray always, and not faint; that ye must not perform any thing unto the Lord save in the first place ye shall pray unto the Father in the name of Christ, that he will consecrate thy performance unto thee, that thy performance may be for the welfare of thy soul. (2 Nephi 32:9)

Behold, I say unto you they are made known unto me by the Holy Spirit of God. Behold, I have fasted and prayed many days that I might know these things of myself. And now I do know of myself that they are true; for the Lord God hath made them manifest unto me by his Holy Spirit; and this is the spirit of revelation, which is in me. (Alma 5:46)

But it is by the prayers of the righteous that ye are spared; now therefore, if ye will cast out the righteous from among you then will not the Lord stay his hand; but in his fierce anger he will come out against you; then ye shall be smitten by famine, and by pestilence, and by the sword; and the time is soon at hand except ye repent. (Alma 10:23)

Therefore may God grant unto you, my brethren, that ye may begin to exercise your faith unto repentance, that ye begin to call upon his holy name, that he would have mercy upon you;
Yea, cry unto him for mercy; for he is mighty to save.
Yea, humble yourselves, and continue in prayer unto him.
Cry unto him when ye are in your fields, yea, over all your flocks.
Cry unto him in your houses, yea, over all your household, both morning, mid-day, and evening.
Yea, cry unto him against the power of your enemies.

Yea, cry unto him against the devil, who is an enemy to all righteousness.

Cry unto him over the crops of your fields, that ye may prosper in them.

Cry over the crops of your fields, that they may increase.

But this is not all; ye must pour out your souls in your closets, and your secret places, and in your wilderness.

Yea, and when you do not cry unto the Lord, let your hearts by full, drawn out in prayer unto him continually for your welfare, and also for the welfare of those who are around you.

And now behold, my beloved brethren, I say unto you, do not suppose that this is all; for after ye have done all these things, if ye turn away the needy, and the naked, and visit not the sick and afflicted, and impart of your substance, if ye have, to those who stand in need—I say unto you, if ye do not any of these things, behold, your prayer is vain, and availeth you nothing, and ye are as hypocrites who do deny the faith.

Therefore, if ye do not remember to be charitable, ye are as dross, which the refiners do cast out, (it being of no worth) and is trodden under foot of men. (Alma 34:17–29)

And if thou wilt inquire, thou shalt know mysteries which are great and marvelous; therefore thou shalt exercise thy gift, that thou mayest find out mysteries, that thou mayest bring many to the knowledge of the truth, yea, convince them of the error of their ways. (D & C 6:11)

MEDITATION

Meditation has a different meaning for some than it does for others. *Webster's Dictionary* defines meditation as "the act of meditating; thought; reflection; contemplation; a thinking over."

We can and should meditate about the many important things in life, but we should never confuse meditation with fantasizing. The fantasies, many of us practice at times, should be controlled and only used for our growth toward perfection. Sexual and other negative fantasies should be entirely avoided as they are destructive to our growth and often become an acceptable part of our real lives. They can destroy relationships just as surely as actions. They leave us with not only a need for bigger and better fantasies but actions that match them. "For as he thinketh in his heart, so is he" (Proverbs 23:7) or to paraphrase, "As a man thinketh in his heart he is sure to become." Also, "For where your treasure is, there will your heart be also" (Matthew 6:21).

Meditating is one of the most powerful forces on earth. Meditation brings us closer to inspiration, guidance, and revelation than any other activity we can engage in. Every human accomplishment has been planned for in men's minds. It is through the spirit of God that man obtains all righteous thoughts, ideas, and inventions. Nothing of any value will come from man unless it is first studied out in his mind. Anything righteous we wish to do can be accomplished if it is desired with our whole heart, reflected on, and acted upon.

Thought is the precursor to success in every endeavor. Any achievement depends on eight things. First, comes the thought, idea, concept, or goal. Second, a burning desire and determination to accomplishment. Third, intention and willingness. Fourth, gaining the knowledge and expertise. Fifth, effective study and planning. Sixth, hope and belief. Seventh, acting decisively upon our plans, having a positive faith that it will happen. Eighth, sustained effort and perseverance, never give up on righteous endeavors.

Once the desire has jelled, once the planning has been completed, and by following the outline above, success is almost guaranteed, except for doubt. Our thoughts and plans (including the blueprint) are tantamount to "spiritual creation." (Study Moses 3:4–9.) Paraphrased, these scriptures tell us that God first created all things spiritually before he created them literally or temporally.

By thought and concentration (meditation) we plan all our accomplishments, whether they are great or small, physical, or spiritual. These thoughts and plans are the "spiritual creation" of what we wish to accomplish spiritually or physically. If we have a strong desire to do something, whether it be the elimination of a destructive trait or actually building a physical object, we must first plan it out in our minds and then, put it on paper. Examples are the 3"×5" cards with our goals written on them, a blueprint for a house, etc. Without these elements, nothing of any value can be created.

Meditation, then, is the thought process preceding the accomplishment of any action we pursue, whether it is good or evil. Satan would have us meditate on those things which are destructive to our physical, mental, emotional, and spiritual development. Again, we have our agency to choose whichever path we desire. Choosing Satan's path continually assures our destruction. Select righteousness continually and our salvation and exaltation may be assured.

The following scriptures are offered for further study:

> This book of the law shall not depart out of thy mouth; but thou shalt meditate therein day and night, that thou mayest observe to do according to all that is written therein: for then thou shalt make thy way prosperous, and then thou shalt have good success. (Joshua 1:8)

> Give ear to my words, O Lord, consider my meditation. (Psalms 5:1)

> Let the words of my mouth, and the meditation of my heart, be acceptable in thy sight, O Lord, my strength, and my redeemer. (Psalms 19:14)

> I will meditate also of all thy work, and talk of thy doings. (Psalms 77:12)

> And all the people were in expectation, and all men mused in their hearts of John, whether he were the Christ, or not; (Luke 3:15)

> Settle it therefore in your hearts, not to meditate before what ye shall answer: (Luke 21:14)

> Let no man despise thy youth; but be thou an example of the believers, in word in conversation, in charity, in spirit, in faith, in purity.
> Till I come, give attendance to reading, to exhortation, to doctrine.
> Neglect not the gift that is in thee, which was given thee by prophecy, with the laying on of the hands of the presbytery.

Meditate upon these things; give thyself wholly to them; that thy profiting may appear to all.

Take heed unto thyself, and unto the doctrine; continue in them: for in doing this thou shalt both save thyself, and them that hear thee. (1 Timothy 4:12–16)

Behold, you have not understood; you have supposed that I would give it unto you, when you took no thought save it was to ask me.

But, behold, I say unto you, that you must study it out in your mind; then you must ask me if it be right, and if it is right I will cause that your bosom shall burn within you; there-fore, you shall feel that it is right.

But if it be not right you shall have no such feelings, but you shall have a stupor of thought that shall cause you to forget the thing which is wrong; therefore you cannot write that which is sacred save it be given you from me. (D & C 9:7–9)

Hearken ye to these words. Behold I am Jesus Christ, the Savior of the world. Treasure these things up in your hearts, and let the solemnities of eternity rest upon your minds. (D & C 43:34)

And while we meditated upon these things, the Lord touched the eyes of our understandings and they were opened, and the glory of the Lord shone round about.

And we beheld the glory of the Son, on the right hand of the Father, and received of his fullness;

And saw the holy angels, and them who are sanctified before his throne, worshiping (D & C 76:19–21)

21

DESTRUCTIVE SYNDROMES

There are several very destructive psychological syndromes that are generated in our early formative years. As individuals, we need to be familiar with them so we can overcome the effect they have our lives. As parents, we need to be aware of their roots in order to protect our children from being crippled by them. Most of these disablers are generated when our children first become curious at the crawling or toddling age. For babies who are chronic criers and wailers, it may begin much earlier because of the intolerance many parents have to baby noise.

The natural curiosity of babies often leads them into the investigation of new and interesting objects. They may damage one of them while examining it. Sometimes, they do things that place them in a dangerous situation like running out into a busy street, touching a hot stove, attempting to pull something heavy down on their heads, etc. Prior to this pivotal incident, the parents are loving and kind and fulfilling the child's every need, love, nourishment, physical support, etc. Then without warning, the child is presented with a frenzied giant who is a caricature of their beloved parent. This giant yells, screams, and may inflict some kind of painful physical punishment such as a spanking, slapping of the hands, or even a smack across the face.

This authority figure that has been loving and kind, a haven against the world, and a supplier of needs has now turned into a demonic monster that thunders and causes pain. Confused and frightened, the child screams in terror having the scene indelibly etched on its mind forever. Love is or appears to be withdrawn. For a time, the need to be cuddled and cherished just isn't satisfied. The child is unable to understand any of this. At first, there is no connection between the "danger" or the damaged object and the punishment. It may take several such incidents before an association is made. The parent often reinforces the physical discipline with emotionally charged words such as "bad boy," "bad girl," "how could you be so stupid," or "no, no, that's a bad thing to do." The more often these or other similar phrases are uttered as the child grows, the more he believes them. Eventually, even the subconscious mind will accept them as facts.

The more frequently love is withheld and anger demonstrated, the more confused and worthless the child feels. This may lead to a belief that no one loves them, that they can't do anything right, and that a wall has been erected between them and their parents. This is especially true when there are immature mothers and fathers involved, those who may have been trapped by teenage marriage or pregnancy. In effect, these children are raising children. Many times, these young teenage parents are badly impaired by their own life experiences and have no idea what is expected of them as individuals, much less as parents. They have been told that they should expect very little from life, that they could progress only to certain levels, or some other misinformation because of their station in life. Most of them have lost even before they begin. As is often the case, the sins of the parents are passed on to the child.

These syndromes are not just confined to or passed on by teenage parents. Anyone who has not studied books on child rearing, meditated, and prayed about their responsibility to their families may fall into the trap. I know that Satan is the instigator of this reasoning. If we could just shake off the effects of these traumatic experiences and realize our true potential, it would be much easier to grasp the meaning of life and hold on to the plans that God has for us. We could then take the steps necessary to nullify the effects of our childhood, thereby breaking the cycle that has been perpetuated, perhaps for many generations. The truth is that most people do not want us to succeed in their efforts to be rid of these encumbrances. Therefore, most of us are content to be just like everyone else. Some people just don't want to be reminded that they have the responsibility of overcoming their imperfections. Their jealousy and envy keep them from rejoicing in our progress and we in theirs.

At first, we promote these misconceptions so that our offspring will not be hurt by their failures. Later, we promote them so our children won't judge us harshly for our failures. We teach them as we were taught and do not expect them to give their best efforts. We encourage them to be *normal, average, conforming, standard, or to follow the "pattern"* not realizing that these are all words to make us satisfied with staying mediocre, being ordinary, and curtailing our desire to attain excellence.

We teach our children to go with the flow, be one of the crowd, don't make waves, try to blend in, do what is expected, be careful, don't be different, and the list is endless.

Our beautiful spirits are sent to earth to become as perfect as our environment and thinking will allow. They are constantly being held back by the very people who should be doing all that is within their power to inspire the imagination, stretch the thinking, and create a desire to attain the goal of perfection. By not encouraging excellence and withholding love, approval, and praise, we give the child more problems than he/she can handle. This is sure to retard their spiritual growth and increase their need for recognition. Under these circumstances, they are likely to continue doing things that will incur the wrath of their parents; even the attention of a yelling mother or father is better than nothing.

As time goes by, the desire to act in unacceptable ways becomes deeply ingrained in the child. His peers easily lead him into undesirable pathways such as alcoholism, drugs, crime, gaming, etc. just to get noticed, to be accepted, and be one of the gang. Of course, all these things increase his estrangement from his parents; bringing more punishment down on him; and increases his need to even a greater extent to be wanted, needed, understood, and loved. It is a vicious cycle that never seems to end or get better. There are a few who, with proper help, are able to break out of the mold, very few. What makes the difference? Many times, it is the intervention of an outsider who has taken notice, given time, and has been willing to share. Sometimes, it is the parents who recognizes the folly of their ways and make the effort to break the bonds of these stifling syndromes. It is not easy to recognize these patterns, let alone do something about them. That is why it is always necessary to call on God and a professional for help.

There are times when parents have had additional children later in life, second families so to speak, who have recognized the errors in the way they have handled the first family and who have been able to break the bonds of this vicious cycle and give more love and understanding to the latest children. Though this newer family is better adjusted and emotionally more stable, there is a great deal of anger and resentment directed at them by their older siblings.

Some of these former children run away to a "better life" but not many find it. In fact, what they do find is unbelievable horror, drugs, become prostitutes, become addicted to pornography, and some even seek the tranquility of death. Some children can't cope at all and turn to autism—they withdraw from reality in order to survive. The very least that can happen is that most will become losers in life.

As the child matures, he finds that others are just waiting to reinforce the many elements of these syndromes. Teachers, preachers, and peers are noted for doing it. The message left by these people and accepted by the child is one of low self-esteem of not being able to do anything right, one that conformity is the only way to go. When children are busy just trying to get their basic emotional needs met by whoever is available, it becomes extremely difficult to try for excellence. Their peers meet some of these needs and, since this association is absolutely necessary for their sanity, they will cling to it. There is safety, acceptance, recognition, and love from these peers. To break away and try for excellence would be a form of death for them. As a result, they refuse to even consider it. And so, it is much easier to bend with the wind than to try for excellence. After all, it would take less effort to not try at all than risk failure by stretching their limitations. So, they cling to that with which they are comfortable, never generating the desire or courage to make the separation.

Our society perpetuates the myth that being normal or average is better than being exceptional, which incurs the disapproval or jealousy of those within their social circle. The final stage of rebellion is when they become so hurt by their parents, teachers, and preachers that they can no longer tolerate the world that is trying to be forced on them. They no longer want to be normal at all. They do not want to conform or want to try for excellence because it is unacceptable to their peers. So, they try to be *different* by exaggerated activities, antisocial behavior, drugs, or anything that tends to set them apart. Trying to be normal is too painful for them and nothing is known about trying for excellence, so what other path is there? They become different.

I'm not advocating the elimination of punishment as a means of discipline. What I am suggesting is that the approach should be carefully thought out in advance and then tempered with an abundance of love, touching, and communicating. Without them, as an ongoing part of the child-parent relationship regardless of the circumstances, an unbalanced emotional growth may occur. In a gentle, persuasive manner, we must try to give the child an understanding of why we feel it is necessary for their behavior to change and, if possible, what the consequences will be if they persist in the undesired behavior. It is imperative that the child understands the consequence of unacceptable behavior before punishment is exacted. God gives us the same consideration, even giving us an opportunity for repentance. Should we not give our children the same opportunity?

Following through with threatened punishment is just as important for the child's growth as giving the needed love afterwards. Idle threats are very damaging to our children's emotional balance. Could there be any trust in God if His threats were idle? Our children cannot believe or trust us either when we do not follow through with the punishment we promise for an infraction of the rules. But we must endeavor to prevent loud traumatic angry outbursts when we do have to exact punishment. Our voices must remain calm but firm. We must not give the impression that love is not present that we don't care for them. Our uncontrolled anger can be very traumatic for our children, leaving scars that last a lifetime and which may precipitate the same sort of behavior in their offspring.

22

THE KAMIKAZE SYNDROME

One of the syndromes that begins early in our childhood and having much the same genesis as most of the others, which I have named the kamikaze syndrome.

During the last months of World War II, the Japanese, in a last-ditch effort, called for volunteers to go on suicide missions in which the pilots would fly their planes loaded with large amounts of explosives into our naval convoys. These self-destruct missions were not as successful as they thought they should be. For the most part, the pilots were young and inexperienced but were nevertheless willing to give their lives for the cause. These suicide flights were called kamikaze missions because of the acceptance of self-destruction. I have chosen the term *kamikaze* not as a means to deride the great nation of Japan, for I have a tremendous admiration for their industry and the structure of their loving family relationships. I have chosen it because of the demoralizing influence these kamikaze runs had on our navy at the time, and because of the nature of the self-destructive mechanisms involved, nothing more.

The kamikaze syndrome arises during the early formative years. It is a complex weapon generated and used by Satan to attack our self-esteem, our worthiness. People having a low self-worth spend so much of their time just trying to cope with the everyday pressures that they have little time to devote to others or to the plan of salvation and perfection. They become overly concerned about the way they believe that others view them and, subsequently, are apt to withdraw from society to a great extent. This prevents them from interacting with others and giving of themselves as Christ has admonished. This is a good plan Satan has developed to keep us from helping others and prevent growth in ourselves; he uses it often.

This complex syndrome begins very early in life, when we are told by various people— especially our parents, teachers, and preachers—that we are bad, will go to hell, and never amount to anything. Constant criticism instead of love is the order of the day. We can't seem to do anything right. Love is or appears to be withheld. When we are punished—spankings, privileges reduced or withdrawn, possessions taken away, groundings, etc.—the message received is that we are not worth or even deserve being loved, that we are losers and failures. Throughout our lives, this feeling is reinforced when love is excluded from relationships and we are subjected to punishment. When our playmates cast us aside, we have additional proof. When our first love rejects us, this feeling is driven home even more forcefully. This is the basic scenario that Satan sets up in our lives that affects our families for generations. There may be variations from family to family, and due to the differences in our personalities, our responses may differ, but the basic premise is sound. Satan will spare no effort and will use anyone and anything to make us lose faith and confidence in ourselves, destroy our self-esteem, and make us surrender to this kamikaze syndrome.

By the time we are adults, this ritualistic response has become so deeply embedded in our personalities that our subconscious minds not only believe it but also forces us to act on it in very undesirable ways. When this happens a self-destruct mechanism is set up that controls many aspects of our lives and which may defy every effort we can make to rid ourselves of it. Our subconscious mind, believing we are not worth being loved, will attempt in every way to set up situations in which relationships will fail and situations in which we will fail, so that we can say to ourselves, "See, I really am not worth being loved after all."

Until rooted out, this syndrome may cause us to respond in very destructive ways, especially to praises or gifts. When someone says or does something nice to us, our subconscious will respond by whispering to us, "We are really not worth the love this person has shown us because we do not deserve it, we are not worthy of it." Still in control, our subconscious may cause us to underplay or negate in some way the praise or gift we have received. Example, to complements given to us on a new dress we may respond, "Oh, this is just an old rag I've had hanging in the closet for years." We try and do the things that will justify in our subconscious mind this feeling that we are not worth being loved, that the complements are not deserved.

A woman whom I know well who is very overweight once received a dozen beautiful red roses for a love gift—no other reason, just for love. This challenged her subconscious view of herself. She reacted by putting the roses aside with no water where they soon wilted and died. She then went on an eating binge to make her more undesirable, thus, in her mind, proving to herself and everyone else she really wasn't deserving of love. One of the sad but true side effects of this syndrome is the feeling of sick satisfaction we get in feeling sorry for ourselves, admitting that we really are too undesirable to warrant any love, attention, or consideration.

This syndrome is not just a manifestation of the obese. I firmly believe we all have it to one degree or another. The alcoholic, the rapist, the thief, the womanizer, the loser, or anyone who reacts in a self-destructive way to praise, gifts, or niceties of any kind is reacting to this syndrome. The more often we respond, the deeper it becomes facilitated or ingrained as part of our personality. It can become a very destructive habit to which we soon become a slave.

Just recognizing and admitting that we play this terrible game can help us negate many of the reinforcement encounters we have had down through the years. This syndrome has made cripples of many of us and retarded our progression. To reduce their effects on us, we must attack each of these episodes on a one-on-one basis. As clearly as possible, we need to recall each undesirable occurrence that has demeaned us and remember that there were many who did love us at the time of the encounter, therefore we were *worth* being loved. As we recall each painful experience of punishment, rejection, and withheld love, just remember all the other times that same person did show forth love. We then realize that individual punishments do not justify the feeling that we don't deserve being loved by anyone. Maybe at that specific moment, there appeared to be evidence that we were not worth being loved by that one individual. But many other times we have enjoyed the love of that same person. Concentrate on how we feel about that person's love for us right now. Is there anything that would signal that love is not present? In most cases, there is an indication that it is there. If not, then we need to find out if we are indeed responsible and take the necessary corrective action. Just remember that the multiplicity of reinforcements down through the years has created in us a tendency to generalize these feelings, and Satan would have us believe that we don't deserve to be loved by anyone anymore.

Something else that promotes and feeds this syndrome is unresolved guilt. What makes us feel less worthwhile than guilt that has festered and has become a part of our lives since we were children? How can we feel good about ourselves when we know that we are not perfect, that we have committed some terrible sin when we were very young, and that we are presenting to the world a perfection that doesn't exist? Many of the episodes that have occurred in our childhood are just too painful to talk about. We don't go to those who could help us because we don't deserve to. So, we put up a facade, a false front. In our minds, we believe we are living a lie. Therefore, we are not worth the trust that others place in us, regardless of whether or not we keep the trust.

One thing that creates the most guilt in children is molestation. They know it is wrong but often don't have the courage to change or stop it. Many believe that they have done something that has encouraged it, and therefore, they are somehow responsible. They fear the punishment that may come their way, so they remain silent. Some, who may not be getting love and attention from any other source, may find a sick kind of enjoyment in it. Whatever the cause or reason, there is bound to be a great deal of guilt associated with it. This unresolved guilt creates a feeling of self-abhorrence, worthlessness. This, combined with the lack of love in the home, magnifies the problem beyond their capabilities. Because of this, they must seek the services of someone within the church or a professional who can help them. They must rid themselves of the guilt by repentance so they can get on with their lives. They *can* become productive, worthwhile members of our society, members who cannot only help themselves but others as well.

Our recognition of the destructive power of this syndrome should put us all on guard with respect to our children. It may be wise to approach their punishments as outlined in the Doctrine and Covenants Section 121:41–45:

> "No power or influence can or ought to be maintained by virtue of the priesthood, (or parents) only by persuasion, by long-suffering, by gentleness and meekness, and by love unfeigned;" (Parenthesis added for comprehension.)
>
> By kindness, and pure knowledge, which shall greatly enlarge the soul without hypocrisy, and without guile –
>
> Reproving betimes with sharpness, when moved upon by the Holy Ghost; and then showing forth afterwards an increase of love toward him whom thou hast reproved, lest he esteem thee to be his enemy;
>
> That he may know that thy faithfulness is stronger than the cords of death.
>
> Let thy bowels also be full of charity towards all men, and to the household of faith, and let virtue garnish thy thoughts unceasingly; then shall thy confidence wax strong in the presence of God; and the doctrine of the priesthood shall distil upon thy soul as the dews from heaven.

Remember that God's love for us is real and infinite and that He is immensely more knowledgeable about us than anyone on this earth, and if we are worth His love, then we are certainly worth being loved by all the inferior beings on earth. If someone does not love us, it is because they do not know us as God does. When we do things to others to destroy their love for us, it is simply a manifestation of the kamikaze syndrome at work within us—the desire Satan puts in our hearts to destroy us.

Bear in mind that the only force preventing a loving friendly relationship between God and us and between anyone else and us is the satanic force of evil. This force has the primary goal of destroying every relationship we develop, especially the eternal marriage relationship. Satan is *relentless* and cunning. If one weapon or method won't work for our destruction, another will be tried. The war is not over until we either give up, in which case we are lost, or we live unto the Lord. The obtaining of the celestial kingdom is worth every effort we can possibly make, and the price we must pay is to make ourselves whole and pure in the eyes of our Savior. We may win a few and lose a few. When we lose one, we must go through the process of repentance, *and never give up on ourselves*; in other words, persevere to the end.

23

ANGER

WHAT IS ANGER?

The *New Webster's Dictionary of the English Language* defines anger as: "A violent, revengeful passion or emotion, excited by a real or supposed injury to oneself or others; passion; ire; choler; rage; wrath. Anger is more general and expresses a less strong feeling than wrath and rage, both of which imply a certain outward manifestation, and the latter, violence and want of self-command."

As mentioned above, anger, wrath, and rage are different degrees or stages of the same emotion. This chapter will not differentiate between them but will concentrate on some of the problems with which they are associated and the troubles they bring into our lives. It will also discuss some methods of eliminating the effects they have on the growth and maturity of our personalities.

First of all, anger is a choice we make in response to learned stimuli. We all experience the many things that create anger in our parents or society in general. Television and the entertainment field, in general, are two of the most prevalent media that affect us and teach us the things that make anger acceptable to us. However, we still have our agency and may choose or not to express anger.

Of all the counterproductive traits, anger stands out as one of the top three in being the most destructive. The other two are greed and hatred. If left uncontrolled and unconquered until judgment day, these three harbingers of spiritual death must relegate us to one of the lesser degrees or kingdoms of glory. One method of purging them has been discussed in chapter 2. Hopefully, this chapter will give some new insights into coping with all of the facets of anger in order to increase the effectiveness of our efforts in eliminating this character flaw.

There are many different kinds of anger, each having its own peculiar problems. It is not the intent of this book to identify each and every one of them but rather identify a few and show methods that can be effective in coping with them all. Nevertheless, it matters not how many types we identify if we then do nothing to control them. We should generate an intense desire by every means available to make the commitment to rid ourselves of this terrible trait. Last but not least, we must persevere until we have won.

Self-anger is a type of anger that, when used wisely, can give us a growth opportunity. I often become angry with myself when I do something dumb or stupid. Learning from these mistakes is a productive part of life. It's when these errors are made repeatedly that we must take a closer look at the motivating factors. Self-anger can only be justified if we are growing and learning from our blunders.

Frustration causes another type of anger. We all get upset with nonworking inanimate objects. My wife says she gets angry at nonworking animate objects, our children, and me. I once petrified my wife by beating the hood of our old Buick because the vacuum operated windshield wipers didn't work properly. It happened during a heavy rainstorm in Gallup, New Mexico, while trying unsuccessfully to find a route through the town during interstate highway construction and heavy rains. We had gone around in circles for what seemed to be hours. For some unknown reason, the windshield wipers worked only intermittently, and when they stopped, it necessitated my having to get out into the deluge to restart them. Each time I left the car I was being soaked to the bone. Finally, my frustration got the better of me. I had been in and out of the car at least three times in less than two minutes and had painfully bumped my head on the door frame while getting back in the car only to find that the wipers had stopped again! I became so frustrated that I totally lost control. I got out of the car and started beating on the hood with all of that pent-up emotion raging in my fists. Finally, drenched to the skin and having released most of my anger, I got back into the car and glared at my wife, Geri, "Don't you say a word, not one word!" I said between clenched teeth. She didn't. I don't think I would have done anything had she said something, but the intensity of my emotions and not being married for very long at the time allowed me to use anger as a tool or weapon to frighten her unnecessarily. My wife tells this story with much more eloquence and fervor than I do.

As distressing as this experience was, there was still no excuse for losing my temper that way and putting fear into my wife and children. There are many more acceptable ways of handling a situation such as this, but because of various reinforcements, down through the years, I responded as I had been conditioned. Frustration anger is an integral part of our lives. We allow it to upset us, causing loss of control over our thoughts and actions. Just how intelligent is it to let some mindless inanimate object dominate our emotions? And then, we put the blame on it rather than on us. It is a very convenient way of not accepting the responsibility for our anger. Of course, we do this with all types of anger—he made me lose control, that makes me so mad, or anything to switch the blame for our anger to someone or something else. After all, if it weren't for these things, I would be in perfect control. Ha!

WHY DO WE GET ANGRY?

We seem to enjoy using frustration as an excuse for our loss of self-control and venting our emotional steam. We become irritated at pets, farm animals, hobbies, children, mates, jobs, friends, housework, and too many demands on our time, circumstances, and many other things. In fact, we can become angry at almost anything with the right provocation. Anger is universal.

We all get angry each for our own reasons; however, all the reasons we can come up with point to a common denominator. *We do it because we feel justified.* If we didn't, we would not allow ourselves to be provoked. When we view the circumstance as being acceptable, we get angry to the extent that our self-justification allows. There is a built-in computer in our brains that constantly monitors the current situation, always alert for an opportunity to force a demonstration of our anger, making sure that all reasons are valid. Some examples of the excuses that usually provoke us are: he swore at me, she betrayed me, the noise in this house is just too much for me to bear, she spilled the milk, you've always hated my mother, he kicked the cat, why can't he ever agree with me, you don't earn enough, you're not the man my first husband was, you didn't do what I told you to do, etc.

There are thousands of excuses for anger and few have any validity. They all attempt to shift the blame on something or someone else. I personally feel there is little justification for anger, although at times nothing else seems to work, especially when we are trying to get one of the children to do what we have asked them to do. Often, we condition them to react only when we display anger against them. We seldom take the time to explore other avenues that may work just as well or better and not leave the scars that are associated with anger. In the final analysis, what righteous purpose can it possibly serve that other more effective methods such as love will not? Will it help us to get to the celestial kingdom? Will it help us to grow spiritually? Does it create the serenity we desire for our home or business environment?

Under the influence of anger, our thinking can become so irrational that often we are unable to control our actions, causing physical or mental pain and suffering that can last a lifetime. There is little difference between being under the influence of alcohol or drugs and anger. We are simply not in full control of our faculties. I'm sure our Savoir would not want us to react in this manner.

HOW CAN WE CONTROL ANGER?

The name of the game in this life is learning to control, to discipline all of our disruptive emotions and to control, conquer, and rise above them. We must not allow ourselves to be controlled by them nor permit them to put us in the bondage of sin. It is imperative we learn total self-discipline. We must strive to master the perfection that is necessary to enable us to enter the celestial kingdom. To strive for anything less is to admit that for us mediocrity is good enough; that it is far too much trouble to strive for excellence; and that complacency and procrastination is, after all, easier than the commitment and dedication needed to gain residence with God. It is not uncommon for any of us to lose our tempers just as we lose control of many of the other undesirable traits. It is this loss of restraint that will inevitably cause our spiritual demise.

Anger, if unchecked for a number of years and if no attempt is made to bring it under control, can explode into fits of physical violence. Its use becomes so automatic that we make no real effort at learning to subdue or control it—we just strike out. Then pain, fear, sorrow, and hatred are the results. In this state, we are in the bondage of sin. It has become an uncontrollable habit, like gossip, smoking, or drinking; we are slaves to it. This is the final state of the wicked—being controlled by Satan and our lusts, habits, traits, and having no real command over our lives just being tossed to and fro by the winds of our over ripe emotions. Satan knows his weapons well.

There are those who try and justify their temper by calling it a righteous anger. The use of righteous anger may be justified in certain circumstances; but since it is almost impossible to differentiate between it and regular anger, it may be wise to leave righteous anger to God.

Uncontrolled rage is the cause of many violent crimes. What is anger? Why are we so prone to use it? Why is it so hard to control? Often, these questions are difficult to answer but an understanding of the basic fabric of anger may help us in its ultimate control. Perhaps control is not the word we should use in conjunction with anger because it gives the impression that it is still there simmering beneath the surface just waiting for an opportunity to erupt. The state for which we should strive is not just control but the total elimination of this destructive emotion. We must cultivate a mindset that completely prevents it from welling up within us. We must learn the steps to take that prevent us from responding to those stimuli that cause the loss of our temper.

Anger, like many of the destructive traits arising from our childhood, is picked up from our parents, siblings, friends, television, etc. When we watch people get what they desire by the use of angry outbursts, it is no small wonder that we quickly learn to do the same. Using anger to create fear in others seems to give us the position of top dog, makes us the dominant figure, the leader, or the boss.

For most of us, the expression of anger is a conditioned response we learn during the formative years. Very early, we learn that we can get what we want by angry outbursts. We see our parents use it as a coercive tool against us and against each other. We see it used as an instrument of emotional blackmail to force some inconsequential point and to win an argument. In practice, it appears that the one who can create the most noise, shout the loudest, create the most impressive scene, and display the greatest degree of uncontrolled anger usually wins—or perhaps not?

Sometimes, we display our anger by total silence, deliberately ignoring the needs of those around us. However it is used, it is always destructive. We use it to force and to emotionally punish, blackmail, or coerce someone into acting or thinking in a way that is not in keeping with their own experiences, opinions, or, many times, best interests. Much of the time anger is used as emotional punishment or even expressed as physical punishment. Often, it is used to create guilt feelings in others to force them to agree with us.

I believe anger and selfishness to be the underlying cause of most divorces.

The heart of an argument is anger. In a heated atmosphere, we argue about money, sex, children, anything, and everything. How serene a marriage would be if there were no anger present. Without it, all problems could be discussed in a calm, coherent manner. Serenity would reign supreme, and it would be hard to destroy a marriage or any other relationship under these conditions. Serenity is an expression of love!

In most relationships, especially in marriage, there are two roles—dominant and submissive. In some, the division is not clear to either party. When this occurs, a power struggle will inevitably arise and anger will be the primary tool used to gain dominance. I have seen this struggle go on for the lifetime of some couples. They argue continually (displaying anger) about anything and everything (the right-wrong conflict). The underlying thought seems to be, "If I can win this argument, I have gained a dominant role, won a victory, proved that I'm better than the other, and I have demonstrated my superior intelligence and knowledge."

Each of us should look inward to examine the motives we use or the excuses we put forth to justify the anger we exhibit when various stimuli are applied. Restraint is much easier when we understand the underlying factors that have programmed us to respond in these uncontrolled episodes. We see our parents become angry when things are done that displease them, mistakes, accidents, or whatever. We log these occurrences into our minds as being acceptable and when the same or similar situations arises in our lives, we program ourselves to respond in the same manner.

Another method used to develop anger is trial and error. As children or even as babies, we find what works for us. Anger tantrums seem to work well in most families. Typically, though, our parents, who have been conditioned by their parents who had been trained by their families, condition us, and so it goes. It is our responsibility to recognize that these "traditions" have been going on for generations, and that we must make every effort to break the cycle and eliminate them from our personalities. Satan will endeavor using every faculty and weapon at his disposal to prevent this from happening.

Making an anger log can be a very effective way to accomplish our control of anger. Write down every time you get angry, regardless of how mild or how violent the episode. Then write down what you believe to be the stimulus and why you felt justified in getting angry under that circumstance. In a short period, perhaps a week or two, you will see the patterns emerging, patterns that relate to your past. This greater understanding of what provokes you and why you feel justified in your anger will help you to gain the control you desire.

Jimmy D. Williams, MCSW, gives a rule for handling anger that is one of the most effective methods we can use. It goes something like this: "You may only hold on to anger for ten days. At the end of that time, you must decide to either go to war over the hurt or find some way to resolve and rid yourself of its influence." This may mean talking it out with the person, forgetting the slight, using a mediator, writing a letter stating all the angry things that you feel and then burning it, smashing old dishes, beating a stuffed toy, going into a closet or an area where your voice will not carry and screaming your heart out, going for a walk, cleaning out that drawer or basement, hammering on a board, making bread and kneading it to death, counting your blessings, etc. Using this method, my wife has almost stopped allowing herself to become angry. When she feels that pressure is building up, she asks, "Is this important enough for me go to war over?" If not, she tries to understand the motivation for her anger and deals with it immediately. It should also mean praying and asking God for help. You may have to try many different methods before you find one that will work for you, but this one has certainly helped in our family relationship.

We must be careful in using the above method because it could reinforce anger, making it acceptable.

One of the prime things to remember is that anger is not caused by anyone; each of us chooses our own response to the presented situation. The stimuli may take the form of someone acting in an unacceptable manner, unkind words, or frustrating situations. How often have we heard this statement; "He or she makes me so mad." In essence, what we are saying is that we lack control over what upsets us. Anger is always a choice! We're also admitting that we don't care, that it is too much trouble to change. Satan's influence can easily be seen here. If we allow him to do so, he will program us in such a way that generations may be affected by our uncontrolled actions. He also magnifies our emotion of anger making it more than we intend. *The secret is choosing not to be angry, not to respond to anything anyone can say or do. To not respond to the many frustrating circumstances that occur from day to day. This is repentance in action.* It is not an easy thing to do, but the rewards will far outweigh the effort it takes.

Anger is one of the most destructive forces on the face of the earth. This being true, why do we pay so little attention to it? Why do we spend so little time trying to control it? Why do we make it so acceptable in our society? For one thing, Satan implants in our minds complacency, an uncaring attitude, a lethargy that discourages us from acting on any desire to gain dominance over it. No one else seems to want to control it, so why should I?

We do have our agency to choose to use anger or not. The rewards for eliminating it from our personalities are many: peace of mind, serenity, calmness, and the knowledge that we will harm no one physically, mentally, emotionally, or spiritually by not giving in to it.

The ability to think clearly and act rationally eludes us in our fits of rage.

There are volumes that could be written about anger. All we need do is to look in the daily newspapers, watch it on the TV news, and the other programs that are foisted off on us as entertainment. Anger is everywhere. It seems to be the very essence of our lives.

It is completely infused into our society as an acceptable means of expressing ourselves and getting our way. Why should we want to root out such a "desirable" trait? Instead, we actually nurture it and teach our children how to use it effectively so they can teach their children to do the same. Satan has made it appear to be a necessity in our daily living. Our lackadaisical attitude in generating a desire to overcome this terrible trait comes directly from him. Are we going to let him win? If so, we have joined his ranks.

There are those dictators and despots who use anger as a tool to accomplish their evil designs. Hitler used it to make acceptable the destruction of over six million Jews, plus all his political enemies and all the rest who were killed as a result of the war. Are we not able to see through the facade of the propaganda presented to us by our leaders and the media? What makes it acceptable to mankind for them to perpetrate these and other great atrocities on mankind? Obviously, we, as the human race, haven't deemed it necessary nor matured enough to overcome this terribly counterproductive trait. We just don't stop to analyze the dreadful consequence of allowing others to control our anger.

We can choose to be ruled by it if we wish. We can choose not to respond to those who use it as a weapon against us. We can also choose to be master over it, to be serene and calm under all circumstances. There is no doubt that we can think and function on a much higher plane if we follow this path than if we choose to act or react in anger. We alone can make the choice that will bring us closer to God.

In summary, anger develops into a habit that is an uncontrollable, a destructive, and a detestable emotion. It is used to blackmail, coerce, or punish others, forcing them into performing acts against their wishes. *It is an attempt to reduce or take away any or part of their agency.* Since agency is one of God's greatest gifts, it's no small wonder that anger is one of the most effective weapons Satan uses to destroy us.

Unfortunately, I'm afraid it will take a world crisis, a cataclysmic destruction of most of the inhabitants of the world by global nuclear war to make them aware of the terrible effects of the many aspects of uncontrolled anger and hatred. This will probably occur just prior to the millennium and will be wasted except as a reminder to those who live on into it of what the consequences are for the lack of a desire to control our anger. It is my prayer that we all take seriously our responsibility of conquering this terrible trait before it's too late.

Here are some scriptural references that show how God feels about anger:

> A wrathful man stirreth up strife: but he that is slow to anger appeaseth strife. (Proverbs 15:18)

> He that is slow to anger is better than the mighty; and he that ruleth his spirit than he that taketh a city. (Proverbs 16:32)

> Wrath is cruel, and anger is outrageous; but who is able to stand before envy. (Proverbs 27:4)

> But I say unto you, That whosoever is angry with his brother without a cause shall be in danger of the judgment: and whosoever shall say to his brother, Raca, shall be in danger of the council: but whosoever shall say, thou fool, shall be in danger of hell fire. (Matthew 5:22)

> Let all bitterness, and wrath, and anger, and clamor, and evil speaking, be put away from you, with all malice:
> And be ye kind one to another, tenderhearted, forgiving one another, even as God for Christ's sake hath forgiven you. (Ephesians 4:31–32)

> But now ye also put off all these; anger, wrath, malice, blasphemy, filthy communication out of your mouth. (Colossians 3:8)

> Fathers, provoke not your children to anger, lest they be discouraged. (Colossians 3:21)

> For the kingdom of the devil must shake, and they which belong to it must needs be stirred up unto repentance, or the devil will grasp them with his everlasting chains, and they be stirred up to anger, and perish;

For behold, at that day shall he rage in the hearts of the children of men, and stir them up to anger against that which is good. (2 Nephi 28:19–20)

And now behold, my son, I fear lest the Lamanites shall destroy this people; for they do not repent, and Satan stirreth them up continually to anger one with another.

Behold, I am laboring with them continually; and when I speak the word of God with sharpness they tremble and anger against me; and when I use no sharpness they harden their hearts against it; wherefore, I fear lest the Spirit of the Lord hath ceased striving with them.

For so exceedingly do they anger what it seemeth me that they have no fear of death; and they have lost their love, one towards another; and they thirst after blood and revenge continually.

And now, my beloved son, notwithstanding their hardness, let us labor diligently; for if we should cease to labor, we should be brought under condemnation; for we have a labor to perform whilst in this tabernacle of clay, that we may conquer the enemy of all righteousness, and rest our souls in the kingdom of God. (Moroni 9:3–6)

24

HATRED AND PREJUDICE

From the *New Webster's Dictionary*:

> *Hatred*: Great dislike or aversion; detestation antipathy; animosity.

> *Prejudice:* An opinion or judgment, favorable or more often unfavorable, conceived without proof or competent evidence; a bias against race, creed, group, or the like; the holding of such feelings.

In terms of human behavior, these are certainly not desirable traits. Yet the world appears to be a boiling cesspool of hatred and prejudice. We embrace and use these terms as if they were coveted above all traits.

A few years ago, I was reading in the newspaper about the death of an African American in New York City. He and some of his friends had accidently stalled their car on the highway and had tried to get help in a local establishment. Several "whites" who were present preceded to terrorize them resulting in the death of one of the men. An automobile struck him as he fled across a busy highway to escape their threats.

The terrorists gave no thought for the welfare of their fellow man. No love or compassion was present, just blind, unjustified, hatred and prejudice. Is it possible they claimed to be Christians? Is it possible they had never been taught the simple principles of love and tolerance? Or is this a case where the sins of the fathers were passed on to the children by telling off colored jokes, by making unkind remarks, and categorizing the faults of a few and applying them to a whole race?

If this were just an isolated incident, we could look upon it as a case of madness or insanity. But it isn't! And it isn't just confined to whites being prejudiced against blacks. All races are involved. Prejudices, distrusts, and hatreds are all part of the human persona. Are we justified in clinging to these destructive traits?

Perhaps if we view it in another perspective it will make more sense. Are other races, religions, or groups of any kind, justified in being prejudiced against us regardless of who we are? No, of course not! Then how can we justify our prejudice against others? Our prejudice should be saved for the evil actions of those who are in the bondage of sin but not against the individuals themselves. If we feel the overpowering need to have and display our hatreds and prejudices, then display them against Satan, the force behind all of our troubles and woes. We are all prejudiced in one way or another, perhaps against the poor, the rich, the intelligent, the stupid, the handicapped, and so on.

God doesn't care what color of skin we have or to what nation or organization we belong. He only cares about the application of the principles He has taught us and the love we need to show one to another. He cares about the progress and growth we experience. It doesn't matter to what race we belong if we demonstrate love for our fellow man. Those who do will far surpass in spiritual growth the bigoted and prejudiced that show their hatred for any race, nationality, religion, creed, or organization. In the final analysis, it is what we finally become that counts. What really matters is the degree of our repentance, our tolerance for man's weaknesses and national origin, and the love, desire, and willingness to serve all mankind. The demonstration of these Christ-like traits places our souls in the hands of God.

A news item followed up an article that appeared in a newspaper and on television. It showed an angry mob and the hatred in the faces of the participants. Accusations and fists were flying on both sides. The media was there in force making sure that no sordid detail was missed. It appeared that the mob had completely relinquished the control of their emotions to Satan. There was no love present. Christ's teachings for the past two thousand years meant nothing. If this were an isolated case, it would not be so difficult to cope with it, but it isn't. It is with us every day and everywhere.

Beware of those who incite political and other types of riots. They always have an agenda that is mostly engendered by the satanic forces of destruction. Those who participate in them have joined the army of Lucifer. They are henchmen who do his bidding in all things. The evil behind these rioters is the one paying them to do so. Follow the money, and we may find the evil one behind it all.

It is hard to believe that the majority of the human race has not matured beyond the stage of childhood during these past six thousand years. The maturity and oneness of mankind depends on the spiritual health of each individual within our society. Just like the functional integrity of each person depends on the health of every cell within their bodies. When enough cells malfunction, the body is reduced to illness, demonstrating symptoms that are related to the type of cell involved. This same thing applies to the human race.

When enough people demonstrate their prejudices and hatreds, symptoms of unrest and violence will inevitably appear. These are the manifestations of a sick and immature society. When this occurs in the body, it protects itself by generating other cells that attack and kill the offending ones. Our armies and law enforcement agencies are similar to these cells and should be doing much the same job for the human race. Unfortunately, many of our laws seem to be lacking in their ability to protect us. It does protect many of the malfunctioning units, the hardened criminal, by placing them in an environment which teaches them to be an even greater destructive force against society. Before our race can progress and mature the way God intends, we must find a way that will either destroy these cancerous units or find a way to teach and encourage them to become functional members of our society again. Until we do this, our societies will remain immature, radiating its problems from one end of the world to the other. Unfortunately, most of the leaders of our nations who should be most concerned about these problems are themselves flawed and will do nothing but perpetuate and magnify the problems that already exist. It is like calling on one deadly bacterium to help another deadly bacterium to heal the body; it just can't be done.

Generally speaking, much of the media throughout the world plays a big part in fostering the attitudes that allow these disruptive people to perpetrate their miseries on mankind. I realize the media must depend to a great extent on the public for their ratings and success, but the sensationalism that accompanies most violent news items should be dampened rather than magnified. The media has the tendency to feed the fires of unrest, increasing the likelihood of creating other related incidents which is then played for all it is worth in the media. In this way, the media is creating its own news then using it to build its own circulation. To say that all of the media falls into this category is wrong. There are many who take their responsibility to mankind seriously, endeavoring always to give us their best and promote the standards upon which this great nation was built.

Most people who harbor hatreds and prejudices are easily led and swayed by the media, which in turn is swayed by Satan, and so it goes. Some are even paid to create riots and unrest for the sake of politics. Many see it as a form of justification for their beliefs, and the physical violence they use against those of whom they are prejudiced. I don't mean to isolate just the media because all facets of our society are involved in the deterioration of the righteous standards of America.

All of the professions should monitor themselves and do all within their power to control those within their ranks who would create degeneration or the mental and emotionally pollution of our society.

Hatred and prejudice are much the same as anger and the other counterproductive traits. When they control our lives, we can't. We are in the bondage of sin; we are slaves to the powers of evil, and our hope of ever gaining the kingdom of God is lessened. We need to gain complete control and never relinquish it to any of those traits with which Satan tries so hard to bind us.

Hatred is one of the top three major counterproductive traits that afflict mankind. There are those who say it is the base from which all destructive characteristics originate. Personally, I believe that anger is the base. I cannot picture hatred or prejudice existing without first there having been anger.

We see the destructive effects of hatred so many times in our lives that its presence fails to impress us; we become inured to it. Every day, we see marriages dissolved, friendships broken, brother against brother, people against people, or race against race. Once started, it is like a cancer that eats at the very roots of our world societies, destroying all relationships in which it is allowed to exist. It can devastate both the hated and hater and often those caught in the crossfire. Mankind needs to bring love to bear on this great evil to nullify its effects.

Hatred and prejudice usually stem from an anger conflict related to low self-esteem directed at someone in an attempt to show superiority, gain dominance, or to punish them. We learn these traits from our associates and parents who may have had them passed down from generation to generation, and finally are affecting us. We learn them at school and even in our churches. Often, these biases are created when we have suffered some physical or mental anguish as a result of someone's actions, either real or imagined. The reasons we possess these undesirable traits are so many and so varied that it would be impossible to list them all. Ultimately the reasons are unimportant, what does matter is that we do everything we can to cleanse ourselves of these destructive traits so that we, again, can live with our Father in heaven.

We try in many ways to justify our hatreds and biases. It is the other guy's fault, he started it, he did that to me, and a thousand other excuses. In truth there is no justification. Our hatred is present because of an unforgiving attitude. If we cannot or will not forgive, then neither will we be forgiven in the eternities to come, unless we repent. This is one of the basic laws of heaven; we cannot bypass it by any means whatsoever. God is very explicit on this principle in all the scriptures. Our hatreds, prejudices, and bigotries must be purged from our personalities, by repentance before we can live in His presence. Cleansing ourselves of them is not easy because of the hurt and emotion that is associated with them. But just because it seems impossible does not absolve us from the responsibility of doing it by asking help of our heavenly Father.

Going to our Father in heaven is not always easy either because we have a tendency to nurture these detestable traits. They have become a comfortable part of our lives. Besides, the other fellow started it, so he should take the first step. I'll forgive him when he forgives me. And so, we go on with our lives trying not to think about the problem for fear we will have to do something about it. It takes a great deal of courage to correct some of these long-lasting hatreds and prejudices, but our Father in heaven will give us the courage if we pursue it with an intense desire, persevering until it is accomplished.

It appears to me that most counterproductive traits have their roots in anger and maybe hatred. Since love is the opposite of hate, we need to generate a desire to cultivate it to replace the hate. This is essential for our salvation. If we harbor any hatred toward anyone, a review of chapter 9 on forgiveness may help.

Although love is the major weapon ordained to fight our hatreds and prejudices, there are others that will help. It is important to go through the list of productive traits in chapter 2 and then using our wisdom, intelligence, and prayer to select those that will be effective against the hatreds and prejudices we are attempting to expunge. We cannot be passive or complacent about eliminating any of our counterproductive traits; intensive effort is needed on a continuing basis to rid ourselves of them. Satan knows the power of habit, and he makes it almost impossible for us to break old habits, but we can do it if we rely on the power of God and the weapons He has ordained to help us win. We need to approach God in prayer, go to our bishops or branch presidents, our home and visiting teachers, or maybe a close trustworthy friend. Even therapy may be in order to accomplish our goal.

We do have our agency to choose between love and hate. No one makes us hate anyone. When someone does something unkind to us and we choose to hate them, it is our choice not theirs. If anyone had a right to hate, it was Christ who suffered as no man has ever suffered; but as he hung on the cross, he said, "Father forgive them for they know not what they do." I believe that when we hate and cannot forgive, we just don't realize the effect or magnitude of what we are doing.

Forgiving is an integral part of relinquishing our hatreds and prejudices. Hatred is merely the nurturing of an unforgiven trespass or maybe a grudge, whether it is real or imagined. Prejudice is basically the same thing except we often listen to and act on false information we get from our parents or peers rather than forming our opinions on true concepts. We allow our emotions to respond to what others say and do instead of thinking for ourselves. We need to stop feeding our emotions and start feeding our minds with the food of forgiveness. Stop dwelling on the offenses of others and look for something we can love or appreciate about those who have offended us. We can start doing things for them instead of to them. It is hard to hate someone that we have become close to. Bring them into our circle of influence, our circle of light, and expand our light; become their friend, their confidant, and the hatred will fall away.

When hatred becomes uncontrollable, we must take a close look at the influences that surround it. Without Satan's influence, there would be no hatred. He directly affects our thinking and magnifies our emotions. First, he creates a situation that produces hatred, and then he perpetuates it by directly increasing our negative emotions. We need to recognize this as fact or our efforts to conquer our hatreds will be futile. We need to create a mindset in which we always recognize that it is Satan who causes all of our suffering, pain, anger, hatred, and all other destructive traits. Satan is the root of all of our problems and if we concentrate on making him ineffective by studying and heeding the words of God and listening to the still small voice, we can make love the center of our lives instead of hatred and prejudice.

When we begin to harbor a prejudice or hatred against some race, group, or individual, we should ask ourselves these questions, "Do I really want to become a tool or weapon that Satan uses to accomplish his goals?" "Do I really want to turn control of my life over to him and become his slave or soldier?" If we did ask these questions and act righteously on them, we would soon have the problem under control. Just reading and agreeing with these concepts will do nothing for us. We must make a serious effort and commitment to take the action necessary for our salvation and exaltation.

Prayer and supplication are always essential in conquering any of our counterproductive traits. It is my prayer that each of us will look inward at the prejudices and hatreds we harbor and make the commitments necessary to eliminate them from our personalities. This is what God would have us do. Satan would have us nurture and magnify our hatreds and prejudices to the point where we are no longer in control. He would have us murder and do all manner of evil, all in what we consider *justifiable* hatred and prejudice. He would tell us that our evil was justified by our hatreds and prejudices. His goal is to prevent us from gaining the celestial kingdom. God has given us our agency, and we have the choice of being what we want to be, God's servant or Satan's slave.

Here are some scriptural references to study and contemplate. They should help give us the strength and desire to overcome these destructive traits and replace them with love.

> Thou shalt not hate thy brother in thine heart: Thou shalt not in any wise rebuke thy neighbor, and not suffer sin upon him.
> Thou shalt not avenge, nor bear any grudge against the children of thy people, but thou shalt love thy neighbor as thyself: I am the Lord. (Leviticus 19:17–18)

> Ye that love the Lord, hate evil: he preserveth the souls of his saints; he delivereth them out of the hand of the wicked. (Psalms 97:10)

> These six things doth the Lord hate: yea seven are an abomination unto him.
> A proud look, a lying tongue, and hands that shed innocent blood,
> An heart that deviseth wicked imaginations, feet that be swift in running to mischief,
> A false witness that speaketh lies, and he that seweth discord among thy brethren. (Proverbs 6:16–19)

> He that spareth the rod hateth his son, but he that loveth him chasteneth him betimes. (Proverbs 13:24)

> But I say unto you, love your enemies, bless them that curse you, do good to them that hate you, and pray for them which despitefully use you; (Matthew 5:44)

> Blessed are ye, when men shall hate you and when they shall separate you from their company, and shall reproach you and cast out your name as evil, for the son of man's sake. (Luke 5:22)

He that loveth his life shall lose it: and he that hateth his life in this world shall keep it unto life eternal. (John 12:25)

If the world hates you, ye know that it hated me before it hated you. (John 15:18)

Whosoever hateth his brother is a murderer: and ye know that no murderer hath eternal life abiding in him. (1 John 3:15)

If a man say, I love God, and hateth his brother, he is a liar: for he that loveth not his brother whom he hath seen, how can he love God whom he hath not seen? (1 John 4:20)

And now my son, remember the words which I have spoken unto you; trust not those secret plans unto this people, but teach them an everlasting hatred against sin and iniquity.
Preach unto them repentance, and faith on the Lord Jesus Christ; teach them to humble themselves and to be meek and lowly in heart; teach them to withstand every temptation of the devil, with their faith on the Lord Jesus Christ. (Alma 37:32–34)
Teach them to never be weary of good works but to be meek and lowly in heart; for such shall find rest to their souls.

25

GREED

Greed is the inordinate desire or yearning for things, especially money and power, that goes beyond our needs. Greed is the emotional trait opposite to charity, and charity is the pure love of Christ. Greed always manifests itself in the drive to get gain, to accumulate money and obtain power over others, to present one's self as better than other people, and seldom manifests humility.

It is my opinion that Satan uses greed to control people, to incite most of the worlds wars, and is the cause of most misery in the world. Those who are in its clutches can never be satisfied. These are they who will not inherit any of the higher degrees of glory in God's kingdom unless they truly repent.

Many of those who accumulate great wealth will use it as a destructive force, to subjugate, control, enslave, and have unrighteous dominion over those who depend and rely on them.

According to Jacob in the Book of Mormon, great wealth will come to the righteous if they seek and use it charitably and wisely. Their use of this wealth will always be productive and a source of blessings to those who are in need. They do not hesitate to share their wealth with others and are always willing to sacrifice all if called upon to do so. They know that death leaves all physical accumulations behind. They understand that the greatest wealth to be amassed on earth is spiritual. In fact, they know that wealth exists only within and not without. This is the wealth gained through service, sharing, caring, and by accumulating knowledge and wisdom, and by perfecting every facet of their personalities.

Greed is a destructive emotion. Like any other counterproductive trait, we have the power to accept or reject it as part of our persona. Each of us knowingly makes the choice to be greedy or not. The responsibility lies only within us. No one else can make us greedy, angry, or hateful. We can choose to allow these emotions to control us or we can control them. God will hold only us responsible.

When greed becomes a part of our personality controlling our destiny, it is almost impossible to get rid of it. However, if we can create a strong enough desire, we can overcome its terrible influence. This can be accomplished by cultivating charity, which is opposite to greed. We are capable of retraining ourselves to be charitable and to help others in every way possible. I believe God would be happy if we expunged this extremely destructive trait. We could search for people to help find ways to make the lives of others more pleasant, more meaningful. Remember, charity and greed cannot coexist, so if we are helping others, greed cannot be present. We must always remember that God's help is essential in overcoming any of the destructive traits.

Pondering these scriptures may give us the strength to overcome this horrible trait:

> He that is greedy of gain troubleth his own house; but he that hateth gifts shall live. (Proverbs 15:27)

> All ye beasts of the field, come to devour, yea, all ye beasts in the forest.
> His watchmen are blind: they are all ignorant, they are all dumb dogs, they cannot bark; sleeping, lying down, loving to slumber.
> Yea, they are greedy dogs which can never have enough, and they are shepherds that cannot understand: they all look to their own way, everyone for his gain, from his quarter.
> Come ye, say they, I will fetch wine, and we will fill ourselves with strong drink; and tomorrow shall be as this day, and much more abundant. (Isaiah 56:9–12)

Mortify therefore your members which are upon the earth; fornication, uncleanness, inordinate affection, evil concupiscence, and covetousness, which is idolatry: (Colossians 3:5)

Woe to him that coveteth an evil covetousness to his house, that he may set his nest on high, that he may be delivered from the power of evil! (Habakkuk 2:9)

And he said unto them, Take heed, and beware of covetousness: for a man's life consisteth not in abundance of the things which he possesseth.
And he spake a parable unto them, saying, the ground of a certain rich man brought forth plentifully:
And he thought within himself, saying, what shall I do, because I have no room where to bestow my fruits?
And he said, this will I do: I will pull down my barns, and build greater; and there will I bestow all my fruits and my goods.
And I will say to my soul, Soul, thou hast much goods laid up for many years; take thine ease, eat, drink, and be merry.
But God said unto him, thou fool, this night thy soul shall be required of thee: then whose shall those things be, which thou hast provided?
So is he that layeth up treasure for himself, and is not rich toward God. (Luke 12:15–21)

For this, thou shalt not commit adultery, Thou shalt not kill, Thou shalt not steal, Thou shalt not bear false witness, Thou shalt not covet; and if there be any other commandment, it is briefly comprehended in this saying, namely, Thou shalt love thy neighbor as thyself.
Love worketh no ill to his neighbor: therefore love is the fulfilling of the law. (Romans 13:9–10)

For the love of money is the root of all evil: Which while some coveted after, they have erred from the faith, and pierced themselves through with many sorrows.

But thou, O man of God, flee these things; and follow after righteousness, godliness, faith, love, patience, meekness.

Fight the good fight of faith, lay hold on eternal life, whereunto thou art also called, and hast professed a good profession before many witnesses. (1 Timothy 6:10–12)

Now my son, I would that ye should repent and forsake your sins, and go no more after the lusts of your eyes, but cross yourself in all these things; for except ye do this ye can in nowise inherit the kingdom of God. Oh, remember, and take it upon you, and cross yourself in these things. (Alma 39:9)

Wo unto you rich men, that will not give your substance to the poor, for your riches will canker your souls; and this shall be your lamentation in the day of visitation, and of judgment, and of indignation: The harvest is past, the summer is ended, and my soul is not saved!

Wo unto you poor men, whose hearts are not broken, whose spirits are not contrite, and whose bellies are not satisfied, and whose hands are not stayed from laying hold upon other men's goods, whose eyes are full of greediness, and who will not labor with your own hands!

But blessed are the poor who are pure in heart, whose hearts are broken, and whose spirits are contrite, for they shall see the kingdom of God coming in power and great glory unto their deliverance; for the fatness of the earth shall be theirs. (D & C 56:16–18)

See that ye love one another; cease to be covetous; learn to impart one to another as the gospel requires. (D & C 88:123)

26

PROCRASTINATION

We are all procrastinators at times. Putting off undesirable tasks is a worldwide pastime. Often, we just can't be bothered to do them at all. This is especially true when it comes to things pertaining to the gospel. We leave our genealogy undone. We don't read our lessons or scriptures. Missionary responsibilities are not taken seriously. Home and visiting teaching assignments are taken lightly and are often superseded by other activities, such as our favorite TV programs, a football game, a soap opera, etc. According to the scriptures (D & C 130:20), we must obey the commandment pertaining to desired blessings before we can expect their fulfillment. When we complain about prayers not being answered, it may be advisable to take a good hard look at whether or not we deserve and have earned the blessing and whether our zest and enthusiasm warrants them and how do we approach our spiritual duties and responsibilities.

Procrastination is one of the greatest weapons Satan uses against us. The more we submit to its practice, the more counterproductive we become. This makes us less goal oriented. We, then, are more likely to embrace other temptations he uses to destroy us. Today's modern world is full of time wasters and goal discouragers. It is not possible to become goal oriented when we spend hours each day in front of the television. If it isn't television or reading novels, it may be something else that takes precedence. Time is an element for which we must account to our heavenly Father. It may help to treat each hour of each day as a sacred gift from God.

Procrastination is the unwise use of time, which is a vital asset. One method of beating this disruptive trait is to make an expense account of the hours allotted to us each day. Then every morning, determine how much of it we will spend doing our essential work, our chosen profession, church and community responsibilities, etc. The remaining time could be budgeted for other things: time with individual family members, watching an uplifting movie, scripture study, and other worthwhile projects.

Never indiscriminately sit down and watch a TV program. That is like trying to eat one potato chip. The next thing we know the whole evening or day is gone, wasted.

We are each allotted twenty-four hours every day. John doesn't get twenty-six because he has been a good boy or does Jane get only eighteen because she wasted four yesterday. At midnight, our banker allots everyone the same amount. We can be good or bad stewards over each day's allotment. We can spend it wisely or foolishly. We can use it selfishly or charitably. Whatever we do with it is because we have made that choice. Sometimes, there are situations that arise which give us little or no control over how our time is spent. Through an error in judgment we may give command to someone else. For instance, if we were to steal something and get caught, most likely we would give mastery of how it is spent to some penal institution. Under these circumstances, stealing becomes destructive to our stewardship over our time, and we will not only be held accountable for stealing but for the unwise use of our time as well.

Alma 34:33 informs us, "Do not procrastinate the day of your repentance." Once we die, it is too late. Satan has won if our time is spent unwisely. Procrastination touches every aspect of our earthly lives. It is the time wasters way to justify their lack of accomplishment. It is driven by habit and reinforced by our neglect to conquer it. Soon, this trait becomes so entrenched that it is almost impossible to extract.

We all tend to take the paths of least resistance. This can be a form of procrastination except when we use our creative imagination to make a task easier. Sometimes, fear is an intimidating factor, preventing us from trying to accomplish something. "If I don't try no one will look down on me for failing."

Low self-esteem is one of the roots of this evil trait. Satan uses his power to keep it low. When we fail to accomplish a goal, we have the tendency to allow our self-worth to suffer. We then have the inclination to believe that others will look down on us for failing. Actually, people look up to those who have the courage to get up and try again when they occasionally fail. The doer, the man of action, and the achiever, has always been the foundation of our society. So, what do we have to fear for trying? Nothing! To me, the doer the accomplisher, the achiever, and the creator is our hero.

A great man once said, "Out of every failure or adversity comes an equal or greater opportunity." I like to add "for growth." The winner never looks upon a failure as such but merely a temporary setback or a stepping-stone to achieve even greater things.

Procrastinators are not goal setters, hence they have no desire to achieve. They say, "I probably wouldn't succeed anyway, so why try?" It is much easier to take the easy way out, the path of least resistance, and coast through life by letting someone else do it. No worthwhile project was ever completed by sitting in front of a TV set.

This trait should not be taken lightly. It is much easier to just ignore it or let it ride. Maybe it will go away by itself. I'll do something about it later, right now I need to take a nap. Tomorrow, I'll take the time and set some goals. Unfortunately, tomorrow never comes for the procrastinator.

We all try to justify our inactions. We make excuses and often do more work by trying to avoid it. When the kingdom of heaven is at hand, time has run out (death), there is no more time in this life, no more tomorrow. The axe has fallen, and the procrastinator is guilty of heeding the promptings of Satan and not our Savior. No excuse will be good enough. No excuse will be accepted. Procrastinators cannot live with God in the celestial kingdom.

With persistent effort, we can eliminate this destructive trait from our daily lives. Use the motto, *"Do it now."* Make it a part of our personality instead of *"It can wait."* If we review the chapter on repentance, it will help reinforce our desire to control this totally destructive trait.

The following scriptures can help us understand how our Lord and Savior feels about procrastination:

> Watch therefore: for ye know not what hour your Lord doth come.
>
> But know this, that if the good-man of the house had known in what watch the thief would come, he would have watched, and would not have suffered his house to be broken up.
>
> Therefore be ye also ready: for in such an hour as ye think not the Son of man cometh. (Death)
>
> Who then is a faithful and wise servant, whom his lord hath made ruler over his household, to give them meat in due season?
>
> Blessed is that servant, whom his lord when he cometh shall find so doing.
>
> Verily I say unto you, that he shall make him ruler over all his goods.
>
> But and if that evil servant shall say in his heart, My lord delayeth his coming;
>
> And shall begin to smite his fellow servants, and to eat and drink with the drunken;
>
> The lord of that servant shall come in a day when he looketh not for him, and in an hour that he is not aware of,
>
> And shall cut him asunder, and appoint him his portion with the hypocrites: there shall be weeping and gnashing of teeth. (Matthew 24:42–51)

> Then shall the kingdom of heaven be likened unto ten virgins, which took their lamps, and went forth to meet the bridegroom.
>
> And five of them were wise, and five were foolish.
>
> They that were foolish took their lamps, and took no oil with them:
>
> But the wise took oil in their vessels with their lamps.
>
> While the bridegroom tarried, they all slumbered and slept.
>
> And at midnight there was a cry made, Behold the bridegroom cometh; go ye out to meet him.
>
> Then all those virgins arose, and trimmed their lamps.

EXPANDING OUR LIGHT

And the foolish said unto the wise, Give us of your oil; for our lamps have gone out.

But the wise answered, saying, Not so; lest there be not enough for us and you: but go ye rather to them that sell, and buy for yourselves.

And while they went to buy, the bridegroom came; and they that were ready went in with him to the marriage: and the door was shut.

Afterward came also the other virgins, saying, Lord, Lord, open to us.

But he answered and said, Verily I say unto you, I know you not.

Watch therefore, for ye know neither the day nor the hour wherein the Son of man cometh. (Matthew 25:1–13)

And another also said, Lord, I will follow thee; but let me first go bid them farewell, which are at home at my house.

And Jesus said unto him, No man, having put his hand to the plough, and looking back, is fit for the kingdom of God. (Luke 9:61–62)

But and if that servant say in his heart, My lord delayeth his coming; and shall begin to beat the men-servants and the maidens, and to eat and drink, and to be drunken;

The lord of that servant will come in a day when he looketh not for him, and at an hour when he is not aware, and will cut him in sunder, and will appoint him his portion with the unbelievers.

And that servant, which knew his lord's will, and prepared not himself, neither did according to his will, shall be beaten with many stripes.

But he that knew not, and did commit things worthy of stripes, shall be beaten with few stripes. For unto whomsoever much is given, of him shall much be required: and to whom men have committed much, of him they will ask the more. (Luke 12:45–48)

And take heed to yourselves, lest at any time your hearts be overcharged with surfeiting, and drunkenness, and cares of this life, and so that day come upon you unawares.

For as a snare shall it come on all them that dwell on the face of the whole earth.

Watch ye therefore, and pray always, that ye may be accounted worthy to escape all these things that shall come to pass, and to stand before the Son of man. (Luke 21:34–36)

Have ye walked, keeping yourselves blameless before God? Could ye say, if ye were called to die at this time, within yourselves, that ye have been sufficiently humble? That your garments have been cleansed and made white through the blood of Christ, who will come to redeem his people from their sins?

4Behold, are ye stripped of pride? I say unto you, if ye are not ye are not prepared to meet God. Behold ye must prepare quickly; for the kingdom of heaven is soon at hand, and such an one hath not eternal life.

Behold, I say, is there one among you who is not stripped of envy? I say unto you that such an one is not prepared; and I would that he should prepare quickly, for the hour is close at hand, and he knoweth not when the time shall come; for such an one is not found guiltless.

And again I say unto you, is there one among you that doth make a mock of his brother, or that heapeth upon him persecutions?

Wo unto such an one, for he is not prepared, and the time is at hand that he must repent or he cannot be saved!

Yea, even wo unto all ye workers of iniquity; repent, repent, for the Lord God hath spoken it!

Behold, he sendeth an invitation unto all men, for the arms of mercy are extended towards them, and he saith: Repent, and I will receive you. (Alma 5:27–33)

Yea, I would that ye would come forth and harden not your hearts any longer; for behold, now is the time and the day of your salvation; and therefore, if ye will repent and harden not your hearts, immediately shall the great plan of redemption be brought about unto you.

For behold, this life is the time for men to prepare to meet God; yea, behold the day of this life is the day for men to perform their labors.

And now, as I said unto you before, as ye have had so many witnesses, therefore, I beseech of you that ye do not procrastinate the day of your repentance until the end; for after this day of life, which is given us to prepare for eternity, behold, if we do not improve our time while in this life, then cometh the night of darkness wherein there can be no labor performed.

Ye cannot say, when ye are brought to that awful crisis, that I will repent, that I will return to my God. Nay, ye cannot say this; for that same spirit which doth possess your bodies at the time that ye go out of this life, that same spirit will have power to possess your body in that eternal world.

For behold, if ye have procrastinated the day of your repentance even until death, behold, ye have become subjected to the spirit of the devil, and he doth seal you his; therefore, the Spirit of the Lord hath withdrawn from you, and hath no place in you, and the devil hath all power over you; and this is the final state of the wicked.

Helaman 13:38 But behold, your days of probation are past; ye have procrastinated the day of your salvation until it is everlastingly too late, and your destruction is made sure; yea, for ye have sought all the days of your lives for that which ye could not obtain; and ye have sought for happiness in doing iniquity, which thing is contrary to the nature of that righteousness which is in our great and Eternal Head. (Alma 34:31-35)

And in one place they were heard to cry, saying: O that we had repented before this great and terrible day, and then would our brethren have been spared, and they would not have been burned in that great city Zerahemla. (3 Nephi 8:24)

27

IDOLATRY

> Therefore take no thought, saying, What shall we eat? or, What shall we drink? or wherewithal shall we be clothed?
>
> (For after all these things do the Gentiles seek:) for your heavenly Father knoweth that ye have need of all these things.
>
> But seek ye first the kingdom of God, and his righteousness; and all these things shall be added unto you. (Matthew 6:31–33)

When we are in the process of seeking after the things of the world without thought for our spiritual welfare, we are setting our goals on those things which will take us farther and farther away from the kingdom of God. We are, in effect, worshiping our accumulations and collectibles instead of God. This can be idolatry.

When we buy a new sports car, boat, or anything to show off or give the impression we are better than others, are we not worshiping these items instead of God? "For where your treasure is, there will your heart be also" (Matthew 6:21).

If our hearts are on the things of the world, that is where our treasure is. If our hearts are on the things of God, we will reap the spiritual treasures of eternal life with our heavenly Father.

Idol worship is rampant in the world today. We don't have to set an idol on our mantle and bow down to it morning and night to worship it. All we need to do is to place the accumulation of worldly goods or place activities such as golf, fishing, watching TV, etc., ahead of worshiping God, and we are worshiping idols. When we choose to stay home from our church services to watch the World Series or Super Bowl, we are telling God that these things are more important than He is.

There is plenty of room in our lives for these activities. It is when we place their importance above our duties to God that we are breaking the commandments and making idols of them. It is by excessively involving ourselves in worldly activities, especially on the Sabbath, instead of worshiping God that we err. We worship idols when we fail to extend a helping hand to the poor, feed the hungry, or care for the needy but instead purchase the luxuries of life for our own greedy, self-centered, egotistical desires.

We all live by a set of established priorities. Whatever we do is because we have chosen to do it above all other things for that period of time. We do the things that are important to us at the moment. The choices we make are because of the priorities we have set beforehand. Sometimes, these priorities are set because of attitudes we have learned in our childhood. Once in a while, they are set because we place fun and pleasure above duty and responsibility. There are times when they are determined by emergency situations. Whatever the reason we need to re-evaluate our priorities and place them in perspective. The scriptures inform us to "Seek first the kingdom of God." This, then, should be first on our list of priorities. By placing God first, we not only obey His commandments but also place ourselves in a position to receive the many blessings associated with obedience.

There is plenty of room in our lives for such activities as boating, fishing, golfing, bridge, etc., but we need to establish the order on our list in which they should fall. We shouldn't go out and play bridge while we neglect the family or go fishing when other important duties remain unfinished like home teaching, church attendance, etc. To change the order of importance from material to spiritual is not always easy. This is a physical world in which we live and to change from tangible to intangible or physical to spiritual goals and attitudes takes extended, focused effort. Until we can make this change, we are likely to find ourselves worshiping the physical things of this world instead of the spiritual things that will bring us eternal life with God and Jesus Christ.

The following list depicts an order of priorities that works for many people. I try to follow it as closely as possible. Sometimes, I stray, as we all will at times, but I always come back to it to get on the right track. The exact order may be changed to meet individual family needs. Each of us should have a list to which we refer at times to help place our lives in proper perspective:

1. Duty and love for God. (Church responsibilities.)
2. Duty and love to marriage.
3. Duty and love to spouse.
4. Duty and love to children.
5. Duty and love to fellow man.
6. Duty and love to self.
7. Duty to a vocation or profession.
8. Service to home. (Home repairs, etc.)
9. Recreational activities and hobbies for family and then for oneself.

The exact order of some things on the list may vary according to immediate needs, such as emergencies, but generally speaking, it covers the basics. The order of priorities in this list takes all selfishness out of our lives. This alone is worth much in the eyes of God and will bring us many blessings.

We may need some help to place duty to God first on our list of priorities, especially where finances are concerned. I have found that if I ask the following questions it helps: "Is what I am doing or buying necessary for my salvation and growth toward perfection?" "Will it help others achieve their salvation and encourage their growth toward perfection?"

Our growth and salvation depends on the priorities we set. If they are set on the things of the world, we will suffer. If they are set on the things of God, we will be blessed.

If I had to choose a day of the week that idol worship is most prevalent in the world, I would have to choose the Sabbath. Since this is the day God has consecrated for worship, I find it most interesting that rather than worship God, visit the sick, and help the poor, we choose to go fishing, golfing, shopping, boating, etc. Why is it that the majority of us feel these things are OK? Why do we place so little value on the things of righteousness and so much on the lure of the world? Everyone else does it so it must be OK, right? Is it right when we stay home and watch TV instead of going to church? Is it right when we place *anything* above the worship of God on the Sabbath? Infirmity and illness are good reasons to stay home, especially, if they pose a health hazard to those with whom we come in contact or when we are so infirmed that to do so would cause greater pain; if not, they are just excuses.

Placing the worship of God lower than number one on our list of priorities endangers our opportunities for growth and for attaining salvation and exaltation. Allowing other things to take priority over our duties and responsibilities to the gospel places our souls in jeopardy of everlasting misery with Satan, to whose temptations we often value more than life itself. We must always remember that *God really is our eternal Father in heaven!*

The following scriptures will help us evaluate our worship of idols:

> No man can serve two masters: for either he will hate the one, and love the other; or else he will hold to the one, and despise the other. Ye cannot serve God and Mammon. (Matthew 6:24)

> Wherefore, my dearly beloved, flee from idolatry.
> I speak as to wise men; judge ye what I say.
> The cup of blessing which we bless, is it not the communion of the blood of Christ? The bread which we break, is it not the communion of the body of Christ?
> For we being many are one bread, and one body: for we are all partakers of that one bread.
> Behold Israel after the flesh: are not they which eat of the sacrifices partakers of the altar?
> What say I then? that the idol is any thing, or that which is offered in sacrifice to idols is any thing?

But I say, that the things, which the Gentiles sacrifice, they sacrifice to devils, and not to God: and I would not that ye should have fellowship with devils.

Ye cannot drink the cup of the Lord, and the cup of devils: ye cannot be partakers of the Lord's table, and of the table of devils.

Do we provoke the Lord to jealousy? are we stronger than he?

All things are lawful for me, but all things are not expedient: all things are lawful for me, but all things edify not.

Let no man seek his own, but every man another's wealth.

Whatsoever is sold in the shambles, that eat, asking no question for conscience sake:

For the earth is the Lord's and the fulness thereof.

If any of them that believe not bid you feast, and ye be disposed to go; whatsoever is set before you, eat, asking no question for conscience sake.

But if any man say unto you, this is offered in sacrifice unto idols, eat not for his sake that shewed it, and for the conscience sake: for the earth is the Lord's and the fulness thereof:

Conscience, I say, not thine own, but of the other: for why is my liberty judged of another man's conscience?

For if I by grace be a partaker, why am I evil spoken of for that for which I give thanks?

Whether therefore ye eat, or drink, or whatsoever ye do, do all to the glory of God.

Give none offense, neither to the Jews, nor to the Gentiles, nor to the church of God:

Even as I please all men in all things, not seeking mine own profit, but the profit of many, that they may be saved. (1 Corinthians 10:14–33)

Mortify therefore your members which are upon the earth; fornication, uncleanness, inordinate affection, evil concupiscence, and covetousness, which is idolatry:

For which things' sake the wrath of God cometh on the children of disobedience: (Colossians 3:5–6)

Blessed art thou and thy children; and they shall be blessed, inasmuch as they shall keep my commandments they shall prosper in the land. But remember, inasmuch as they will not keep my commandments they shall be cut off from the presence of the Lord.

And we see that these promises have been verified to the people of Nephi; for it has been their quarlings and their contentions, yea, their murderings, and their plunderings, their idolatry, their whoredoms, and their abominations, which were among themselves, which brought upon them their wars and their destructions. (Alma 50:20–21)

They seek not the Lord to establish his righteousness, but every man walketh in his own way, and after the image of his own god, whose image is in the likeness of the world, and whose substance is that of an idol, which waxeth old and shall perish in Babylon, even Babylon the great, which shall fall. (D & C 1:16; emphasis added)

28

PRIDE

From *Webster's New World Dictionary*:

Pride:

1. An overly high opinion of oneself, exaggerated self-esteem.
2. Haughtiness; arrogance.
3. An *exaggerated* sense of one's own dignity; self-respect.
4. One's i*nflated* delight or satisfaction in his achievements, children etc.
5. A person or thing in which, pride is taken.
6. *Bragging about being* the best in class, group, etc.
7. The best part; prime as in pride of manhood. (Italics denotes my addition)

From the above description, it's not hard to understand why Christ has put such an emphasis on not being prideful. Feeling good about oneself is better than feeling bad about one's self, but increasing our feeling to the extent that it is exaggerated and makes us feel like we're better than someone else is being prideful. The same goes for self-respect and dignity. It's also acceptable to feel happy about ours or our children's accomplishments, but when we brag about them or place bumper stickers on our vehicles, it then becomes prideful. Our feelings of being exceptional, which tends to elevate us above someone else for any reason is contrary to God's wishes for our spiritual growth and advancement. To exhibit arrogance and haughtiness, in any thought or action, is even carrying pride to its limits. Essentially, pride is excluding God from any accomplishment, activity, speech, event, deed, endeavor, or achievement by ourselves, family members and friends, even our thoughts.

How often have we heard the saying "pride goeth before the fall?" Perhaps when we exclude God or Christ from any of our activities, they will not include us in their blessings. We should never condone pride in any of its forms because it is not acceptable to God and Christ.

The following scriptures should drive this point home even more. Please enjoy.

> Behold, this was the iniquity of bread, and abundance of idleness was in her and her daughters, neither did she strengthen the hand of the poor and needy.
> And they were haughty, and committed abomination before me: therefore, I took them away as I saw good. (Ezekiel 16:49–50)

> The wicked in the pride of hid countenance, will not seek after the will of God: God is not in all his thoughts. (Psalms 10:4)

> For the day of hosts shall be upon every one that is proud and lofty, and upon every one that is lifted up; and he shall be brought low. (Isaiah 2:12)

> Woe unto them that are wise in their own eyes, and prudent in their own sight. (Isaiah 5:21)

> We have heard of the pride of Moab; he is very proud: even his haughtiness, and his pride, and his wrath: but his lies shall not be so. (Isaiah 16:6)

> We have heard the pride of Moab, (he is exceeding proud) his loftiness and his arrogancy, and his pride, and the haughtiness of heart. (Jeremiah 48:29)

DR. LAUREN J. BALL

Thus saith the Lord, after this manner will mar the pride of Judah, and the great pride of Jerusalem. (Jeremiah 13:9)

Now I Nebuchadnezzar praise and extol and honor the King of heaven, all whose works are truth, and his ways judgment: and those that walk in pride he is able to abase. (Daniel 4:37)

The pride of thine heart hath deceived thee, thou that dwellest in the clefts of the rock, whose habitation is high; that saith in his heart, who shall bring me down to the ground? (Obadiah 1:3)

For, behold, the day cometh, that shall burn as an oven; and all the proud, yea all that do wickedly, shall burn as stubble: and the day that cometh shall burn them up, saith the Lord of hosts, that it shall leave them neither root nor branch. (Malachi 4:1)

And he said unto them in his doctrine, Beware of the scribes, which love to go in long clothing, and love salutations in the marketplaces,
And the chief seats in the synagogues, and the uppermost rooms at feasts:
Which devour widows' houses, and for a pretense make long prayers: these shall receive greater damnation. (Mark 12:38–40)

And whosoever shall exalt himself shall be abased; and he that shall humble himself shall be exalted. (Matthew 23:12)

Backbiters, haters of God, despiteful, proud, boasters, inventors of evil things, disobedient to parents,
Without understanding, covenant breakers, without natural affection, implacable, unmerciful:
Who knowing the judgment of God, that they which commit such things are worthy of death, not only do the same, but have pleasure in them that do them. (Romans 1:30–32)

EXPANDING OUR LIGHT

Not a novice, lest being lifted up with pride he fall into the condemnation of the devil. (1 Timothy 3:6)

He is proud, knowing nothing, but doting about questions and strifes of words, whereof cometh envy, strife, railings, evil surmisings,

Perverse disputations of men of corrupt minds, and destitute of the truth, supposing that gain is Godliness: from such withdraw thyself. (1 Timothy 6:4–5)

This know also, that in the last days perilous times shall come.

For men shall be lovers of their own selves, covetous, boasters, proud, blasphemers, disobedient to parents, unthankful, unholy,

Without natural affection, trucebreakers, false accusers, incontinent, fierce, despisers of those that are good. (2 Timothy 3:1–3)

But he giveth more grace. Wherefore he saith, od resisteth the proud, but giveth grace unto the humble. (James 4:6)

And it came to pass that I saw and bear record, that the great and spacious building was the pride of the world; and it fell, and the fall thereof was exceedingly great. And the angel of the Lord spake unto me again saying; Thus shall be the destruction of all nations, kindreds, tongues and people, that shall fight against the twelve apostles of the Lamb. (1 Nehemiah 11:36)

And the Gentiles are lifted up in the pride of their eyes, and have stumbled, because of the greatness of their stumbling block, that they have built up many churches; nevertheless, they put down miracles of God, and preach up unto themselves their own wisdom and their own learning, that they may get gain and grind upon the face of the poor. (2 Nehemiah 26:20)

Because of the pride, and because of false teachers, and false doctrine, their churches have become corrupted, and their churches are lifted up; because of the pride they are puffed up. (2 Nehemiah 28:12)

O the wise, and learned, and the rich, that are puffed up in the pride of their hearts, and all those who preach doctrine, and all those who commit whoredoms, and pervert the right way of the Lord, wo, wo, wo, be unto them, saith the Lord God almighty, for they shall be thrust down to hell! (2 Nehemiah 28:15)

O that he would rid you from this iniquity and abomination, and, O that ye would listen unto the word of his commands, and let not this pride of your hearts destroy your souls. (Jacob 2:16)

Behold are ye stripped of pride? I say unto ye, if ye are ye are not prepared to meet God. Behold ye must prepare quickly; for the kingdom of heaven is soon at hand, and such an one hath not eternal life. (Alma 5:28)

There are many more powerful scriptures pertaining to pride that we all would well to study and put into practice.

29

AFTERTHOUGHTS

As I have reviewed this book, I find that I have been very preachy at times. My intent has not been to preach at anyone, except to myself which this book was mostly written for, but rather to convey to the reader the necessity for us all to continually progress toward perfection using the process of repentance when we go astray. Man's way is the way of the world, and man's teachings cannot be relied upon. God's way is the eternal way, and His word can always be trusted implicitly.

When we are born into this world, we are given six empty barrels to fill as we choose. Others may influence us regarding the contents we put in each one, but in the final analysis, we and we alone are responsible for what we put in each one or allow others to put in. They are as follows:

1. The first barrel is labeled *physical collectibles*. In this one, we place all our physical accumulations: houses, boats, money, automobiles, power over others, etc. When we die, they all remain on earth!
2. The second is labeled *knowledge*. All of our experiences and all of our knowledge, good or bad, that we acquire are placed herein. We take this barrel with us when we die, except the things of which we have truly repented, whether

the knowledge is productive or counterproductive to our growth toward perfection.
3. The third is labeled *spirituality*. This is the receptacle for anything of a spiritual nature: prayer, repentance, scripture study, fasting, anything that brings us closer to God. This we also take with us.
4. The fourth, although it is related to the third, is by its very nature worthy of a container of its own. This is *service to mankind*. Here, we deposit charity, love, compassion, kindness, consideration, good deeds, etc. We take the results of these actions with us.
5. The fifth one is labeled *unresolved sin*. This is related to the third also but is deserving of a separate container because we need to be able to view it continually for its contents both qualitatively and quantitatively. Since we have the means to keep it empty here on earth, if we die with any contents left in this container whatsoever, we have to answer directly to the one who gave us the means to empty it, Jesus Christ. Most righteous, intelligent people recognize the necessity for keeping this one empty and so, through repentance, they transfer its contents to the spirituality container.
6. The last container is the barrel of *achievement*. We can have all the knowledge in the universe, but if we choose not to use it to achieve anything of spiritual value, we are lost. Our developed talents, our mastery over destructive traits, humility, faith, self-discipline, etc., are placed in this last container, which we also take with us.

There may be other barrels the reader may wish to place on this list. To become aware of the need to fill or empty each of the barrels is a very personal thing, but with this awareness comes the desire and responsibility to control our own destiny with the help of Him who was sent here for that very purpose—Jesus Christ. This world was not designed to progress toward perfection without Him, and those who try will eventually realize that Satan has doped them. When this realization comes, hope and pray it is not too late.

All but the first container goes with us when we depart this life. We will be judged not only on the contents in each container and the amount therein but the method used to fill or empty each one. *At some time in our lives, we must pause and ponder how we are filling our containers and estimate which ones will be the fullest when we die.* If we come to understand this before it's too late, we can *brighten and expand our light,* which then can touch others and help to brighten theirs.

I bear you my testimony that God and Christ live and are in control of this world, and what they do is for the benefit of the world at large to help us attain the highest possible kingdom in God's realm. The limitless knowledge of God, Christ, and the Holy Ghost are so far above and superior to ours that we cannot even begin to comprehend what and why they do in and to this world. When we become angry at what they do, are we not trying to tell them that we know what is best for their creations? Our thoughts are so far below theirs and so limited that to try to interfere with their judgments is the very epitome of pride.

I testify that this church, The Church of Jesus Christ of Latter Day Saints, was established by both the Father and the Son by appearing to Joseph Smith, Jr. and personally choosing him to be the prophet to bring the gospel to the world in this, the dispensation of the fullness of times. That it includes the fullness of the restored Gospel of Jesus Christ.

I testify that Jesus Christ chose all of the succeeding prophets and that our current prophet, Russell M. Nelson, was also chosen and called to be a prophet seer and revelator by Christ and administers all of the keys and authority necessary for the salvation and exaltation of all who desire to live with God the Father and His Son Jesus Christ in the celestial kingdom.

It is my prayer that everyone who reads this work, including me, will take it seriously and advance to the celestial kingdom where all that God hath will be given them.

30

LIVING THE GOSPEL OF JESUS CHRIST REQUIRES US TO:

1. Have the power and authority traceable to Jesus Christ through a line of authority from prophet to prophet to all church leaders for officiating in all priesthood, ordinances, duties, and responsibilities. (For males only.)
2. Always be obedient to all commandments, participate in all ordinances, and accept and righteously fulfill all callings.
3. Overcome, conquer, and rise above every temptation, prompting, influence, illness, and affliction generated by Lucifer and his minions.
4. Embrace and perfect every righteous trait, such as love, compassion, humility, kindness, etc.
5. Expunge and eradicate all unrighteous traits from our lives, such as hate, anger, greed, avarice, lust, etc.
6. Love everyone and be of service to those in need.
7. Have faith in God the Father, Jesus Christ, and the Holy Ghost and rely on their promptings, influences, and revelation.
8. Continually remain in a state of complete repentance by participating in the sacrament as often as possible.

9. Develop the faith, hope, charity, and humility that will carry us through to the end.
10. Pay an honest tithe, offerings, missionary, and humanitarian aid.
11. Complete a mission for the Church of Jesus Christ of Latter-day Saints when possible.
12. Study, embrace, and put into action the precepts found in the scriptures.
13. Heed the words of our current prophets and church leaders.
14. Work on our genealogy and attend the temple on a consistent basis.
15. Embrace the law of love and practice it daily.
16. Prepare each of us to receive revelations from God in our personal lives.
17. Through prayer, fasting, and meditation seek for and embrace the blessing of being able to discern between the promptings of the Holy Ghost and the influences of the satanic forces of evil.
18. Always seek God's help to brighten and expand our light!
19. May God bless our best efforts in attaining the celestial kingdom!

As I have written and edited this work, I realize that I have written it mostly for my own edification and benefit to help me along the way to salvation and exaltation. If by chance, it helps others who are interested in spiritual growth toward the perfection commanded in Matthew 5:48, I will be very happy to have been helpful, and I hope they find the road they are looking for.

I alone, could never have written this book. I have relied on the powers above to help me every step of the way, I am most thankful for this help!

www.ingramcontent.com/pod-product-compliance
Lightning Source LLC
Chambersburg PA
CBHW020522080526
44583CB00013B/694